JOB: A CASE STUDY

JOB: A CASE STUDY

Selected and Edited

by

Raymond Breakstone

BOOKMAN ASSOCIATES, INC.

New York

In Loving Memory
of
Papa Ben and Papa David

ACKNOWLEDGMENTS

Works included in this collection are used by permission and arrangement with copyright holders as follows:

The Bible text in this publication is from the *Revised Standard Version of the Bible,* copyrighted 1946 and 1952 by the Division of Christian Education of the National Council of Churches, and used by permission; *J.B.* by Archibald MacLeish, copyright 1958 by Archibald MacLeish, Houghton Mifflin Company, publishers, by arrangement; "Masque of Reason" by Robert Frost, from *Complete Poems of Robert Frost,* copyright 1945 by Holt, Rinehart and Winston, Inc. Reprinted by permission of Holt, Rinehart and Winston, Inc.

TABLE OF CONTENTS

INTRODUCTION

No one person may perhaps be qualified to state that a single book of the Bible is more important than any other, but few Biblical scholars would disagree that Job and the tale of his suffering still reflect a universal dilemma of the human condition.

As is well known, the Book of Job contains what amounts to a lengthy discussion between Job and three friends who symbolize the normal and anticipated explanations for human experience and suffering. Job and his friends are concerned with a single issue—they seek to discover an answer to the question of the justice of God in His dealings with men. Job's friends explain and understand physical evil, disease, poverty, and sudden death as divine punishment for sin or error. As was the custom in the Biblical era, men sacrificed animals in an effort to placate a supposedly angry God who had punished them for sins that possibly were not apparent. Later, as man and his religion became more sophisticated, good deeds, love, justice, and humility were substituted for sacrifices as means of insuring the favor of God.

The *quid pro quo,* cause-and-effect logic is apparent in these acts. Unfortunately, the good deeds did not reward Job any more than modern man. The story of Job is the confrontation of man with this fact. Job considers the frightening experience of man when he *does* live a good life only to know suffering, destruction, and death. How can a just God whom the prophets have told us has mercy "unto the thousandth generation" of those who love Him and keep His commandments, renege on His promises and indicate to man that life is nothing more than an impossible mystery and that man is ever denied the opportunity to understand the purpose of what goes on about him? How can a just God permit injustice and horror to reign in a world that is presumably of His creation? This is the problem of Job.

Interestingly, Job seeks insight and understanding into the nature of man and the world by "demanding" an explanation for what has occurred. He cannot see the justice for his treatment. He struggles then for spiritual integrity to match his personal integrity, and in this struggle faces three possibilities offered by his friends.

The playwright Archibald MacLeish has skillfully dramatized these possibilities in his play *J.B.* He uses the basic problems of Job and extends them into our time to show their relation to what we know and the development of what we know from our past. *J.B.* confronts three individuals, each of whom symbolizes a religious and semi-religious answer to human problems, while presenting a utilitarian response to spiritual conflicts. *J.B.* meets the religious professional who urges him to confess his sins and humble himself before God; the social reformer who sees society as the corrupter of man; and the psychologically oriented religionist who sees *J.B.* as ridden by guilt and anxiety which can be cleansed only by his coming to terms with his personality. *J.B.*'s friends, like Job's, never come close to the issue *J.B.* knew. Job and *J.B.* recognize that the answers to their suffering do not lie in cutting and shaping God to the goals of man. They see human fulfillment in an awareness of the mighty rhythms of the universe and in man's struggle against them when possible. Without exhortation, promise, or threat, the Book of Job beckons to man to consider himself, the world, the intimations of God that he senses about him, and to be aware of his human opportunity to attain the truth of himself in his response to the truths of his existence.

Readers of the companion volume to this book, *Job's Encounter*, will see in the excerpts from several of the writers of centuries past, an indication of the effects of the Jobian struggle on our times and thought. The focus of thought in this volume and in *Job's Encounter* is both literary and philosophical. With the presentation of the works in this collection, in addition to the guide to the Book of Job, we feel that the fledgling in this area will have sufficient material to comprehend the universal theme that still exists in every man.

The highest form of religion and philosophy—denominational symbols or forms aside—is the questioning of one's reason for existence. When man does so, as He says in *Masque of Reason:* "You are the Emancipator of your God."

THE BOOK OF JOB

T HERE was a man in the land of Uz, whose name was Job; and that man was blameless and upright, one who feared God, and turned away from evil. 2 There were born to him seven sons and three daughters. 3 He had seven thousand sheep, three thousand camels, five hundred yoke of oxen, and five hundred she-asses, and very many servants; so that this man was the greatest of all the people of the east. 4 His sons used to go and hold a feast in the house of each on his day; and they would send and invite their three sisters to eat and drink with them. 5 And when the days of the feast had run their course, Job would send and sanctify them, and he would rise early in the morning and offer burnt offerings according to the number of them all; for Job said, "It may be that my sons have sinned, and cursed God in their hearts." Thus Job did continually.

6 Now there was a day when the sons of God came to present themselves before the LORD, and Satan also came among them. 7 The LORD said to Satan, "Whence have you come?" Satan answered the LORD, "From going to and fro on the earth, and from walking up and down on it." 8 And the LORD said to Satan, "Have you considered my servant Job, that there is none like him on the earth, a blameless and upright man, who fears God and turns away from evil?" 9 Then Satan answered the LORD, "Does Job fear God for nought? 10 Hast thou not put a hedge about him and his house and all that he has, on every side? Thou hast blessed the work of his hands, and his possessions have increased in the land. 11 But put forth thy hand now, and touch all that he has, and he will curse thee to thy face." 12 And the LORD said to Satan, "Behold, all that he has is in your power, only upon himself do not put forth your hand." So Satan went forth from the presence of the LORD.

13 Now there was a day when his sons and daughters were eating and drinking wine in their eldest brother's house; 14 and there came a messenger to Job, and said, "The oxen were plowing and the asses feeding beside them; 15 and the Sabe'ans fell upon them and took them, and slew the servants with the edge of the sword; and I alone have escaped to tell you." 16 While he was yet speaking, there came another, and said, "The fire of God fell from heaven and burned

up the sheep and the servants, and consumed them; and I alone have escaped to tell you." *17* While he was yet speaking, there came another, and said, "The Chalde'ans formed three companies, and made a raid upon the camels and took them, and slew the servants with the edge of the sword; and I alone have escaped to tell you." *18* While he was yet speaking, there came another, and said, "Your sons and daughters were eating and drinking wine in their eldest brother's house; *19* and behold, a great wind came across the wilderness, and struck the four corners of the house, and it fell upon the young people, and they are dead; and I alone have escaped to tell you."

20 Then Job arose, and rent his robe, and shaved his head, and fell upon the ground, and worshipped. *21* And he said, "Naked I came from my mother's womb; and naked shall I return; the LORD gave, and the LORD has taken away; blessed be the name of the LORD."

22 In all this Job did not sin or charge God with wrong.

2 Again there was a day when the sons of God came to present themselves before the LORD, and Satan also came among them to present himself before the LORD. *2* And the LORD said to Satan, "Whence have you come?" Satan answered the LORD, "From going to and fro on the earth, and from walking up and down on it." *3* And the LORD said to Satan, "Have you considered my servant Job, that there is none like him on the earth, a blameless and upright man, who fears God and turns away from evil? He still holds fast his integrity, although you moved me against him, to destroy him without cause." *4* Then Satan answered the LORD "Skin for skin! All that a man has he will give for his life. *5* But put forth thy hand now, and touch his bone and his flesh, and he will curse thee to thy face." *6* And the LORD said to Satan, "Behold, he is in your power; only spare his life."

7 So Satan went forth from the presence of the LORD, and afflicted Job with loathsome sores from the sole of his foot to the crown of his head. *8* And he took a potsherd with which to scrape himself, and sat among the ashes.

9 Then his wife said to him, "Do you still hold fast to your integrity? Curse God, and die." *10* But he said to her, "You speak as one of the foolish women would speak. Shall we receive good at the hand of God, and shall we not receive evil?" In all this Job did not sin with his lips.

11 Now when Job's three friends heard of all this evil that had come upon him, they came each from his own place, Eli'phaz the Te'manite, Bildad the Shuhite, and Zophar the Na'amathite. They made an appointment together to come to condole with him and comfort him. *12* And when they saw him from afar, they did not recognize him; and they raised their voices and wept; and they rent their robes and sprinkled dust upon their heads toward heaven. *13* And they sat with him on the ground seven days and seven nights, and no one spoke a word to him, for they saw that his suffering was very great.

3 After this Job opened his mouth and cursed the day of his birth.

2 And Job said:

3 "Let the day perish wherein I was born,
  and the night which said,
  'A man-child is conceived.'

4 Let that day be darkness!
  May God above not seek it,
  nor light shine upon it.

5 Let gloom and deep darkness claim it.
  Let clouds dwell upon it;
  let the blackness of the day terrify it.

6 That night—let thick darkness seize it!
  let it not rejoice among the days of the year,
  let it not come into the number of the months.

7 Yea, let that night be barren;
  let no joyful cry be heard in it.

8 Let those curse it who curse the day,
  who are skilled to rouse up Leviathan.

9 Let the stars of its dawn be dark;
  let it hope for light, but have none,
  nor see the eyelids of the morning;

10 because it did not shut the doors of my mother's womb,
  nor hide trouble from my eyes.

11 "Why did I not die at birth,
  come forth from the womb and expire?

12 Why did the knees receive me?
  Oh why the breasts, that I should suck?

13 For then I should have lain down and been quiet;
  I should have slept; then I should have been at rest.

14 with kings and counselors of the earth who rebuilt ruins for
    themselves,
15 or with princes who had gold,
    who filled their houses with silver.
16 Or why was I not as a hidden untimely birth,
    as infants that never see the light?
17 There the wicked cease from troubling,
    and there the weary are at rest.
18 There the prisoners are at ease together;
    they hear not the voice of the task-master.
19 The small and the great are there,
    and the slave is free from the master.

20 Why is light given to him that is in misery,
    and life to the bitter in soul,
21 who long for death, but it comes not,
    and dig for it more than for hid treasures;
22 who rejoice exceedingly,
    and are glad, when they find the grave?
23 Why is light given to a man whose way is hid,
    whom God has hedged in?
24 For my sighing comes as my bread,
    and my groanings are poured out like water.
25 For the thing that I fear comes upon me,
    and what I dread befalls me.
26 I am not at ease, nor am I quiet;
    I have no rest; but trouble comes."

4 Then Eli'phaz the Te'manite answered:
  2 "If one ventures a word with you, will you be offended?
    Yet who can keep from speaking?
3 Behold, you have instructed many,
    and you have strengthened the weak hands.
4 Your words have upheld him who was stumbling,
    and you have made firm the feeble knees.
5 But now it has come to you, and you are impatient;
    it touches you, and you are dismayed.
6 Is not your fear of God your confidence,
    and the integrity of your ways your hope?
7 "Think now, who that was innocent ever perished?
    Or where were the upright cut off?

8 As I have seen, those who plow iniquity
 and sow trouble reap the same.
9 By the breath of God they perish,
 and by the blast of his anger they are consumed.
10 The roar of the lion, the voice of the fierce lion,
 the teeth of the young lions, are broken.
11 The strong lion perishes for lack of prey,
 and the whelps of the lioness are scattered.

12 "Now a word was brought to me stealthily,
 my ear received the whisper of it.
13 Amid thoughts from visions of the night,
 when deep sleep falls on men,
14 dread came upon me, and trembling,
 which made all my bones shake.
15 A spirit glided past my face;
 the hair of my flesh stood up.
16 It stood still,
 but I could not discern its appearance.
 A form was before my eyes;
 there was silence, then I heard a voice:
17 'Can mortal man be righteous before God?
 Can a man be pure before his Maker?
18 Even in his servants he puts no trust,
 and his angels he charges with error;
19 how much more those who dwell in houses of clay,
 whose foundation is in the dust,
 who are crushed before the moth.
20 Between morning and evening they are destroyed;
 they perish for ever without any regarding it.
21 If their tent-cord is plucked up within them,
 do they not die, and that without wisdom?'

5 "Call now; is there any one who will answer you?
 To which of the holy ones will you turn?
2 Surely vexation kills the fool,
 and jealousy slays the simple.
3 I have seen the fool taking root,
 but suddenly I cursed his dwelling.
4 His sons are far from safety,
 they are crushed in the gate,
 and there is no one to deliver them.

5 His harvest the hungry eat,
   and he takes it even out of thorns;
   and the thirsty pant after his wealth.
6 For affliction does not come from the dust,
   nor does trouble sprout from the ground;
.7 but man is born to trouble
   as the sparks fly upward.

8 "As for me, I would seek God,
   and to God would I commit my cause;
9 who does great things and unsearchable,
   marvelous things without number:
10 he gives rain upon the earth
   and sends waters upon the fields;
11 he sets on high those who are lowly,
   and those who mourn are lifted to safety.
12 He frustrates the devices of the crafty,
   so that their hands achieve no success.
13 He takes the wise in their own craftiness;
   and the schemes of the wily are brought to a quick end.
14 They meet with darkness in the daytime,
   and grope at noonday as in the night.
15 But he saves the fatherless from their mouth,
   the needy from the hand of the mighty.
16 So the poor have hope,
   and injustice shuts her mouth.

17 "Behold, happy is the man whom God reproves;
   therefore despise not the chastening of the Almighty.
18 For he wounds, but he binds up,
   he smites, but his hands heal.
19 He will deliver you from six troubles;
   in seven there shall no evil touch you.
20 In famine he will redeem you from death,
   and in war from the power of the sword.
21 You shall be hid from the scourge of the tongue,
   and shall not fear destruction when it comes.
22 At destruction and famine you shall laugh,
   and shall not fear the beasts of the earth.
23 For you shall be in league with the stones of the field,
   and the beasts of the field shall be at peace with you.

16

24 You shall know that your tent is safe,
 and you shall inspect your fold and miss nothing.
25 You shall know also that your descendants shall be many,
 and your offspring as the grass of the earth.
26 You shall come to your grave in ripe old age,
 as a shock of grain comes up to the threshing floor in its season.
27 Lo, this we have searched out; it is true.
 Hear, and know it for your good."

6 Then Job answered:
 2 "O that my vexation were weighed,
 and all my calamity laid in the balances!
3 For then it would be heavier than the sand of the sea;
 therefore my words have been rash.
4 For the arrows of the Almighty are in me;
 my spirit drinks their poison;
 the terrors of God are arrayed against me.
5 Does the wild ass bray when he has grass,
 or the ox low over his fodder?
6 Can that which is tasteless be eaten without salt,
 or is there any taste in the slime of the purslane?
7 My appetite refuses to touch them;
 they are as food that is loathsome to me.

8 "O that I might have my request,
 and that God would grant my desire;
9 that it would please God to crush me,
 that he would let loose his hand and cut me off!
10 This would be my consolation;
 I would even exult in pain unsparing;
 for I have not denied the words of the Holy One.
11 What is my strength, that I should wait?
 And what is my end, that I should be patient?
12 Is my strength the strength of stones,
 or is my flesh bronze?
13 In truth I have no help in me,
 and any resource is driven from me.

14 "He who withholds kindness from a friend
 forsakes the fear of the Almighty.
15 My brethren are treacherous as a torrent-bed,
 as freshets that pass away,

16 which are dark with ice,
  and where the snow hides itself.
17 In time of heat they disappear;
  when it is hot, they vanish from their place.
18 The caravans turn aside from their course;
  they go up into the waste, and perish.
19 The caravans of Tema look,
  the travelers of Sheba hope.
20 They are disappointed because they were confident;
  they come thither and are confounded.
21 Such you have now become to me;
  you see my calamity, and are afraid.
22 Have I said, 'Make me a gift'?
  Or, 'From your wealth offer a bribe for me'?
23 Or, 'Deliver me from the adversary's hand'?
  Or, 'Ransom me from the hand of oppressors'?

24 Teach me, and I will be silent;
  make me understand how I have erred.
25 How forceful are honest words!
  But what does reproof from you reprove?
26 Do you think that you can reprove words,
  when the speech of a despairing man is wind?
27 You would even cast lots over the fatherless,
  and bargain over your friend.

28 "But now, be pleased to look at me;
  for I will not lie to your face.
29 Turn, I pray, let no wrong be done.
  Turn now, my vindication is at stake.
30 Is there any wrong on my tongue?
  Cannot my taste discern calamity?

7 "Has not man a hard service upon earth,
  and are not his days like the days of a hireling?
2 Like a slave who longs for the shadow,
  and like a hireling who looks for his wages,
3 so I am allotted months of emptiness,
  and nights of misery are apportioned to me.
4 When I lie down I say, 'When shall I arise?'
  But the night is long,
  and I am full of tossing till the dawn.

5 My flesh is clothed with worms and dirt;
   my skin hardens, then breaks out afresh.
6 My days are swifter than a weaver's shuttle,
   and come to their end without hope.

7 "Remember that my life is a breath;
   my eye will never again see good.
8 The eye of him who sees me will behold me no more;
   while thy eyes are upon me, I shall be gone.
9 As the cloud fades and vanishes,
   so he who goes down to Sheol does not come up;
10 he returns no more to his house,
   nor does his place know him any more.
11 "Therefore I will not restrain my mouth;
   I will speak in the anguish of my spirit;
   I will complain in the bitterness of my soul.
12 Am I the sea, or a sea monster,
   that thou settest a guard over me?
13 When I say, 'My bed will comfort me,
   my couch will ease my complaint,'
14 then thou dost scare me with dreams
   and terrify me with visions,
15 so that I would choose strangling
   and death rather than my bones.
16 I loathe my life; I would not live for ever.
   Let me alone, for my days are a breath.
17 What is a man, that thou dost make so much of him,
   and that thou dost set thy mind upon him,
18 dost visit him every morning,
   and test him every moment?
19 How long wilt thou not look away from me,
   nor let me alone till I swallow my spittle?
20 If I sin, what do I do to thee, thou watcher of men?
   Why hast thou made me thy mark?
   Why have I become a burden to thee?
21 Why dost thou not pardon my transgression
   and take away my iniquity?
For now I shall lie in the earth;
   thou wilt seek me, but I shall not be."

8   Then Bildad the Shuhite answered:
   2 "How long will you say these things,
   and the words of your mouth be a great wind?

3 Does God pervert justice?
  Or does the Almight pervert right?
4 If your children have sinned against him,
  he has delivered them into the power of their transgression.
5 If you will seek God
  and make supplication to the Almighty,
6 if you are pure and upright,
  surely then he will rouse himself for you
  and reward you with a rightful habitation.
7 And though your beginning was small,
  your latter days will be very great.

8 "For inquire, I pray you, of bygone ages,
  and consider what the fathers have found;
9 for we are but of yesterday, and know nothing,
  for our days on earth are a shadow.
10 Will they not teach you, and tell you,
  and utter words out of their understanding?

11 "Can papyrus grow where there is no marsh?
   Can reeds flourish where there is no water?
12 While yet in flower and not cut down,
   they wither before any other plant.
13 Such are the paths of all who forget God;
   the hope of the godless man shall perish.
14 His confidence breaks in sunder,
   and his trust in a spider's web.
15 He leans against his house, but it does not stand;
   he lays hold of it, but it does not endure.
16 He thrives before the sun,
   and his shoots spread over his garden.
17 His roots twine about the stoneheap;
   he lives among the rocks.
18 If he is destroyed from his place,
   then it will deny him, saying, 'I have never seen you.'
19 Behold, this is the joy of his way;
   and out of the earth others will spring.

20 "Behold, God will not reject a blameless man,
   nor take the hand of evildoers.
21 He will yet fill your mouth with laughter,
   and your lips with shouting.

22 Those who hate you will be clothed with shame,
    and the tent of the wicked will be no more."

9   Then Job answered:
     2 "Truly I know that it is so:
     But how can a man be just before God?
  3 If one wished to contend with him,
       one could not answer him once in a thousand times.
  4 He is wise in heart, and mighty in strength
   —who has hardened himself against him, and succeeded?—
  5 he who removes mountains, and they know it not,
       when he overturns them in his anger;
  6 who shakes the earth out of its place,
       and its pillars tremble;
  7 who commands the sun, and it does not rise;
       who seals up the stars;
  8 who alone stretched out the heavens,
       and trampled the waves of the sea;
  9 who made the Bear and Orion,
       the Plei'ades and the chambers of the south;
 10 who does great things beyond understanding;
       and marvelous things without number.
 11 Lo, he passes by me, and I see him not;
       he moves on, but I do not perceive him.
 12 Behold, he snatches away; who can hinder him?
       Who will say to him, 'What doest thou'?

 13 "God will not turn back his anger;
       beneath him bowed the helpers of Rahab.
 14 How then can I answer him,
       choosing my words with him?
 15 Though I am innocent, I cannot answer him;
       I must appeal for mercy to my accuser.
 16 If I summoned him and he answered me,
       I would not believe that he was listening to my voice.
 17 For he crushes me with a tempest,
       and multiplies my wounds without cause;
 18 he will not let me get my breath,
       but fills me with bitterness.
 19 If it is a contest of strength, behold him!
       If it is a matter of justice, who can summon him?

20 Though I am innocent, my own mouth would condemn me;
   though I am blameless, he would prove me perverse.
21 I am blameless; I regard not myself;
   I loathe my life.
22 It is all one; therefore I say,
   he destroys both the blameless and the wicked.
23 When disaster brings sudden death,
   he mocks at the calamity of the innocent.
24 The earth is given into the hand of the wicked;
   he covers the faces of its judges--
   if it is not he, who then is it?

25 "My days are swifter than a runner;
   they flee away, they see no good.
26 They go by like skiffs of reed,
   like an eagle swooping on the prey.
27 If I say, 'I will forget my complaint,
   I will put off my sad countenance, and be of good cheer,'
28 I become afraid of all my suffering,
   for I know thou wilt not held me innocent.
29 I shall be condemned;
   why then do I labor in vain?
30 If I wash myself with snow,
   and cleanse my hands with lye,
31 yet thou wilt plunge me into a pit,
   and my own clothes will abhor me.
32 For he is not a man, as I am, that I might answer him,
   that we should come to trial together.
33 There is no umpire between us,
   who might lay his hand upon us both.
34 Let him take his rod away from me,
   and let not dread of him terrify me.
35 Then I would speak without fear of him,
   for I am not so in myself.

10 "I loathe my life;
   I will give free utterance to my complaint;
   I will speak in the bitterness of my soul.
2 I will say to God, Do not condemn me;
   let me know why thou dost contend against me.
3 Does it seem good to thee to oppress,
   to despise the work of thy hands
   and favor the designs of the wicked?

4 Hast thou eyes of flesh?
   Dost thou see as man sees?
5 Are thy days as the days of man,
   or thy years as man's years,
6 that thou dost seek out my iniquity
   and search for my sin,
7 although thou knowest that I am not guilty,
   and there is none to deliver out of thy hand?
8 Thy hands fashioned and made me;
   and now thou dost turn about and destroy me.
9 Remember that thou hast made me of clay;
   and wilt thou turn me to dust again?
10 Didst thou not pour me out like milk
   and curdle me like cheese?
11 Thou didst clothe me with skin and flesh,
   and knit me together with bones and sinews.
12 Thou hast granted me life and steadfast love;
   and thy care has preserved my spirit.
13 Yet these things thou didst hide in thy heart;
   I know that this was thy purpose.
14 If I sin, thou dost mark me,
   and dost not acquit me of my iniquity.
15 If I am wicked, woe to me!
   If I am righteous, I cannot lift up my head,
   for I am filled with disgrace
   and look upon my affliction.
16 And if I lift myself up, thou dost hunt me like a lion,
   and again work wonders against me;
17 thou dost renew thy witnesses against me,
   and increase thy vexation toward me;
   thou dost bring fresh hosts against me.

18 Why didst thou bring me forth from the womb?
   Would that I had died before any eye had seen me,
19 and were as though I had not been,
   carried from the womb to the grave.
20 Are not the days of my life few?
   Let me alone, that I may find a little comfort
21 before I go whence I shall not return,
   to the land of gloom and deep darkness,
22 the land of gloom and chaos,
   where light is as darkness."

11 Then Zophar the Na'amathite answered:
2 "Should a multitude of words go unanswered,
and a man full of talk be vindicated?
3 Should your babble-silence men,
and when you mock, shall no one shame you?
4 For you say, 'My doctrine is pure,
and I am clean in God's eyes.'
5 But oh, that God would speak,
and open his lips to you,
6 and that he would tell you the secrets of wisdom!
For he is manifold in understanding.
Know then that God exacts of you less than your guilt deserves.
7 "Can you find out the deep things of God?
Can you find out the limit of the Almighty?
8 It is higher than heaven—what can you do?
Deeper than Sheol—what can you know?
9 Its measure is longer than the earth,
and broader than the sea.
10 If he passes through, and imprisons,
and calls to judgment, who can hinder him?
11 For he knows worthless men;
when he sees iniquity, will he not consider it?
12 But a stupid man will get understanding,
when a wild ass's colt is born a man.

13 "If you set your heart aright,
you will stretch out your hands toward him.
14 If iniquity is in your hand, put it far away,
and let not wickedness dwell in your tents.
15 Surely then you will lift up your face without blemish;
you will be secure, and will not fear.
16 You will forget your misery;
you will remember it as waters that have passed away.
17 And your life will be brighter than the noonday;
its darkness will be like the morning.
18 And you will have confidence, because there is hope;
you will be protected and take your rest in safety.
19 You will lie down, and none will make you afraid;
many will entreat your favor.
20 But the eyes of the wicked will fail;
all way of escape will be lost to them,
and their hope is to breathe their last."

12 Then Job answered:
2 "No doubt you are the people,
and wisdom will die with you.
3 But I have understanding as well as you;
I am not inferior to you.
Who does not know such things as these?
4 I am a laughingstock to my friends;
I, who called upon God and he answered me,
a just and blameless man, am a laughingstock.
5 In the thought of one who is at ease there is contempt for misfortune;
it is ready for those whose feet slip.
6 The tents of robbers are at peace,
and those who provoke God are secure,
who bring their god in their hand.

7 "But ask the beasts, and they will teach you;
the birds of the air, and they will tell you;
8 or the plants of the earth, and they will teach you;
and the fish of the sea will declare to you.
9 Who among all these does not know
that the hand of the LORD has done this?
10 In his hand is the life of every living thing
and the breath of all mankind.
11 Does not the ear try words
as the palate tastes food?
12 Wisdom is with the aged,
and understanding in length of days.

13 "With God are wisdom and might;
he has counsel and understanding,
14 If he tears down, none can rebuild;
if he shuts a man in, none can open.
15 If he withholds the waters, they dry up;
if he sends them out, they overwhelm the land.
16 With him are strength and wisdom;
the deceived and the deceiver are his.
17 He leads counselors away stripped,
and judges he makes fools.
18 He looses the bonds of kings,
and binds a waistcloth on their loins.

19 He leads priests away stripped,
and overthrows the mighty.
20 He deprives of speech those who are trusted,
and takes away the discernment of the elders.
21 He pours contempt on princes,
and looses the belt of the strong.
22 He uncovers the deeps out of darkness,
and brings deep darkness to light.
23 He makes nations great, and he destroys them;
he enlarges nations, and leads them away.
24 He takes away understanding from the chiefs of the people of the
earth,
and makes them wander in a pathless waste.
25 They grope in the dark without light;
and he makes them stagger like a drunken man.

13

"Lo, my eye has seen all this,
my ear has heard and understood it.
2 What you know, I also know;
I am not inferior to you.
3 But I would speak to the Almighty,
and I desire to argue my case with God.
4 As for you, you whitewash with lies;
worthless physicians are you all.
5 Oh that you would keep silent,
and it would be your wisdom!
6 Hear now my reasoning,
and listen to the pleading of my lips.
7 Will you speak false for God,
and speak deceitfully for him?
8 Will you show partiality toward him,
will you plead the case for God?
9 Will it be well with you when he searches you out?
Or can you deceive him, as one deceives a man?
10 He will surely rebuke you
if in secret you show partiality.
11 Will not his majesty terrify you,
and the dread of him fall upon you?
12 Your maxims are proverbs of ashes,
your defenses are defenses of clay.

13 "Let me have silence, and I will speak,
   and let come on me what may.
14 I will take my flesh in my teeth,
   and put my life in my hand.
15 Behold, he will slay me; I have no hope;
   yet I will defend my ways to his face.
16 This will be my salvation,
   that a godless man shall not come before him.
17 Listen carefully to my words,
   and let my declaration be in your ears.
18 Behold, I have prepared my case;
   I know that I shall be vindicated.
19 Who is there that will contend with me?
   For then I would be silent and die.
20 Only grant two things to me,
   then I will not hide myself from thy face:
21 withdraw thy hand far from me,
   and let not dread of thee terrify me.
22 Then call, and I will answer;
   or let me speak, and do thou reply to me.
23 How many are my iniquities and my sins?
   Make me know my transgression and my sin.
24 Why dost thou hide thy face,
   and count me as thy enemy?
25 Wilt thou frighten a driven leaf
   and pursue dry chaff?
26 For thou writest bitter things against me,
   and makest me inherit the iniquities of my youth.
27 Thou puttest my feet in the stocks,
   and watchest all my paths;
   thou settest a bound to the soles of my feet.
28 Man wastes away like a rotten thing,
   like a garment that is moth-eaten.

14 "Man that is born of a woman
   is of few days, and full of trouble.
2 He comes forth like a flower, and withers;
   he flees like a shadow, and continues not.
3 And dost thou open thy eyes upon such a one
   and bring him into judgment with thee?
4 Who can bring a clean thing out of an unclean?
   There is not one.

5 Since his days are determined,
>   and the number of his months is with thee,
>   and thou hast appointed his bounds that he cannot pass,
6 look away from him, and desist,
>   that he may enjoy, like a hireling, his day.

7 "For there is hope for a tree,
>   if it be cut down, that it will sprout again,
>   and that its shoots will not cease.
8 Though its root grow old in the earth,
>   and its stump die in the ground,
9 yet at the scent of water it will bud
>   and put forth branches like a young plant.
10 But man dies, and is laid low;
>   man breathes his last, and where is he?
11 As waters fail from a lake,
>   and a river wastes away and dries up,
12 so man lies down and rises not again;
>   till the heavens are no more he will not awake,
>   or be roused out of his sleep.
13 Oh that thou wouldest hide me in Sheol,
>   that thou wouldest conceal me until thy wrath be past,
>   that thou wouldest appoint me a set time, and remember me!
14 If a man die, shall he live again?
>   All the days of my service I would wait,
>   till my release should come.
15 Thou wouldest call, and I would answer thee;
>   thou wouldest long for the work of thy hands.
16 For then thou wouldest number my steps,
>   thou wouldest not keep watch over my sin;
17 my transgression would be sealed up in a bag,
>   and thou wouldest cover over my iniquity.

18 "But the mountain falls and crumbles away,
>   and the rock is removed from its place;
19 the waters wear away the stones;
>   the torrents wash away the soil of the earth;
>   so thou destroyest the hope of man.
20 Thou prevailest for ever against him, and he passes;
>   thou changest his countenance, and sendest him away.
21 His sons come to honor, and he does not know it;
>   they are brought low, and he perceives it not.

22 He feels only the pain of his own body,
   and he mourns only for himself."

15 Then Eli'phaz the Te'manite answered:
   2 "Should a wise man answer with windy knowledge,
   and fill himself with the east wind?
3 Should he argue in unprofitable talk,
   or in words with which he can do no good?
4 But you are doing away with the fear of God,
   and hindering meditation before God.
5 For your iniquity teaches your mouth,
   and you choose the tongue of the crafty.
6 Your own mouth condemns you, and not I;
   your own lips testify against you.

7 "Are you the first man that was born?
   Or were you brought forth before the hills?
8 Have you listened in the council of God?
   And do you limit wisdom to yourself?
9 What do you know that we do not know?
   What do you understand that is not clear to us?
10 Both the gray-haired and the aged are among us,
   older than your father.
11 Are the consolations of God too small for you,
   or the word that deals gently with you?
12 Why does your heart carry you away,
   and why do your eyes flash,
13 that you turn your spirit against God,
   and let such words go out of your mouth?
14 What is man, that he can be clean?
   Or he that is born of a woman, that he can be righteous?
15 Behold, God puts no trust in his holy ones,
   and the heavens are not clean in his sight;
16 how much less one who is abominable and corrupt,
   a man who drinks iniquity like water!

17 "I will show you, hear me;
   and what I have seen I will declare
18 (what wise men have told,
   and their fathers have not hidden,
19 to whom alone the land was given,
   and no stranger passed among them).

20 The wicked man writhes in pain all his days,
    through all the years that are laid up for the ruthless.
21 Terrifying sounds are in his ears;
    in prosperity the destroyer will come upon him.
22 He does not believe that he will return out of darkness,
    and he is destined for the sword.
23 He wanders abroad for bread, saying, 'Where is it?'
    He knows that a day of darkness is ready at his hand;
24 distress and anguish terrify him;
    they prevail against him, like a king prepared for battle.
25 Because he has stretched forth his hand against God,
    and bids defiance to the Almighty,
26 running stubbornly against him
    with a thick-bossed shield;
27 because he has covered his face with his fat,
    and gathered fat upon his loins,
28 and has lived in desolate cities,
    in houses which no man should inhabit,
    which were destined to become heaps of ruins;
29 he will not be rich, and his wealth will not endure,
    nor will he strike root in the earth;
30 he will not escape from darkness;
    the flame will dry up his shoots,
    and his blossom will be swept away by the wind.
31 Let him not trust in emptiness, deceiving himself;
    for emptiness will be his recompense.
32 It will be paid in full before his time,
    and his branch will not be green.
33 He will shake off his unripe grape, like the vine,
    and cast off his blossom, like the olive tree.
34 For the company of the godless is barren,
    and fire consumes the tents of bribery.
35 They conceive mischief and bring forth evil
    and their heart prepares deceit."

16 Then Job answered:
    2 "I have heard many such things;
    miserable comforters are you all.
3 Shall windy words have an end?
    Or what provokes you that you answer?
4 I also could speak as you do,
    if you were in my place;

I could join words together against you,
and shake my head at you.
5 I could strengthen you with my mouth,
and the solace of my lips would assuage your pain.

6 "If I speak, my pain is not assuaged,
and if I forbear, how much of it leaves me?
7 Surely now God has worn me out;
he has made desolate all my company.
8 And he has shriveled me up,
which is a witness against me;
and my leanness has risen up against me,
it testifies to my face.
9 He has torn me in his wrath, and hated me;
he has gnashed his teeth at me;
my adversary sharpens his eyes against me.
10 Men have gaped at me with their mouth,
they have struck me insolently upon the cheek,
they mass themselves together against me.
11 God gives me up to the ungodly,
and casts me into the hands of the wicked.
12 I was at ease, and he broke me asunder;
he seized me by the neck and dashed me to pieces;
he set me up as his target,
13   his archers surround me.
He slashes open my kidneys, and does not spare;
he pours out my gall on the ground.
14 He breaks me with breach upon breach;
he runs upon me like a warrior.
15 I have sewed sackcloth upon my skin,
and have laid my strength in the dust.
16 My face is red with weeping,
and on my eyelids is deep darkness;
17 although there is no violence in my hands,
and my prayer is pure.

18 "O earth, cover not my blood,
and let my cry find no resting place.
19 Even now, behold, my witness is in heaven,
and he that vouches for me is on high.
20 My friends scorn me;
my eye pours out tears to God,

21 that he would maintain the right of a man with God,
  like that of a man with his neighbor.
22 For when a few years have come
  I shall go the way whence I shall not return.

17 My spirit is broken, my days are extinct,
  'the grave is ready for me.
2 Surely there are mockers about me,
  and my eye dwells on their provocation.

3 "Lay down a pledge for me with thyself;
  who is there that will give surety for me?
4 Since thou hast closed their minds to understanding,
  therefore thou wilt not let them triumph.
5 He who informs against his friends to get a share of their property,
  the eyes of his children will fail.

6 "He has made me a byword of the peoples,
  and I am one before whom men spit.
7 My eye has grown dim from grief,
  and all my members are like a shadow.
8 Upright men are appalled at this,
  and the innocent stirs himself up against the godless.
9 Yet the righteous holds to his way,
  and he that has clean hands grows stronger and stronger.
10 But you, come on again, all of you,
  and I shall not find a wise man among you.
11 My days are past, my plans are broken off,
  the desires of my heart.
12 They make night into day;
  'The light,' they say, 'is near to the darkness.'
13 If I look for Sheol as my house,
  if I spread my couch in darkness,
14 if I say to the pit, 'You are my father,'
  and to the worm, 'My mother,' or 'My sister,'
15 where then is my hope?
  Who will see my hope?
16 Will it go down to the bars of Sheol?
  Shall we descend together into the dust "

18 Then Bildad the Shuhite answered:
  2 "How long will you hunt for words?
  Consider, and then we will speak.

3 Why are we counted as cattle?
   Why are we stupid in your sight?
4 You who tear yourself in your anger,
   shall the earth be forsaken for you,
   or the rock be removed out of its place?

5 "Yea, the light of the wicked is put out,
   and the flame of his fire does not shine.
6 The light is dark in his tent,
   and his lamp above him is put out.
7 His strong steps are shortened
   and his own schemes throw him down
8 For he is cast into a net by his own feet,
   and he walks on a pitfall.
9 A trap seizes him by the heel,
   a snare lays hold of him.
10 A rope is hid for him in the ground,
   a trap for him in the path.
11 Terrors frighten him on every side,
   and chase him at his heels.
12 His strength is hunger-bitten,
   and calamity is ready for his stumbling.
13 By disease his skin is consumed,
   the first-born of death consumes his limbs.
14 He is torn from the tent in which he trusted,
   and is brought to the king of terrors.
15 In his tent dwells that which is none of his;
   brimstone is scattered upon his habitation.
16 His roots dry up beneath,
   and his branches wither above.
17 His memory perishes from the earth,
   and he has no name in the street.
18 He is thrust from light into darkness,
   and driven out of the world.
19 He has no offspring or descendant among his people,
   and no survivor where he used to live.
20 They of the west are appalled at his day,
   and horror seizes them of the east.
21 Surely such are the dwellings of the ungodly,
   such is the place of him who knows not God."

19 Then Job answered:
2 "How long will you torment me,
   and break me in pieces with words?
3 These ten times you have cast reproach upon me;
   are you not ashamed to wrong me?
4 And even if it be true that I have erred,
   my error remains with myself.
5 If indeed you magnify yourselves against me,
   and make my humiliation an argument against me,
6 know then that God has put me in the wrong,
   and closed his net about me.
7 Behold, I cry out, 'Violence!' but I am not answered;
   I call aloud, but there is no justice.
8 He has walled up my way, so that I cannot pass,
   and he has set darkness upon my paths.
9 He has stripped from me my glory,
   and taken the crown from my head.
10 He breaks me down on every side, and I am gone,
   and my hope has he pulled up like a tree.
11 He has kindled his wrath against me,
   and counts me as his adversary.
12 His troops come on together;
   they have cast up siegeworks against me,
   and encamp round about my tent.

13 "He has put my brethren far from me,
   and my acquaintances are wholly estranged from me.
14 My kinsfolk and my close friends have failed me;
15   the guests in my house have forgotten me;
   my maidservants count me as a stranger;
   I have become an alien in their eyes.
16 I call to my servant, but he gives me no answer;
   I must beseech him with my mouth.
17 I am repulsive to my wife,
   loathsome to the sons of my own mother.
18 Even young children despise me;
   when I rise they talk against me.
19 All my intimate friends abhor me,
   and those whom I loved have turned against me.
20 My bones cleave to my skin and to my flesh,
   and I have escaped by the skin of my teeth.

21 Have pity on me, have pity on me, O you my friends,
   for the hand of God has touched me!
22 Why do you, like God, pursue me?
   why are you not satisfied with my flesh?

23 "Oh that my words were written!
   Oh that they were inscribed in a book!
24 Oh that with an iron pen and lead
   they were graven in the rock for ever!
25 For I know that my Redeemer lives,
   and at last he will stand upon the earth;
26 and after my skin has been thus destroyed,
   then from my flesh I shall see God,
27 whom I shall see on my side,
   and my eyes shall behold, and not another.
   My heart faints within me!
28 If you say, 'How we will pursue him!'
   and, 'The root of the matter is found in him';
29 be afraid of the sword,
   for wrath brings the punishment of the sword,
   that you may know there is a judgment."

20 Then Zophar the Na'amathite answered:
   2 "Therefore my thoughts answer me,
   because of my haste within me.
3 I hear censure which insults me,
   and out of my understanding a spirit answers me.
4 Do you not know this from of old,
   since man was placed upon earth,
5 that the exulting of the wicked is short,
   and the joy of the godless but for a moment?
6 Though his height mount up to the heavens,
   and his head reach to the clouds,
7 he will perish for ever like his own dung;
   those who have seen him will say, 'Where is he?'
8 He will fly away like a dream, and not be found;
   he will be chased away like a vision of the night.
9 The eye which saw him will see him no more,
   nor will his place any more behold him.
10 His children will seek the favor of the poor,
   and his hands will give back his wealth.

11 His bones are full of youthful vigor,
   but it will lie down with him in the dust.

12 "Though wickedness is sweet in his mouth,
   though he hides it under his tongue,
13 though he is loath to let it go,
   and holds it in his mouth,
14 yet his food is turned in his stomach;
   it is the gall of asps within him.
15 He swallows down riches and vomits them up again!
   God casts them out of his belly.
16 He will suck the poison of asps;
   the tongue of a viper will kill him.
17 He will not look upon the rivers,
   the streams flowing with honey and curds.
18 He will give back the fruit of his toil,
   and will not swallow it down;
from the profit of his trading
   he will get no enjoyment.
19 For he has crushed and abandoned the poor,
   he has seized a house which he did not build.

20 "Because his greed knew no rest,
   he will not save anything in which he delights.
21 There was nothing left after he had eaten;
   therefore his prosperity will not endure.
22 In the fulness of his sufficiency he will be in straits;
   all the force of misery will come upon him.
23 To fill his belly to the full
   God will send his fierce anger into him,
   and rain it upon him as his food.
24 He will flee from an iron weapon;
   a bronze arrow will strike him through.
25 It is drawn forth and comes out of his body,
   the glittering point comes out of his gall;
   terrors come upon him.
26 Utter darkness is laid up for his treasures;
   a fire not blown upon will devour him;
   what is left in his tent will be consumed.
27 The heavens will reveal his iniquity,
   and the earth will rise up against him.

28 The possessions of his house will be carried away,
   dragged off in the day of God's wrath.
29 This is the wicked man's portion from God,
   the heritage decreed for him by God."

21

Then Job answered:
2 "Listen carefully to my words,
and let this be your consolation.
3 Bear with me, and I will speak,
   and after I have spoken, mock on.
4 As for me, is my complaint against man?
   Why should I not be impatient?
5 Look at me, and be appalled,
   and lay your hand upon your mouth.
6 When I think of it I am dismayed,
   and shuddering seizes my flesh.
7 Why do the wicked live,
   reach old age, and grow mighty in power?
8 Their children are established in their presence,
   and their offspring before their eyes.
9 Their houses are safe from fear,
   and no rod of God is upon them.
10 Their bull breeds without fail;
   their cow calves, and does not cast her calf.
11 They send forth their little ones like a flock,
   and their children dance.
12 They sing to the tambourine and the lyre,
   and rejoice to the sound of the pipe.
13 They spend their days in prosperity,
   and in peace they go down to Sheol.
14 They say to God, 'Depart from us!
   We do not desire the knowledge of thy ways.
15 What is the Almighty, that we should serve him?
   And what profit do we get if we pray to him?
16 Behold, is not their prosperity in their hand?
   The counsel of the wicked is far from me.

17 "How often is it that the lamp of the wicked is put out?
   That their calamity comes upon them?
   That God distributes pains in his anger?
18 That they are like straw before the wind,
   and like chaff that the storm carries away?

19 You say, 'God stores up their iniquity for their sons.'
  Let him recompense it to themselves, that they may know it.
20 Let their own eyes see their destruction,
  and let them drink of the wrath of the Almighty.
21 For what do they care for their houses after them,
  when the number of their months is cut off?
22 Will any teach God knowledge,
  seeing that he judges those that are on high?
23 One dies in full prosperity,
  being wholly at ease and secure,
24 his body full of fat
  and the marrow of his bones moist.
25 Another dies in bitterness of soul,
  never having tasted of good.
26 They lie down alike in the dust,
  and the worms cover them.

27 "Behold, I know your thoughts,
  and your schemes to wrong me.
28 For you say, 'Where is the house of the prince?
  Where is the tent in which the wicked dwelt?'
29 Have you not asked those who travel the roads,
  and do you not accept their testimony
30 that the wicked man is spared in the day of calamity,
  that he is rescued in the day of wrath?
31 Who declares his way to his face,
  and who requites him for what he has done?
32 When he is borne to the grave,
  watch is kept over his tomb.
33 The clods of the valley are sweet to him;
  all men follow after him,
  and those who go before him are innumerable.
34 How then will you comfort me with empty nothings?
  There is nothing left of your answers but falsehood."

22 Then Eli'phaz the Te'manite answered:
  2 "Can a man be profitable to God?
  Surely he who is wise is profitable to himself.
3 Is it any pleasure to the Almighty if you are righteous,
  or is it gain to him if you make your ways blameless?
4 Is it for your fear of him that he reproves you,
  and enters into judgment with you?

5 Is not your wickedness great?
    There is no end to your iniquities.
6 For you have exacted pledges of your brothers for nothing,
    and stripped the naked of their clothing.
7 You have given no water to the weary to drink,
    and you have withheld bread from the hungry.
8 The man with power possessed the land,
    and the favored man dwelt in it.
9 You have sent widows away empty,
    and the arms of the fatherless were crushed.
10 Therefore snares are round about you,
    and sudden terror overwhelms you;
11 your light is darkened, so that you cannot see,
    and a flood of water covers you.

12 "Is not God high in the heavens?
    See the highest stars, how lofty they are!
13 Therefore you say, 'What does God know?
    Can he judge through the deep darkness?
14 Thick clouds enwrap him, so that he does not see,
    and he walks on the vault of heaven.'
15 Will you keep to the old way
    which wicked men have trod?
16 They were snatched away before their time;
    their foundation was washed away.
17 They said to God, 'Depart from us,
    and 'What can the Almighty do to us?'
18 Yet he filled their houses with good things—
    but the counsel of the wicked is far from me.
19 The righteous see it and are glad;
    the innocent laugh them to scorn,
20 saying, 'Surely our adversaries are cut off,
    and what they left the fire has consumed.'

21 "Agree with God, and be at peace;
    thereby good will come to you.
22 Receive instruction from his mouth,
    and lay up his words in your heart.
23 If you return to the Almighty and humble yourself,
    if you remove unrighteousness far from your tents,
24 if you lay gold in the dust,
    and gold of Ophir among the stones of the torrent bed,

25 and if the Almighty is your gold,
   and your precious silver;
26 then you will delight yourself in the Almighty,
   and lift up your face to God.
27 You will make your prayer to him, and he will hear you;
   and you will pay your vows.
28 You will decide on a matter, and it will be established for you,
   and light will shine on your ways.
29 For God abases the proud,
   but he saves the lowly.
30 He delivers the innocent man;

   you will be delivered through the cleanness of your hands."

23   Then Job answered:
   2 "Today also my complaint is bitter,
   his hand is heavy in spite of my groaning.
 3 Oh, that I knew where I might find him,
   that I might come even to his seat!
 4 I would lay my case before him
   and fill my mouth with arguments.
 5 I would learn what he would answer me,
   and understand what he would say to me.
 6 Would he contend with me in the greatness of his power?
   No; he would give heed to me.
 7 There an upright man could reason with him,
   and I should be acquitted for ever by my judge.

 8 "Behold, I go forward, but he is not there;
   and backward, but I cannot perceive him;
 9 on the left hand I seek him, but I cannot behold him;
   I turn to the right hand, but I cannot see him.
10 But he knows the way that I take;
   when he has tried me, I shall come forth as gold.
11 My foot has held fast to his steps;
   I have kept his way and have not turned aside.
12 I have not departed from the commandment of his lips;
   I have treasured in my bosom the words of his mouth.
13 But he is unchangeable and who can turn him?
   What he desires, that he does.
14 For he will complete what he appoints for me;
   and many such things are in his mind.

15 Therefore I am terrified at his presence;
   when I consider, I am in dread of him.
16 God has made my heart faint;
   the Almighty has terrified me;
17 for I am hemmed in by darkness,
   and thick darkness covers my face.

24

"Why are not times of judgment kept by the Almighty,
and why do those who know him never see his days?
2 Men remove landmarks;
   they seize flocks and pasture them.
3 They drive away the ass of the fatherless;
   they take the widow's ox for a pledge.
4 They thrust the poor off the road;
   the poor of the earth all hide themselves.
5 Behold, like wild asses in the desert
      they go forth to their toil,
   seeking prey in the wilderness
      as food for their children.
6 They gather their fodder in the field
   and they glean the vineyard of the wicked man.
7 They lie all night naked, without clothing,
   and have no covering in the cold.
8 They are wet with the rain of the mountains,
   and cling to the rock for want of shelter.
9 (There are those who snatch the fatherless child from the breast,
   and take in pledge the infant of the poor.)
10 They go about naked, without clothing;
   hungry, they carry the sheaves;
11 among the olive rows of the wicked they make oil;
   they tread the wine presses, but suffer thirst.
12 From out of the city the dying groan,
      and the soul of the wounded cries for help;
   yet God pays no attention to their prayer.

13 There are those who rebel against the light,
      who are not acquainted with its ways,
      and do not stay in its paths.
14 The murderer rises in the dark,
      that he may kill the poor and the needy;
      and in the night he is as a thief.

15 The eye of the adulterer also waits for the twilight,
    saying, 'No eye will see me';
    and he disguises his face.
16 In the dark they dig through houses;
    by day they shut themselves up;
    they do not know the light.
17 For deep darkness is morning to all of them;
    for they are friends with the terrors of deep darkness.

18 "You say, 'They are swiftly carried away upon the face of the
       waters;
    their portion is cursed in the land;
    no treader turns toward their vineyards.
19 Drought and heat snatch away the snow waters;
    so does Sheol those who have sinned.
20 The squares of the town forget them;
    their name is no longer remembered;
    so wickedness is broken like a tree.'

21 "They feed on the barren childless woman,
    and do no good to the widow.
22 Yet God prolongs the life of the mighty by his power;
    they rise up when they despair of life.
23 He gives them security, and they are supported;
    and his eyes are upon their ways.
24 They are exalted a little while, and then are gone;
    they wither and fade like the mallow;
    they are cut off like the heads of grain.
25 If it is not so, who will prove me a liar,
    and show that there is nothing in what I say?"

25 Then Bildad the Shuhite answered:
  2 "Dominion and fear are with God;
  3 Is there any number to his armies?
    Upon whom does his light not arise?
  4 How then can man be righteous before God?
    How can he who is born of woman be clean?
  5 Behold, even the moon is not bright
    and the stars are not clean in his sight;
  6 how much less man, who is a maggot,
    and the son of man, who is a worm!"

26   Then Job answered:
           2 "How you have helped him who has no power!
How you have saved the arm that has no strength!
3 How you have counseled him who has no wisdom,
     and plentifully declared sound knowledge!
4 With whose help have you uttered words,
     and whose spirit has come forth from you?
5 The shades below tremble,
     the waters and their inhabitants.
6 Sheol is naked before God,
     and Abaddon has no covering.
7 He stretches out the north over the void,
     and hangs the earth upon nothing.
8 He binds up the waters in his thick clouds,
     and the cloud is not rent under them.
9 He covers the face of the moon,
     and spreads over it his cloud.
10 He has described a circle upon the face of the waters
     at the boundary between light and darkness.
11 The pillars of heaven tremble,
     and are astounded at his rebuke.
12 By his power he stilled the sea;
     by his understanding he smote Rahab.
13 By his wind the heavens were made fair;
     his hand pierced the fleeing serpent.
14 Lo, these are but the outskirts of his ways;
     and how small a whisper do we hear of him!
But the thunder of his power who can understand?"

27   And Job again took up his discourse, and said:
           2 "As God lives, who has taken away my right,
and the Almighty, who has made my soul bitter;
3 as long as my breath is in me,
     and the spirit of God is in my nostrils;
4 my lips will not speak falsehood,
     and my tongue will not utter deceit.
5 Far be it from me to say that you are right;
     till I die I will not put away my integrity from me.
6 I hold fast my righteousness, and will not let it go;
     my heart does not reproach me for any of my days.

7 "Let my enemy be as the wicked,
  and let him that rises up against me be as the unrighteous.
8 For what is the hope of the godless when God cuts him off,
  when God takes away his life?
9 Will God hear his cry,
  when trouble comes upon him?
10 Will he take delight in the Almighty?
  Will he call upon God at all times?
11 I will teach you concerning the hand of God;
  what is with the Almighty I will not conceal.
12 Behold, all of you have seen it yourselves;
  why then have you become altogether vain?

13 "This is the portion of a wicked man with God,
  and the heritage which oppressors receive from the Almighty;
14 If his children are multiplied, it is for the sword;
  and the offspring have not enough to eat.
15 Those who survive him the pestilence buries,
  and their widows make no lamentation.
16 Though he heap up silver like dust,
  and pile up clothing like clay;
17 he may pile it up, but the just will wear it,
  and the innocent will divide the silver.
18 The house which he builds is like a spider's web,
  like a booth which a watchman makes.
19 He goes to bed rich, but will do so no more;
  he opens his eyes, and his wealth is gone.
20 Terrors overtake him like a flood;
  in the night a whirlwind carries him off.
21 The east wind lifts him up and he is gone;
  it sweeps him out of his place.
22 It hurls at him without pity;
  he flees from its power in headlong flight.
23 It claps its hands at him,
  and hisses at him from its place.

28 "Surely there is a mine for silver,
  and a place for gold which they refine.
2 Iron is taken out of the earth,
  and copper is smelted from the ore.
3 Men put an end to darkness,

and search out to the farthest bound
the ore in gloom and deep darkness.
4 They open shafts in a valley away from where men live;
they are forgotten by travelers,
they hang afar from men, they swing to and fro.
5 As for the earth, out of it comes bread;
but underneath it is turned up as by fire.
6 Its stones are the place of sapphires,
and it has dust of gold.

7 "That path no bird of prey knows,
and the falcon's eye has not seen it.
8 The proud beasts have not trodden it;
the lion has not passed over it.

9 "Man puts his hand to the flinty rock,
and overturns mountains by the roots.
10 He cuts out channels in the rocks,
and his eye sees every precious thing.
11 He binds up the streams so that they do not trickle,
and the thing that is hid he brings forth to light.

12 "But where shall wisdom be found?
And where is the place of understanding?
13 Man does not know the way to it,
and it is not found in the land of the living.
14 The deep says, 'It is not in me,'
and the sea says, 'It is not with me.'
15 It cannot be gotten for gold,
and silver cannot be weighed as its price.
16 It cannot be valued in the gold of Ophir,
in precious onyx or sapphire.
17 Gold and glass cannot equal it,
nor can it be exchanged for jewels of fine gold.
18 No mention shall be made of coral or of crystal;
the price of wisdom is above pearls.
19 The topaz of Ethiopia cannot compare with it,
nor can it be valued in pure gold.

20 "Whence then comes wisdom?
And where is the place of understanding?

21 It is hid from the eyes of all living,
   and concealed from the birds of the air.
22 Abaddon and Death say,
   'We have heard a rumor of it with our ears.'

23 "God understands the way to it,
   and he knows its place.
24 For he looks to the ends of the earth,
   and sees everything under the heavens.
25 When he gave to the wind its weight,
   and meted out the waters by measure;
26 when he made a decree for the rain,
   and a way for the lightning of the thunder;
27 then he saw it and declared it;
   he established it, and searched it out.
28 And he said to man,
   "Behold, the fear of the Lord, that is wisdom;
   and to depart from evil is understanding.'"

29 And Job again took up his discourse, and said:
   2 "Oh, that I were as in the months of old,
   as in the days when God watched over me;
3 when his lamp shone upon my head,
   and by his light I walked through darkness;
4 as I was in my autumn days,
   when the friendship of God was upon my tent;
5 when the Almighty was yet with me,
   when my children were about me;
6 when my steps were washed with milk,
   and the rock poured out for me streams of oil!
7 When I went out to the gate of the city,
   when I prepared my seat in the square,
8 the young men saw me and withdrew,
   and the aged rose and stood;
9 the princes refrained from talking,
   and laid their hand on their mouth;
10 the voice of the nobles was hushed,
   and their tongue cleaved to the roof of their mouth.
11 When the ear heard, it called me blessed,
   and when the eye saw, it approved;
12 because I delivered the poor who cried,
   and the fatherless who had none to help him.

13 The blessing of him who was about to perish came upon me,
   and I caused the widow's heart to sing for joy.
14 I put on righteousness, and it clothed me;
   my justice was like a robe and a turban.
15 I was eyes to the blind,
   and feet to the lame.
16 I was a father to the poor,
   and I searched out the cause of him whom I did not know.
17 I broke the fangs of the unrighteous,
   and made him drop his prey from his teeth.
18 Then I thought, 'I shall die in my nest,
   and I shall multiply my days as the sand,
19 My roots spread out to the waters,
   with the dew all night on my branches,
20 my glory fresh with me,
   and my bow ever new in my hand.'

21 "Men listened to me, and waited,
   and kept silence for my counsel.
22 After I spoke they did not speak again,
   and my word dropped upon them.
23 They waited for me as for the rain;
   and they opened their mouths as for the spring rain.
24 I smiled on them when they had no confidence;
   and the light of my countenance they did not cast down.
25 I chose their way, and sat as chief,
   and I dwelt like a king among his troops.
   like one who comforts mourners.

30 "But now they make sport of me,
   men who are younger than I,
   whose fathers I would have disdained
   to set with the dogs of my flock.
2 What could I gain from the strength of their hands,
   men whose vigor is gone?
3 Through want and hard hunger
   they gnaw the dry and desolate ground;
4 they pick mallow and the leaves of bushes,
   and to warm themselves the roots of the broom.
5 They are driven out from among men;
   they shout after them as after a thief.

6 In the gullies of the torrents they must dwell,
  in the holes of the earth and of the rocks.
7 Among the bushes they bray;
  under the nettles they huddle together.
8 A senseless, a disreputable brood,
  they have been whipped out of the land.

9 "And now I have become their song,
  I am a byword to them.
10 They abhor me, they keep aloof from me;
  they do not hesitate to spit at the sight of me.
11 Because God has loosed my cord and humbled me,
  they have cast off restraint in my presence.
12 On my right hand the rabble rise,
  they drive me forth,
  they cast up against me their ways of destruction.
13 They break up my path,
  they promote my calamity;
  no one restrains them.
14 As through a wide breach they come;
  amid the crash they roll on.
15 Terrors are turned upon me;
  my honor is pursued as by the wind,
  and my prosperity has passed away like a cloud.

16 "And now my soul is poured out within me;
  days of affliction have taken hold of me.
17 The night racks my bones,
  and the pain that gnaws me takes no rest.
18 With violence it seizes my garment;
  it binds me about like the collar of my tunic.
19 God has cast me into the mire,
  and I have become like dust and ashes.
20 I cry to thee and thou dost not answer me;
  I stand, and thou dost not heed me.
21 Thou hast turned cruel to me;
  with the might of thy hand thou dost persecute me.
22 Thou liftest me up on the wind, thou makest me ride on it,
  and thou tossest me about in the roar of the storm.
23 Yea, I know that thou wilt bring me to death,
  and to the house appointed for all living.

24 "Yet does not one in a heap of ruins stretch out his hand,
   and in his disaster cry for help?
25 Did not I weep for him whose day was hard?
   Was not my soul grieved for the poor?
26 But when I looked for good, evil came;
   and when I waited for light, darkness came.
27 My heart is in turmoil, and is never still;
   days of affliction come to meet me.
28 I go about blackened, but not by the sun;
   I stand up in the assembly, and cry for help.
29 I am a brother of jackals,
   and a companion of ostriches.
30 My skin turns black and falls from me,
   and my bones burn with heat.
31 My lyre is turned to mourning,
   and my pipe to the voices of those who weep.

31 "I have made a covenant with my eyes;
   how then could I look upon a virgin?
2 What would be my portion from God above,
   and my heritage from the Almighty on high?
3 Does not calamity befall the unrighteous,
   and disaster the workers of iniquity?
4 Does not he see my ways,
   and number all my steps?

5 "If I have walked with falsehood,
   and my foot has hastened to deceit;
6 (Let me be weighed in a just balance,
   and let God know my integrity!)
7 if my step has turned aside from the way,
   and my heart has gone after my eyes,
   and if any spot has cleaved to my hands;
8 then let me sow, and another eat;
   and let what grows for me be rooted out.

9 "If my heart has been enticed to a woman,
   and I have lain in wait at my neighbor's door;
10 then let my wife grind for another,
   and let others bow down upon her.
11 For that would be a heinous crime;
   that would be an iniquity to be punished by the judges;

12 for that would be a fire which consumes unto Abaddon,
and it would burn to the root all my increase.

13 "If I have rejected the cause of my manservant or my maidservant,
when they brought a complaint against me;
14 what then shall I do when God rises up?
When he makes inquiry, what shall I answer him?
15 Did not he who made me in the womb make him?
And did not one fashion us in the womb?

16 "If I have withheld anything that the poor desired,
or have caused the eyes of the widow to fail,
17 or have eaten my morsel alone,
and the fatherless has not eaten of it
18 (for from his youth I reared him as a father,
and from his mother's womb I guided him);
19 if I have seen any one perish for lack of clothing,
or a poor man without covering;
20 if his loins have not blessed me,
and if he was not warmed with the fleece of my sheep;
21 if I have raised my hand against the fatherless,
because I saw help in the gate;
22 then let my shoulder blade fall from my shoulder,
and let my arm be broken from its socket.
23 For I was in terror of calamity from God,
and I could not have faced his majesty.

24 "If I have made gold my trust,
or called fine gold my confidence;
25 if I have rejoiced because my wealth was great,
or because my hand had gotten much;
26 if I have looked at the sun when it shone,
or the moon moving in splendor,
27 and my heart has been secretly enticed,
and my mouth has kissed my hand;
28 this also would be an iniquity to be punished by the judges,
for I should have been false to God above.

29 "If I have rejoiced at the ruin of him that hated me,
or exulted when evil overtook him
30 (I have not let my mouth sin
by asking for his life with a curse);

31 if the men of my tent have not said,
'Who is there that has not been filled with his meat?'
32 (the sojourner has not lodged in the street;
I have opened my doors to the wayfarer);
33 if I have concealed my transgressions from men,
by hiding my iniquity in my bosom,
34 because I stood in great fear of the multitude,
and the contempt of families terrified me,
so that I kept silence, and did not go out of doors—
35 Oh, that I had one to hear me!
(Here is my signature! let the Almighty answer me!)
Oh, that I had the indictment written by my adversary!
36 Surely I would carry it on my shoulder;
I would bind it on me as a crown;
37 I would give him an account of all my steps;
like a prince I would approach him.
38 "If my land has cried out against me,
and its furrows have wept together;
39 if I have eaten its yield without payment,
and caused the death of its owners;
40 let thorns grow instead of wheat, and foul weeds instead of barley."

The words of Job are ended.

32 So these three men ceased to answer Job, because he was righteous in his own eyes. *2* Then Eli'hu son of Bar'achel the Buzite, of the family of Ram, became angry. He was angry at Job because he justified himself rather than God; *3* he was angry also at Job's three friends because they had found no answer, although they had declared Job to be in the wrong. *4* Now Eli'hu had waited to speak to Job because they were older than he. *5* And when Eli'hu saw that there was no answer in the mouth of these three men, he became angry.

6 And Eli'hu the son of Bar'achel the Buzite answered:
"I am young in years,
and you are aged;
therefore I was timid and afraid
to declare my opinion to you.
7 I said, 'Let days speak,
and many years teach wisdom.'
8 But it is the spirit in a man,
the breath of the Almighty,
that makes him understand.

9 It is not the old that are wise,
   nor the aged that understand what is right.
10 Therefore I say, 'Listen to me;
   let me also declare my opinion.'

11 "Behold, I waited for your words,
   I listened for your wise sayings,
   while you searched out what to say.
12 I gave you my attention,
   and, behold, there was none that confuted Job,
   or that answered his words, among you.
13 Beware lest you say, 'We have found wisdom;
   God may vanquish him, not man.'
14 He has not directed his words against me,
   and I will not answer him with your speeches.

15 "They are discomfited, they answer no more;
   they have not a word to say.
16 And shall I wait, because they do not speak,
   because they stand there, and answer no more?
17 I also will give my answer;
   I also will declare my opinion.
18 For I am full of words,
   the spirit within me constrains me.
19 Behold, my heart is like wine that has no vent;
   like new wineskins, it is ready to burst.
20 I must speak, that I may find relief;
   I must open my lips and answer.
21 I will not show partiality to any person
   or use flattery toward any man.
22 For I do not know how to flatter,
   else would my Maker soon put an end to me.

33 "But now, hear my speech, O Job,
   and listen to all my words.
2 Behold, I open my mouth;
   the tongue in my mouth speaks.
3 My words declare the uprightness of my heart,
   and what my lips know they speak sincerely.
4 The spirit of God has made me,
   and the breath of the Almighty gives me life.

5 Answer me, if you can;
  set your words in order before me; take your stand.
6 Behold, I am toward God as you are;
  I too was formed from a piece of clay.
7 Behold, no fear of me need terrify you;
  my pressure will not be heavy upon you.

8 "Surely, you have spoken in my hearing;
  and I have heard the sound of your words.
9 You say, 'I am clean, without transgression;
  I am pure, and there is no iniquity in me.
10 Behold, he finds occasions against me,
   he counts me as his enemy;
11 he puts my feet in the stocks,
   and watches all my paths.'

12 "Behold, in this you are not right. I will answer you.
   God is greater than man.
13 Why do you contend against him,
   saying, 'He will answer none of my words'?
14 For God speaks in one way,
   and in two, though man does not perceive it.
15 In a dream, in a vision of the night,
   when deep sleep falls upon men,
   while they slumber on their beds,
16 then he opens the ears of men,
   and terrifies them with warnings,
17 that he may turn man aside from his deed,
   and cut off pride from man;
18 he keeps back his soul from the Pit,
   his life from perishing by the sword.

19 "Man is also chastened with pain upon his bed,
   and with continual strife in his bones;
20 so that his life loathes bread,
   and his appetite dainty food.
21 His flesh is so wasted away that it cannot be seen;
   and his bones which were not seen stick out.
22 His soul draws near the Pit,
   and his life to those who bring death.
23 If there be for him an angel,
   a mediator, one of the thousand,
   to declare to man what is right for him;

24 and he is gracious to him, and says,
    'Deliver him from going down into the Pit,
    I have found a ransom;
25 let his flesh become fresh with youth;
    let him return to the days of his youthful vigor';
26 then man prays to God, and he accepts him,
    he comes into his presence with joy.
  He recounts to men his salvation,
27   and he sings before men and says:
  'I sinned, and perverted what was right,
    and it was not requited to me.
28 He has redeemed my soul from going down into the Pit,
    and my life shall see the light.'

29 "Behold, God does all these things,
    twice, three times, with a man,
30 to bring back his soul from the Pit,
    that he may see the light of life.
31 Give heed, O Job, listen to me;
    be silent, and I will speak.
32 If you have anything to say, answer me;
    speak, for I desire to justify you.
33 If not, listen to me;
    be silent, and I will teach you wisdom."

34

Then Eli'hu said:
2 "Hear my words, you wise men,
    and give ear to me, you who know;
3 for the ear tests words
    as the palate tastes food.
4 Let us choose what is right;
    let us determine among ourselves what is good.
5 For Job has said, 'I am innocent,
    and God has taken away my right;
6 in spite of my right I am counted a liar;
    my wound is incurable, though I am without transgression.'
7 What man is like Job,
    who drinks up scoffing like water,
8 who goes in company with evildoers
    and walks with wicked men?
9 For he has said, 'It profits a man nothing
    that he should take delight in God.'

10 "Therefore, hear me, you men of understanding,
      far be it from God that he should do wickedness,
      and from the Almighty that he should do wrong.
11 For according to the work of a man he will requite him,
      and according to his ways he will make it befall him.
12 Of a truth, God will not do wickedly,
      and the Almighty will not pervert justice.
13 Who gave him charge over the earth
      and who laid on him the whole world?
14 If he should take back his spirit to himself,
      and gather to himself his breath,
15 all flesh would perish together,
         and man would return to dust.

16 "If you have understanding, hear this;
      listen to what I say.
17 Shall one who hates justice govern?
      Will you condemn him who is righteous and mighty,
18 who says to a king, 'Worthless one,'
      and to nobles, 'Wicked man';
19 who shows no partiality to princes,
      nor regards the rich more than the poor,
      for they are all the work of his hands?
20 In a moment they die;
      at midnight the people are shaken and pass away,
      and the mighty are taken away by no human hand.

21 "For his eyes are upon the ways of a man,
      and he sees all his steps.
22 There is no gloom or deep darkness
      where evildoers may hide themselves.
23 For he has not appointed a time for any man
      to go before God in judgment.
24 He shatters the mighty without investigation,
      and sets others in their place.
25 Thus, knowing their works,
      he overturns them in the night,
         and they are crushed.
26 He strikes them for their wickedness
      in the sight of men,
27 because they turned aside from following him,
      and had no regard for any of his ways,

28 so that they caused the cry of the poor to come to him,
    and he heard the cry of the afflicted—
29 When he is quiet, who can condemn?
    When he hides his face, who can behold him,
    whether it be a nation or a man?—
30 that a godless man should not reign,
    that he should not ensnare the people.

31 "For has any one said to God,
    'I have borne chastisement; I will not offend any more;
32 teach me what I do not see:
    if I have done iniquity, I will do it no more'?
33 Will he then make requital to suit you,
    because you reject it?
  For you must choose, and not I;
    therefore declare what you know.
34 Men of understanding will say to me,
    and the wise man who hears me will say:
35 'Job speaks without knowledge,
    his words are without insight.'
36 Would that Job were tried to the end,
    because he answers like wicked men.
37 For he adds rebellion to his sin;
    he claps his hands among us,
    and multiplies his words against God."

35   And Eli'hu said:
2 "Do you think this to be just?
  Do you say, 'It is my right before God,'
3 that you ask, 'What advantage have I?
    How am I better off than if I had sinned?'
4 I will answer you
    and your friends with you.
5 Look at the heavens, and see;
    and behold the clouds, which are higher than you.
6 If you have sinned, what do you accomplish against him?
    And if your transgressions are multiplied, what do you do to
      him?
7 If you are righteous, what do you give to him;
    or what does he receive from your hand?
8 Your wickedness concerns a man like yourself,
    and your righteousness a son of man.

9 "Because of the multitude of oppressions people cry out;
    they call for help because of the arm of the mighty.
10 But none says, 'Where is God my Maker,
    who gives songs in the night,
11 who teaches us more than the beasts of the earth,
    and makes us wiser than the birds of the air?'
12 There they cry out, but he does not answer,
    because of the pride of evil men.
13 Surely God does not hear an empty cry,
    nor does the Almighty regard it.
14 How much less when you say that you do not see him,
    that the case is before him, and you are waiting for him!
15 And now, because his anger does not punish,
    and he does not greatly heed transgression,
16 Job opens his mouth in empty talk,
    he multiplies words without knowledge."

36

And Eli'hu continued, and said:
2 "Bear with me a little, and I will show you,
    for I have yet something to say on God's behalf.
3 I will fetch my knowledge from afar,
    and ascribe righteousness to my Maker.
4 For truly my words are not false;
    one who is perfect in knowledge is with you.

5 "Behold, God is mighty, and does not despise any;
    he is mighty in strength of understanding.
6 He does not keep the wicked alive;
    but gives the afflicted their right.
7 He does not withdraw his eyes from the righteous,
    but with kings upon the throne
    he sets them for ever, and they are exalted.
8 And if they are bound in fetters
    and caught in the cords of affliction,
9 then he declares to them their work
    and their transgressions, that they are behaving arrogantly.
10 He opens their ears to instruction,
    and commands that they return from iniquity.
11 If they hearken and serve him,
    they complete their days in prosperity,
    and their years in pleasantness.

12 But if they do not hearken, they perish by the sword,
and die without knowledge.

13 "The godless in heart cherish anger;
they do not cry for help when he binds them.
14 They die in youth,
and their life ends in shame.
15 He delivers the afflicted by their affliction,
and opens their ear by adversity.
16 He also allured you out of distress
into a broad place where there was no cramping,
and what was set on your table was full of fatness.

17 "But you are full of the judgment on the wicked;
judgment and justice seize you.
18 Beware lest wrath entice you into scoffing;
and let not the greatness of the ransom turn you aside.
19 Will your cry avail to keep you from distress,
or all the force of your strength?
20 Do not long for the night,
when peoples are cut off in their place.
21 Take heed, do not turn to iniquity,
for this you have chosen rather than affliction.
22 Behold, God is exalted in his power;
who is a teacher like him?
23 Who has prescribed for him his way,
or who can say, 'Thou hast done wrong'?

24 "Remember to extol his work,
of which men have sung.
25 All men have looked on it;
man beholds it from afar.
26 Behold, God is great, and we know him not;
the number of his years is unsearchable.
27 For he draws up the drops of water,
he distils his mist in rain
28 which the skies pour down,
and drop upon man abundantly.
29 Can any one understand the spreading of the clouds,
the thunderings of his pavilion?
30 Behold, he scatters his lightning about him,
and covers the roots of the sea.

31 For by these he judges peoples;
    he gives food in abundance.
32 He covers his hands with the lightning,
    and commands it to strike the mark.
33 Its crashing declares concerning him,
    who is jealous with anger against iniquity.

37

    "At this also my heart trembles,
    and leaps out of its place.
2 Hearken to the thunder of his voice
    and the rumbling that comes from his mouth.
3 Under the whole heaven he lets it go,
    and his lightning to the corners of the earth.
4 After it his voice roars;
    he thunders with his majestic voice
    and he does not restrain the lightnings when his voice is heard.
5 God thunders wondrously with his voice;
    he does great things which we cannot comprehend.
6 For to the snow he says, 'Fall on the earth';
    and to the shower and the rain, 'Be strong.'
7 He seals up the hand of every man,
    that all men may know his work.
8 Then the beasts go into their lairs,
    and remain in their dens.
9 From its chamber comes the whirlwind,
    and cold from the scattering winds.
10 By the breath of God ice is given,
    and the broad waters are frozen fast.
11 He loads the thick cloud with moisture;
    the clouds scatter his lightning.
12 They turn round and round by his guidance,
    to accomplish all that he commands them
    on the face of the habitable world.
13 Whether for correction, or for his land,
    or for love, he causes it to happen.

14 "Hear this, O Job;
    stop and consider the wondrous works of God.
15 Do you know how God lays his command upon them,
    and causes the lightning of his cloud to shine?
16 Do you know the balancings of the clouds,
    the wondrous works of him who is perfect in knowledge,

17 you whose garments are hot
   when the earth is still because of the south wind?
18 Can you, like him, spread out the skies,
   hard as a molten mirror?
19 Teach us what we shall say to him;
   we cannot draw up our case because of darkness.
20 Shall it be told him that I would speak?
   Did a man ever wish that he would be swallowed up?

21 "And now men cannot look on the light
   when it is bright in the skies,
   when the wind has passed and cleared them.
22 Out of the north comes golden splendor;
   God is clothed with terrible majesty.
23 The Almighty—we cannot find him;
   he is great in power and justice,
   and abundant righteousness he will not violate.
24 Therefore men fear him;
   he does not regard any who are wise in their own conceit."

38
Then the LORD answered Job out of the whirlwind:
2 "Who is this that darkens counsel by words without knowledge?
3 Gird up your loins like a man,
   I will question you, and you shall declare to me.

4 "Where were you when I laid the foundation of the earth?
   Tell me, if you have understanding.
5 Who determined its measurements—surely you know!
   Or who stretched the line upon it?
6 On what were its bases sunk,
   or who laid its cornerstone,
7 when the morning stars sang together,
   and all the sons of God shouted for joy?

8 "Or who shut in the sea with doors,
   when it burst forth from the womb;
9 when I made clouds its garment,
   and thick darkness its swaddling band,
10 and prescribed bounds for it,
   and set bars and doors,
11 and said, 'Thus far shall you come, and no further,
   and here shall your proud waves be stayed'?

12 "Have you commanded the morning since your days began,
    and caused the dawn to know its place,
13 that it might take hold of the skirts of the earth,
    and the wicked be shaken out of it?
14 It is changed like clay under the seal,
    and it is dyed like a garment.
15 From the wicked their light is withheld,
    and their uplifted arm is broken.

16 "Have you entered into the springs of the sea,
    or walked in the recesses of the deep?
17 Have the gates of death been revealed to you,
    or have you seen the gates of deep darkness?
18 Have you comprehended the expanse of the earth?
    Declare, if you know all this.

19 "Where is the way to the dwelling of light,
    and where is the place of darkness,
20 that you make take to its territory
    and that you may discern the paths to its home?
21 You know, for you were born then,
    and the number of your days is great!

22 "Have you entered the storehouses of the snow,
    or have you seen the storehouses of the hail,
23 which I have reserved for the time of trouble,
    for the day of battle and war?
24 What is the way to the place where the light is distributed,
    or where the east wind is scattered upon the earth?

25 "Who has cleft a channel for the torrents of rain,
    and a way for the thunderbolt,
26 to bring rain on a land where no man is,
    on the desert in which there is no man;
27 to satisfy the waste and desolate land,
    and to make the ground put forth grass?

28 "Has the rain a father,
    or who has begotten the drops of dew?
29 From whose womb did the ice come forth,
    and who has given birth to the hoarfrost of heaven?
30 The waters become hard like stone,
    and the face of the deep is frozen.

31 "Can you bind the chains of the Pleiades,
     or loose the cords of Orion?
32 Can you lead forth the Maz'zaroth in their season,
     or can you guide the Bear with its children?
33 Do you know the ordinances of the heavens?
     Can you establish their rule on the earth?

34 "Can you lift up your voice to the clouds,
     that a flood of waters may cover you?
35 Can you send forth lightnings, that they may go
     and say to you, 'Here we are'?
36 Who has put wisdom in the clouds,
     or given understanding to the mists?
37 Who can number the clouds by wisdom?
     Or who can tilt the waterskins of the heavens,
38 when the dust runs into a mass
     and the clods cleave fast together?

39 "Can you hunt the prey for the lion,
     or satisfy the appetite of the young lions,
40 when they crouch in their dens,
     or lie in wait in their covert?
41 Who provides for the raven its prey,
     when its young ones cry to God,
     and wander about for lack of food?

39   "Do you know when the mountain goats bring forth?
          Do you observe the calving of the hinds?
2 Can you number the months that they fulfil,
     and do you know the time when they bring forth,
3 when they crouch, bring forth their offspring,
     and are delivered of their young?
4 Their young ones become strong, they grow up in the open;
     they go forth, and do not return to them.

5 "Who has let the wild ass go free?
     Who has loosed the bonds of the swift ass.
6 to whom I have given the steppe for his home,
     and the salt land for his dwelling place?
7 He scorns the tumult of the city;
     he hears not the shouts of the driver.
8 He ranges the mountains as his pasture,
     and he searches after every green thing.

9 "Is the wild ox willing to serve you?
    Will he spend the night at your crib?
10 Can you bind him in the furrow with ropes,
    or will he harrow the valleys after you?
11 Will you depend on him because his strength is great,
    and will you leave to him your labor?
12 Do you have faith in him that he will return,
    and bring your grain to your threshing floor?

13 "The wings of the ostrich wave proudly;
    but are they the pinions and plumage of love?
14 For she leaves her eggs to the earth,
    and lets them be warmed on the ground,
15 forgetting that a foot may crush them,
    and that the wild beast may trample them.
16 She deals cruelly with her young, as if they were not hers;
    though her labor be in vain, yet she has no fear;
17 because God has made her forget wisdom,
    and given her no share in understanding.
18 When she rouses herself to flee,
    she laughs at the horse and his rider.

19 "Do you give the horse his might?
    Do you clothe his neck with strength?
20 Do you make him leap like the locust?
    His majestic snorting is terrible.
21 He paws in the valley, and exults in his strength;
    he goes out to meet the weapons.
22 He laughs at fear, and is not dismayed;
    he does not turn back from the sword.
23 Upon him rattle the quiver,
    the flashing spear and the javelin.
24 With fierceness and rage he swallows the ground;
    he cannot stand still at the sound of the trumpet.
25 When the trumpet sounds, he says 'Aha!'
    He smells the battle from afar,
    the thunder of the captains, and the shouting.

26 "Is it by your wisdom that the hawk soars,
    and spreads his wings toward the south?
27 Is it at your command that the eagle mounts up
    and makes his nest on high?

28 On the rock he dwells and makes his home
   in the fastness of the rocky crag.
29 Thence he spies out the prey;
   his eyes behold it afar off.
30 His young ones suck up blood;
   and where the slain are, there is he."

40

And the LORD said to Job:
2 "Shall a faultfinder contend with the Almighty?
He who argues with God, let him answer it."

3 Then Job answered the LORD:
4 "Behold, I am of small account;
   what shall I answer thee?
   I lay my hand on my mouth.
5 I have spoken once, and I will not answer;
   twice, but I will proceed no further."

6 Then the LORD answered Job out of the whirlwind:
7 "Gird up your loins like a man;
   I will question you, and you declare to me.
8 Will you even put me in the wrong?
   Will you condemn me that you may be justified?
9 Have you an arm like God,
   and can you thunder with a voice like his?

10 "Deck yourself with majesty and dignity;
   clothe yourself with glory and splendor.
11 Pour forth the overflowings of your anger,
   and look on every one that is proud, and abase him.
12 Look on every one that is proud, and bring him low;
   and tread down the wicked where they stand.
13 Hide them all in the dust together;
   bind their faces in the world below.
14 Then will I also acknowledge to you,
   that your own right hand can give you victory.

15 'Behold, Be'hemoth,
   which I made as I made you;
   he eats grass like an ox.
16 Behold, his strength in his loins,
   and his power in the muscles of his belly.

17 He makes his tail stiff like a cedar;
   the sinews of his thighs are knit together.
18 His bones are tubes of bronze,
   his limbs like bars of iron.

19 "He is the first of the works of God;
   let him who made him bring near his sword!
20 For the mountains yield food for him
   where all the wild beasts play.
21 Under the lotus plants he lies,
   in the covert of the reeds and in the marsh.
22 For his shade the lotus trees cover him;
   the willows of the brook surround him.
23 Behold, if the river is turbulent he is not frightened;
   he is confident though Jordan rushes against his mouth.
24 Can one take him with hooks,
   or pierce his nose with a snare?

41 "Can you draw out Leviathan with a fishhook,
   or press down his tongue with a cord?
2 Can you put a rope in his nose,
   or pierce his jaw with a hook?
3 Will he make many supplications to you?
   Will he speak to you soft words?
4 Will he make a covenant with you
   to take him for your servant for ever?
5 Will you play with him as with a bird,
   or will you put him on leash for your maidens?
6 Will traders bargain over him?
   Will they divide him up among the merchants?
7 Can you fill his skin with harpoons,
   or his head with fishing spears?
8 Lay hands on him;
   think of the battle; you will not do it again!
9 Behold, the hope of a man is disappointed;
   he is laid low even at the sight of him.
10 No one is so fierce that he dares to stir him up.
   Who then is he that can stand before me?
11 Who has given to me, that I should repay him?
   Whatever is under the whole heaven is mine.

12 "I will not keep silence concerning his limbs,
   or his mighty strength, or his goodly frame.

13 Who can strip off his outer garment?
  who can penetrate his double coat of mail?
14 Who can open the doors of his face?
  Round about his teeth is terror.
15 His back is made of rows of shields,
  shut up closely as with a seal.
16 One is so near to another
  that no air can come between them.
17 They are joined one to another;
  they clasp each other and cannot be separated.
18 His sneezings flash forth light,
  and his eyes are like the eyelids of the dawn.
19 Out of his mouth go flaming torches;
  sparks of fire leap forth.
20 Out of his nostrils comes forth smoke,
  as from a boiling pot and burning rushes.
21 His breath kindles coals,
  and a flame comes forth from his mouth.
22 In his neck abides strength,
  and terror dances before him.
23 The folds of his flesh cleave together,
  firmly cast upon him and immovable.
24 His heart is hard as a stone,
  hard as the nether millstone.
25 When he raises himself up the mighty are afraid;
  at the crashing they are beside themselves.
26 Though the sword reaches him, it does not avail;
  nor the spear, the dart, or the javelin.
27 He counts iron as straw,
  and bronze as rotten wood.
28 The arrow cannot make him flee;
  for him slingstones are turned to stubble.
29 Clubs are counted as stubble;
  he laughs at the rattle of javelins.
30 His underparts are like sharp potsherds;
  he spreads himself like a threshing sledge on the mire.
31 He makes the deep boil like a pot;
  he makes the sea like a pot of ointment.
32 Behind him he leaves a shining wake;
  one would think the deep to be hoary.
33 Upon earth there is not his like,
  a creature without fear.

34 He beholds everything that is high;
   he is king over all the sons of pride."

42

Then Job answered the Lord:
2 "I know that thou canst do all things,
   and that no purpose of thine can be thwarted.
3 'Who is this that hides counsel without knowledge?'
   Therefore I have uttered what I did not understand,
   things too wonderful for me, which I did not know.
4 'Hear, and I will speak;
   I will question you, and you declare to me.'
5 I had heard of thee by the hearing of the ear,
   but now my eye sees thee;
6 therefore I despise myself,
   and repent in dust and ashes."

7 After the Lord had spoken these words to Job, the Lord said to Eli'phaz the Te'manite: "My wrath is kindled against you and against your two friends; for you have not spoken of me what is right, as my servant Job has. *8* Now therefore take seven bulls and seven rams, and go to my servant Job, and offer up for yourselves a burnt offering; and my servant Job shall pray for you, for I will accept his prayer not to deal with you according to your folly; for you have not spoken of me what is right, as my servant Job has." *9* So Eli'phaz the Te'manite and Bildad the Shuhite and Zophar the Na'amathite went and did what the Lord had told them; and the Lord accepted Job's prayer.

10 And the Lord restored the fortunes of Job, when he had prayed for his friends; and the Lord gave Job twice as much as he had before. *11* Then came to him all his brothers and sisters and all who had known him before, and ate bread with him in his house; and they showed him sympathy and comforted him for all the evil that the Lord has brought upon him; and each of them gave him a piece of money and a ring of gold. *12* And the Lord blessed the latter days of Job more than his beginning; and he had fourteen thousand sheep, six thousand camels, a thousand yoke of oxen, and a thousand she-asses. *13* He had also seven sons and three daughters. *14* And he called the name of the first Jeri'mah; and the name of the second Kezi'ah; and the name of the third Ker'en-hap'puch. *15* And in all the land there were no women so fair as Job's daughters; and their father gave them inheritance among their brothers. *16* And after this Job lived a hundred and forty years, and saw his sons, and his sons' sons, four generations. *17* And Job died, an old man, and full of days.

J.B.

a play in verse

BY ARCHIBALD MacLEISH

The scene throughout is a corner inside an enormous circus tent where a side show of some kind has been set up. There is a rough stage across the corner, on the left of which a wooden platform has been built at a height of six or seven feet. A wooden ladder leans against it. To the right is a deal table with seven straight chairs. There is a door-shaped opening in the canvas to the right rear. Above, a huge, slanted pole thrusts the canvas out and up to make the peak of the corner. Clothes that have the look of vestments of many churches and times have been left about at one side and the other of the stage and the light at the beginning — such light as there is — is provided by bulbs dangling from hanks of wire. The feel is of a public place at late night, the audience gone, no one about but maybe a stage-hand somewhere cleaning up, fooling with the lights.

THE PROLOGUE

Mr. Zuss, followed by Nickles, enters from the dimness off to the left. They stop at the edge of the side-show stage. Both wear the white caps and jackets of circus vendors. Both are old. Mr. Zuss, who has a bunch of balloons hitched to his belt, is large, florid, deep-voiced, dignified, imposing. Nickles is gaunt and sardonic; he has a popcorn tray slung from straps across his shoulders. Both betray in carriage and speech the broken-down actor fallen on evil days but nevertheless and always actor. Throughout the Prologue, from the moment when they mount the side-show stage, they jockey for position, gesture, work themselves up into theatrical flights and rhetorical emotions, play to each other as though they had an actual audience before them in the empty dark.

Mr. Zuss: This is it.

Nickles: This is what?

Mr. Zuss: Where they play the play, Horatio!

Nickles: Bare stage?

Mr. Zuss: Not in the least.
                 Heaven and earth. That platform's Heaven.

They step up onto the stage together

Nickles: Looks like Heaven!

Mr. Zuss: As you remember it?

Nickles: Somebody's got to. You weren't there.
                They never sold balloons in Heaven —
                Not in my time.

Mr. Zuss: Only popcorn.

Nickles shrugs a shudder of disgust, heaving his tray.

Nickles: The two best actors in America
                Selling breath in bags . . .

Mr. Zuss: and bags
                To butter breath with . . .

Nickles: when they sell.

Mr. Zuss: Merchandise not moving, Nickles?

Nickles: Moves wherever I do — all of it.
                No rush to buy your worlds, I notice.

Mr. Zuss: I could sell one to a . . .

Nickles: . . . child!
                You told me. Where's the earth?

Mr. Zuss: Earth?
                Earth is where that table is:

That's where Job sits — at the table.
God and Satan lean above.

Mr. Zuss peers anxiously up into the canvas sky.

I wonder if we'd better?

Nickles: What?

Mr. Zuss: Play it.

Nickles: Why not? Who cares? *They* don't.

Mr. Zuss: At least we're actors. They're not actors.
Never acted anything.

Nickles: That's right.
They only own the show.

Mr. Zuss: I wonder ...

Nickles: They won't care and they won't know.

His eyes follow Mr. Zuss's up to the dangling bulbs.

Those stars that stare their stares at me —
Are those the staring stars I see
Or only lights ...
                    not meant for me?

Mr. Zuss: What's that got to do with anything?

Nickles: Very little. Shall we start?

Mr. Zuss: You think we ought to?

Nickles: They won't care.

Mr. Zuss: Let's start . . .
                    What staring stars?

Nickles: They aren't.
                They're only lights. Not meant.

Mr. Zuss: Why don't we
                Start?

Nickles: You'll play the part of . . .

Mr. Zuss: Naturally!

Nickles: Naturally! And your mask?

Mr. Zuss: Mask!

Nickles: Mask. Naturally. You wouldn't play God in your
                Face would you?

Mr. Zuss: What's the matter with it?

Nickles: God the Creator of the Universe?
                God who hung the world in time?
                You wouldn't hang the world in time
                With a two-days' beard on your chin or a pinky!
                Lay its measure! Stretch the line on it!

Mr. Zuss stares coldly at Nickles, unhitches his balloon belt with

74

magnificent deliberation, drops it, steps forward to the front of the wooden stage, strikes an attitude.

Mr. Zuss: Whatsoever is under the whole
                Heaven is mine!

Nickles: That's what I mean.
            You need a mask.

Mr. Zuss: *heavy irony*   Perhaps a more
                Accomplished actor ...

Nickles: Kiss your accomplishments!
        Nobody doubts your accomplishments — none
           of them —
        The one man for God in the theater!
        They'd all say that. Our ablest actor.
        Nobody else for the part, they'd say.

Mr. Zuss: You make me humble.

Nickles: No! I'm serious.
        The part was written for you.

Mr. Zuss: *gesture of protest*   Oh!

Nickles: But this is God in *Job* you're playing:
        God the Maker: God Himself!
        Remember what He says? — the hawk
        Flies by His wisdom! And the goats —
        Remember the goats? He challenges Job with
          them:

> *Dost thou know the time* of the wild goats?
> What human face knows time like that time?
> You'd need a face of fur to know it.
> Human faces know too much too little.

Mr. Zuss: *suspiciously*
> What kind of mask?

Nickles: You'll find one somewhere.
> *They* never play without the masks.

Mr. Zuss: It's God the Father I play — not
> God the boiling point of water!

Nickles: Nevertheless the mask is imperative.
> If God should laugh
> The mare would calf
> The cow would foal:
> Diddle my soul . . .

Mr. Zuss: *shocked*
> God never laughs! In the whole Bible!

Nickles: That's what I say. *We* do.

Mr. Zuss: *I* don't.

Nickles: *Job* does. He covers his mouth with his hand.

Mr. Zuss: Job is abashed.

Nickles: He says he's abashed.

Mr. Zuss:	He should be abashed: it's rank irreverence — Job there on the earth . . .
Nickles:	On his dung heap . . .
Mr. Zuss:	Challenging God!
Nickles:	Crying to God.
Mr. Zuss:	Demanding *justice* of *God!*
Nickles:	Justice! No wonder he laughs. It's ridiculous. All of it. God has killed his sons, his daughters, Stolen his camels, oxen, sheep, Everything he has and left him Sick and stricken on a dung heap — Not even the consciousness of crime to comfort him — The rags of reasons.
Mr. Zuss:	God is reasons.
Nickles:	For the hawks, yes. For the goats. They're grateful. Take their young away they'll sing Or purr or moo or splash — whatever. Not for Job though.
Mr. Zuss:	And that's why.
Nickles:	Why what?

Mr. Zuss: He suffers.

Nickles: Ah? Because he's . . .
                         Not a bird you mean?

Mr. Zuss: You're frivolous . . .

Nickles: That's precisely what you do mean!
                The one thing God can't stomach is a man,
                That scratcher at the cracked creation!
                That eyeball squinting through into His Eye,
                Blind with the sight of Sight!

Nickles tugs himself free of his tray.

                                    Blast this . . .

Mr. Zuss: God created the whole world.
                Who is Job to . . .

Nickles: Agh! the world!
                The dirty whirler! The toy top!

Mr Zuss: *kicking savagely at the popcorn tray and the balloon
            belt to shove them under the platform*
                What's so wrong with the world?

Nickles: Wrong with it!
                Try to spin one on a dung heap!

Mr. Zuss does not answer. He goes on kicking at the tray.

Nickles sits on a rung of the ladder. After a time he begins to sing to himself in a kind of tuneless tune.

Nickles: I heard upon his dry dung heap
That man cry out who cannot sleep:
"If God is God He is not good,
If God is good He is not God;
Take the even, take the odd,
I would not sleep here if I could
Except for the little green leaves in the wood
And the wind on the water."

There is a long silence.

Mr. Zuss: You are a bitter man.

Nickles: *pompously*   I taste of the world!
I've licked the stick that beat my brains out:
Stock that broke my father's bones!

Mr. Zuss: Our modern hero! Our Odysseus
Sailing sidewalks toward the turd
Of truth and touching it at last in triumph!
The honest, disillusioned man!
You sicken me.

Nickles: *hurt*   All right, I sicken you.
No need to be offensive, is there?
If you would rather someone else...

Mr. Zuss: Did what?

Nickles: Played Job.

Mr. Zuss: What's Job to do with it?

Nickles: Job was honest. He saw God —
                Saw him by that icy moonlight,
                By that cold disclosing eye
                That stares the color out and strews
                Our lives . . . with light . . . for nothing.

Mr. Zuss: Job!
                I never thought of you for Job.

Nickles: You never thought of me for Job!
                What did you think of?

Mr. Zuss: Oh, there's always
                Someone playing Job.

Nickles: There must be
                Thousands! What's that got to do with it?
                Thousands — not with camels either:
                Millions and millions of mankind
                Burned, crushed, broken, mutilated,
                Slaughtered, and for what? For thinking!
                For walking round the world in the wrong
                Skin, the wrong-shaped noses, eyelids:
                Sleeping the wrong night wrong city —
                London, Dresden, Hiroshima.
                There never could have been so many
                Suffered more for less. But where do
                I come in?

Mr. Zuss shuffles uncomfortably.

                            Play the dung heap?

Mr. Zuss:	All we have to do is start.
	Job will join us. Job will be there.

Nickles:	I know. I know. I know. I've seen him.
	Job is everywhere we go,
	His children dead, his work for nothing,
	Counting his losses, scraping his boils,
	Discussing himself with his friends and
	physicians,
	Questioning everything — the times, the stars,
	His own soul, God's providence.
	What do *I* do?

Mr. Zuss: What do *you* do?

Nickles: What do I do? You play God.

Mr. Zuss: I play God. I think I mentioned it.

Nickles: You play God and I play ...

He lets himself down heavily on the rung of the ladder.

                                  Ah!

Mr. Zuss: *embarrassed*
      I had assumed you knew.

Nickles looks up at him, looks away.

Mr. Zuss: You see,
     I think of you and me as ... opposites.

Nickles:	Nice of you.
Mr. Zuss:	I didn't mean to be nasty.
Nickles:	Your opposite! A demanding role!
Mr. Zuss:	I know.
Nickles:	But worthy of me? Worthy of me!
Mr. Zuss:	I have offended you. I didn't mean to.
Nickles:	Did I say I was offended?

There is an awkward silence. Nickles, his face in his hands, begins to hum the tune to his little song. Mr. Zuss looks up and around into the corners of the sky, his head moving cautiously. At length Nickles begins to sing the words.

> I heard upon his dry dung heap
> That man cry out who cannot sleep:
> "If God is God He is not good,
> If God is good He is not God;
> Take the even, take the odd,
> I would not sleep here if I could ..."

Silence.

So I play opposite to God!

Silence.

Father of Lies they call me, don't they?

Mr. Zuss does not answer. He is still searching the dark above. Silence. Nickles goes back to the song.

> "I would not sleep here if I could
> Except for the little green leaves in the wood
> And the wind on the water."

Silence. Then suddenly, theatrically, Nickles is on his feet.

> Who knows enough to know they're lies?
> Show me the mask!

Mr. Zuss: What mask?

Nickles: *attitude*   My mask!

Mr. Zuss: Are you sure you wear a mask?

Nickles: Meaning only God should wear one?

Mr. Zuss: Meaning are you sure it's there.

Nickles: They never play without them.

Mr. Zuss: Yes but
Where?

Nickles: Where? In Heaven probably:
Up on the platform there in Heaven!

Mr. Zuss: Yes ... You wouldn't care to ...

Nickles: What?

Mr. Zuss: Find it for yourself?

Nickles: In Heaven?
               Heaven is your department, Garrick.

Mr. Zuss: My department! I suppose it is.
               Here! Hold this! Hold it! Steady...

*Nickles steadies the ladder. Mr. Zuss climbs warily, keeping his
eye on the canvas darkness; heaves himself over the rail; rum-
mages around on the platform; turns, holding out a huge white,
blank, beautiful, expressionless mask with eyes lidded like the
eyes of the mask in Michelangelo's* Night.

Nickles: That's not mine — not *his*. It's His.
               I've known that face before. I've seen it.
               They find it under bark of marble
               Deep within the rinds of stone:
               God the Creator...(*nastily*) of the animals!

Mr. Zuss: *outraged*   God of
               Everything that is or can!

Nickles: Is or can — but cannot know.

Mr. Zuss: There is nothing those closed eyes
               Have not known and seen.

Nickles: Except
               To know they see: to know they've seen it.
               Lions and dolphins have such eyes.
               They know the way the wild geese know —
               Those pin-point travelers who go home
               To Labradors they never meant to,

Unwinding the will of the world like string.
What would they make of a man, those eyelids?

Mr. Zuss: Make of him! They *made* him.

Nickles: Made him
Animal like any other
Calculated for the boughs of
Trees and meant to chatter and be grateful!
But womb-worm wonders and grows wings —

Nickles breaks off, struck by his own words, goes on:

It actually does! The cock-eyed things
Dream themselves into a buzz
And drown on windowpanes. He made them
Wingless but they learn to wish.
That's why He fumbles Job. Job wishes! —
Thinks there should be justice somewhere —
Beats his bones against the glass.
Justice! In this cesspool! Think of it!
Job knows better when it's over.

Mr. Zuss: Job knows justice when it's over.
Justice has a face like this.

Nickles: Like blinded eyes?

Mr. Zuss: Like skies.

Nickles: Of stone.
Show me the other.

Mr. Zuss ducks away, rummaging in the clutter on the plat-
form; turns again.

Mr. Zuss: You won't find it
                    Beautiful, you understand.

Nickles: I know that.
                    Beauty's the Creator's bait,
                    Not the Uncreator's: his
                    Is Nothing, the no-face of Nothing
                    Grinning with its not-there eyes.
                    Nothing at all! Nothing ever! . . .
                    Never to have been at all!

Mr. Zuss turns, lifts the second mask above Nickles' gesturing.
This is large as the first but dark to the other's white, and
open-eyed where the other was lidded. The eyes, though
wrinkled with laughter, seem to stare and the mouth is drawn
down in agonized disgust.

Mr. Zuss: Well?

Nickles is silent.

Mr. Zuss: *cheerfully*
                    That's it.

Silence.

                                  You don't care for it?
                    It's not precisely the expression
                    Anyone would choose. I know that.
                    Evil is never very pretty:
                    Spitefulness either. Nevertheless it's

His — you'll grant that, won't you? — the
    traditional
Face we've always found for him anyway.
God knows where we go to find it:
Some subterranean memory probably.

Nickles has approached the ladder, staring. He does not reply.

Well, if you won't you won't. It's your
Option. I can't say I blame you.
I wouldn't do it. Fit my face to
That! I'd scrub the skin off afterward!
Eyes to those eyes!

Nickles: *harshly*   You needn't worry.
Your beaux yeux would never bear that
Look of . . .

Mr. Zuss: *smugly*   No. I know.

Nickles: . . . of pity!
Let me have it.

*Nickles starts up the ladder, the mask in Mr. Zuss's hands
above him.*

       Evil you call it!
Look at those lips: they've tasted something
Bitter as a broth of blood
And spat the sup out. Was that evil?

He climbs another rung.

   Was it?

Another rung.

> Spitefulness you say:
> You call that grin of anguish spite?

He pulls himself over the rail, takes the mask in his hands.

> I'd rather wear this look of loathing
> Night after night than wear that other
> Once — that cold complacence...

Mr. Zuss has picked up the first mask again, lifts it.

Nickles: Horrible!
> Horrible as a star above
> A burning, murdered, broken city!
> I'll play the part!...
>   Put your mask on!...
> Give me the lines!...

Mr. Zuss: What lines?

Nickles: His!
> Satan's!

Mr. Zuss: They're in the Bible aren't they?

Nickles: We're supposed to speak the Bible?

Mr. Zuss: *They* do...

The light bulbs fade out, yellow to red to gone. A slow, strong glow spots the platform throwing gigantic shadows up across the canvas. Back to back the shadows of Mr. Zuss and Nickles ad-

just their masks. The masked shadows turn to each other and gravely bow. Their gestures are the stiff formal gestures of pantomime. Their voices, when they speak, are so magnified and hollowed by the masks that they scarcely seem their own.

Godmask: Whence comest thou?

Satanmask: From going to and fro in the earth

There is a snicker of suppressed laughter.

          And from walking up and down in it ...

A great guffaw. Mr. Zuss tears off his mask.

Mr. Zuss: *shouting*   Lights!

The spotlight fades out. The dangling bulbs come feebly on.

        Nobody told you to laugh like that.
        What's so funny? It's irreverent. It's impudent.
        After all, you are talking to God.
        That doesn't happen every Saturday
        Even to kitchen kin like you.
        Take that face off! It's indecent!
        Makes me feel like scratching somewhere!

Nickles painfully removes his mask.

Nickles: Do I look as though I'd laughed?
            If you had seen what I have seen
            You'd never laugh again! ...

89

He stares at his mask.

                                        Weep either . . .

Mr. Zuss: You roared. I heard you.

Nickles: Those eyes *see*.

Mr. Zuss: Of course they see — beneath the trousers
             Stalking up the pulpit stair:
             Under the skirts at tea — wherever
             Decent eyes would be ashamed to.
             Why should you laugh at that?

Nickles: It isn't
             That! It isn't that at all!
             They see the *world*. They do. They see it.
             From going to and fro in the earth,
             From walking up and down, they see it.
             I know what Hell is now — to *see*.
             Consciousness of consciousness . . .

Mr. Zuss: Now
             Listen! This is a simple scene.
             I play God. You play Satan.
             God is asking where you've been.
             All you have to do is tell him:
             Simple as that. "In the earth," you answer.

Nickles: *Satan* answers.

Mr. Zuss: All right — Satan.
             What's the difference?

Nickles: Satan *sees*.
He sees the parked car by the plane tree.
He sees behind the fusty door,
Beneath the rug, those almost children
Struggling on the awkward seat —
Every impossible delighted dream
She's ever had of loveliness, of wonder,
Spilled with her garters to the filthy floor.
Absurd despair! Ridiculous agony!

He looks at the mask in his hands.

What has any man to laugh at!
The panting crow by the dry tree
Drags dusty wings. God's mercy brings
The rains — but not to such as he.

Mr. Zuss: You play your part, I'll say that for you.
In it or out of it, you play.

Nickles: You really think I'm playing?

Mr. Zuss: Aren't you?
Somebody is. Satan maybe.
Maybe Satan's playing *you*.
Let's begin from the beginning.
Ready!

They take their places back to back.

                    Masks!

They raise their masks to their faces.

Lights!

The bulbs go out. Darkness. Silence. In the silence:

A Distant Voice: Whence comest thou?

Mr. Zuss: That's my line.

Nickles: I didn't speak it.

Mr. Zuss: You did. Stop your mischief, won't you?

Nickles: Stop your own! Laughing. Shouting.

Mr. Zuss: Lights, I said!

The spotlight throws the enormous shadows on the canvas sky.

Godmask: Whence comest thou?

Satanmask: From going to and fro in the earth . . .

A choked silence.

               And from walking up and down in it.

Godmask: Hast thou considered my servant Job
                That there is none like him on the earth
                A perfect and an upright man, one
                That feareth God and escheweth evil?

The platform lights sink, the masked shadows fading with them, as a strong light comes on below isolating the table where J.B. stands with his wife and children.

SCENE ONE

The Platform is in darkness, the Table in light. J.B., a big, vigorous man in his middle or late thirties, stands at one end. At the other stands his wife, Sarah, a few years younger than her husband, a fine woman with a laughing, pretty face but a firm mouth and careful eyes, all New England. She is looking reprovingly but proudly at her five blond sons and daughters, who shift from foot to foot behind their chairs, laughing and nudging each other: David, 13; Mary, 12; Jonathan, 10; Ruth, 8; Rebecca, 6. Two buxom, middle-aged maids in frilly aprons stand behind with their hands folded. The children subside under their mother's eyes.

Sarah: J.B. . . .

The heads bow.

J.B.:   Our Father which art in Heaven
                 Give us this day our daily bread.

Rebecca and Ruth: *pulling their chairs out, clattering into them*
                 Amenamen.

The Older Children: *less haste but no less eagerness*
                 Amen!

The Maids: *wheeling majestically but urgently to go out*
                 Amen!

Sarah: *to J.B. over the rattle of dishes and the clatter of talk as she sits down*
>   That was short and sweet, my darling.

J.B.: *sitting down*
>   What was?

Sarah: Grace was.

J.B.: *cheerfully*   All the essentials.

Sarah: Give? Eat?

J.B.:   Besides they're hungry.

Sarah: That's what grace is for — the hunger.
>   Mouth and meat by grace amazed,
>   God upon my lips is praised.

J.B.:   You think they stand in need of it — grace?
>   Look at them!

Sarah: *beaming*   Yes! Look! Oh look!

The maids parade in with a huge turkey on a silver platter, china serving dishes with domed, blue covers, a gravy boat, a bottle of wine in a napkin.

Mary: Papá! Papá! He heard! He heard!

David: Who did?

Ruth: Ourfatherwhichartinheaven.

J.B.: *nudging the bird gently with his finger*
        He did indeed. What a bird He sent us!
        Cooked to a turn!

Ruth: He heard! He heard!

Jonathan: He heard! He heard! He sent a bird!

Sarah: That's enough now, children. Quiet!
        Your father's counting.

J.B.:   Not today.
        Not this gobbler. Feed a regiment.
        Know what I was thinking, Sally?

Sarah: What?

J.B.:   How beautiful you are.

Sarah: With your eye on a turkey? I like that!

J.B.:   Why not? It's an eye-filling bird. Just look at it.

Sarah: Someday you might look at *me*.

J.B.:   I'm always looking at you, Sarah.

He rises, knife and steel in hand, clashing them against each other in a noble rhythm.

        Everywhere I look I see you.

Sarah: *scornfully*
        You never even see my clothes.

J.B.: *a shout of laughter*
    It's true. I don't. But I see *you*.

Sarah: *mock indignation*
    J! B!

J.B.:   And what's wrong with the turkey?
    What's wrong with that bottle of wine, either —
    Montrachet or I'll drink the whole of it!
    What's wrong with the bird or the wine or with
     anything —
    The day either — what's wrong with the day?

He begins carving expertly and rapidly.

    Tell me what day it is.

Jonathan: Turkey Day.

Mary: Cranberry Day.

Ruth: Succotash Day.

David: When we all can have white.

Jonathan: And giblets to bite.

Ruth: And two kinds of pie.

Jonathan: And squash in your eye.

Mary: And mashed potatoes with puddles of butter.

Jonathan: And gravy and such.

Rebecca: . . . and . . . and . . .

The children are screaming with laughter.

Sarah: Children!

Jonathan: *gasping*   And all eat too much.

Sarah: Children!
                Quiet! Quiet every one of you or
                Kate will take it all — everything —
                Knives, forks, turkey, glasses . . .

J.B.:   Not the wine though.

Sarah: Job, I'm serious.
                Answer your father's question, Jonathan.
                Tell him what day it is.

Jonathan: *hushed*   Thanksgiving.

Sarah: What day is that?

Jonathan: Thanksgiving Day.

David: The Day we give thanks to God.

Mary: For His goodness.

Sarah: And did you, David? Did you, Mary?
                Has any one of you thanked God?
                Really thanked Him?

There is an awkward silence.

Thanked Him for everything?

The children's heads are down. J.B. busies himself with his carving.

Sarah: *gently*   God doesn't give all this for nothing:
                       A good home, good food,
                       Father, mother, brothers, sisters.
                       We too have our part to play.
                       If we do our part He does His,
                       He always has. If we forget Him
                       He will forget. Forever. In everything.
                       David!

David raises his head reluctantly.

Did you think of God?

David does not reply.

Did you think, when you woke in your beds this
    morning,
Any one of you, of Him?

Silence.

J.B.: *uncomfortable*
Of course they did. They couldn't have helped
   it . . .

Bit of the breast for you, Rebecca?

Sarah: Please, Job. I want them to answer me.

J.B.:　　　　　How can they answer things like that?

　　　　　　　Gravy? That's the girl...

　　　　　　　　　　　　　　　　They know though.
　　　　　　　Gift of waking, grace of light,
　　　　　　　You and the world brought back together,
　　　　　　　You from sleep, the world from night,
　　　　　　　By God's great goodness and mercy ...

　　　　　　　Wing for Mary? Wing for Mary! ...

　　　　　　　They know all that. It's hard to talk about.

Sarah: *flushed, an edge to her voice*
　　　　　　　Even if it's hard we have to.
　　　　　　　We can't just take, just eat, just — relish!
　　　　　　　Children aren't animals.

J.B.: *he goes on with his serving*　　　　Sweet Sal! Sweet Sal!
　　　　　　　Children know the grace of God
　　　　　　　Better than most of us. They see the world
　　　　　　　The way the morning brings it back to them,
　　　　　　　New and born and fresh and wonderful...

　　　　　　　Ruth? She's always ravenous...

　　　　　　　　　　　　　　　　I remember...

　　　　　　　Jonathan? He never is...

　　　　　　　　　　　　　　...when I was
　　　　　　　Ten I used to stand behind

The window watching when the light began,
Hidden and watching.

That's for David —
Dark and thin.

Mary: Why? Why hidden?

J.B.:   Hidden from the trees of course.
I must have thought the trees would see me
Peeking at them and turn back.

Rebecca: Back where?

J.B.:   Back where they came from, baby.

That's for your mother: crisp and gold.

Ruth: Father, you'd be cold. You didn't.

Sarah: *the edge still there*
He still does. He lies there watching
Long before I see the light —
Can't bear to miss a minute of it:
Sun at morning, moon at night,
The last red apple, the first peas!
I've never seen the dish he wouldn't
Taste and relish and want more of:
People either!

J.B.: *serving himself with heaping spoons*
Come on, Sal!
Plenty of people I don't like.

He sits down. Pours himself a glass of wine.

       I like their being people though . . .

Sips his wine.

       Trying to be.

Sarah: You're hungry for them —
Any kind. People and vegetables:
Any vegetables so long as
Leaves come out on them. He loves leaves!

J.B.:   You love them too. You love them better.
Just because you know their names
You think you choose among your flowers:
Well, you don't. You love the lot of them.

Sarah: I can't take them as a gift though:
I owe for them. We do. We *owe*.

J.B.:   Owe for the greening of the leaves?

Sarah: Please!
Please, Job. I want the children
Somehow to understand this day, this . . .
Feast . . .

Her voice breaks.

J.B.:   Forgive me, Sal. I'm sorry — but
                they
Do. They understand. A little.
Look at me, all of you.

            Ruth, you answer:

Why do we eat all this, these dishes,
All this food?

Ruth twists her napkin.

You say, Rebecca.
You're the littlest of us all.
Why?

Rebecca: Because it's good?

Sarah: Baby!
Ah, my poor baby!

J.B.:   Why your poor baby?
She's right, isn't she? It is. It's good.

Sarah: Good — and God has sent it to us!

J.B.:   She knows that.

Sarah: Does she?

She raises her head sharply.

                         Job! . . .

                                   do *you*?

Their eyes meet; hers drop.

          Oh, I think you do . . .

                              but sometimes —

Times like this when we're together —
I get frightened, Job ...

                                        we have so
Much!

J.B.: *dead serious*   You ought to think I do.
                        Even if no one else should, you should.
                        Never since I learned to tell
                        My shadow from my shirt, not once,
                        Not for a watch-tick, have I doubted
                        God was on my side, was good to me.
                        Even young and poor I knew it.
                        People called it luck: it wasn't.
                        I never thought so from the first
                        Fine silver dollar to the last
                        Controlling interest in some company
                        I couldn't get — and got. It isn't
                        Luck.

Mary: That's in the story.

Jonathan: Tell the
                        Story.

Ruth: Tell the lucky story.

Rebecca: Lucky, lucky, tell the lucky.

J.B.: *getting to his feet again to carve*
                        Tell the story?

                        Drumstick, David?

Man enough to eat a drumstick?
You too, Jonathan?

Rebecca: Story, story.

J.B.:   Fellow came up to me once in a restaurant:
              "J.B.," he says — I knew him . . .

              Mary, want the other wing?

              "Why do you get the best of the rest of us?"
              Fellow named Foley, I think, or Sullivan:
              New-come man he was in town.

Mary: Your turn, Mother.

Sarah: Patrick Sullivan.

J.B. and the children: *together in a shouted chant*
              Patrick Sullivan, that's the man!

J.B.:   "Why do you get the best of the rest of us?
              I've got as many brains as you.
              I work as hard. I keep the lamp lit.
              Luck! That's what it is," says Sullivan.
              "Look!" I said. "Look out the window!"
              "What do you see?" "The street," he tells me.

J.B. and the children: *as before*
              "The street?" says I. "The street," says he.

J.B.:   "What do you want me to call it?" he asks me.
              "What do I want you to call it?" says I.

"A road," says I. "It's going somewhere."
"Where?" says he. "You say," I said to him.

J.B. and the children:
        "God knows!" says Mr. Sullivan.

J.B.:
        "He does," says I. "That's where it's going.
        That's where I go too. That's why."
        "Why what?" says he. "I get the best of you:
        It's God's country, Mr. Sullivan."

J.B. and the children:
        "God forbid!" says Mr. Sullivan.

J.B.:
        I laughed till I choked. He only looked at me.
        "Lucky so-and-so," he yells.

Sarah: Poor Mr. Sullivan.

J.B.: *soberly*   He was wrong.
        It isn't luck when God is good to you.
        It's something more. It's like those dizzy
        Daft old lads who dowse for water.
        They feel the alder twig twist down
        And know they've got it and they have:
        They've got it. Blast the ledge and water
        Gushes at you. And they knew.
        It wasn't luck. They knew. They felt the
        Gush go shuddering through their shoulders,
            huge
        As some mysterious certainty of opulence.
        They couldn't hold it. I can't hold it.

He looks at Sarah.

> I've always known that God was with me.
> I've tried to show I knew it — not
> Only in words.

Sarah: *touched* Oh, you have,
> I know you have. And it's ridiculous,
> Childish, and I shouldn't be afraid . .
> Not even now when suddenly everythin͟
> Fills to overflowing in me
> Brimming the fulness till I feel
> My happiness impending like a danger.
> If ever anyone deserved it, you do.

J.B.: That's not true. I don't deserve it.
> It's not a question of deserving.

Sarah: Oh, it is. That's all the question.
> However could we sleep at night . . .

J.B.: Nobody *deserves* it, Sarah:
> Not the world that God has given us.

There is a moment's strained silence, then J.B. is laughing.

J.B.: But I believe in it, Sal. I trust in it.
> I trust my luck — my life — our life —
> God's goodness to me.

Sarah: *trying to control her voice* Yes! You do!
> I know you do! And that's what frightens me!
> It's not so simple as all that. It's not.

106

They mustn't think it is. God punishes.
God rewards and God can punish.
God is just.

J.B.: *easy again*   Of course He's just.
He'll never change. A man can count on Him.
Look at the world, the order of it,
The certainty of day's return
And spring's and summer's: the leaves' green —
That never cheated expectation.

Sarah: *vehemently*
God can reward and God can punish.
Us He has rewarded. Wonderfully.
Given us everything. Preserved us.
Kept us from harm, each one — each one.
And why? Because of you...

J.B. *raises his head sharply.*

Sarah: No!
Let me say it! Let me say it!
I need to speak the words that say it —
I need to hear them spoken. Nobody,
Nobody knows of it but me.
You never let them know: not anyone —
Even your children. They don't know.

J.B. *heaves himself out of his chair, swings round the table, leans over Sarah, his arms around her.*

J.B.:   Eat your dinner, Sal my darling.
We love our life because it's good:

It isn't good because we love it —
Pay for it — in thanks or prayers. The thanks are
Part of love and paid like love:
Free gift or not worth having.
You know that, Sal...

He kisses her.

                                      better than anyone.
Eat your dinner, girl! There's not a
Harpy on the roof for miles.

She reaches up to touch his cheek with her hand.

Sarah: Nevertheless it's true, Job. You
Can trust your luck because you've earned the
Right to trust it: earned the right
For all of us to trust it.

J.B.: *back at his own place, filling his glass again*
                         Nonsense!
We get the earth for nothing, don't we?
It's given to us, gift on gift:
Sun on the floor, airs in the curtain.
We lie a whole day long and look at it
Crowing or crying in our cribs:
It doesn't matter — crow or cry
The sun shines, the wind blows...

Rebecca! Back for more already?

Rebecca: I want the wishbone please.

J.B.:   Whatever
            For?

Rebecca: To wish.

Sarah: For what, my baby?

Rebecca: For the wishbone.

Sarah: *pulling Rebecca into her lap*
                                Little pig!
                Wishing for wishes!

J.B.: *forking the wishbone onto Rebecca's plate*
                                That's my girl!

Sarah: She is! The spit and image of you!
                Thinking she can eat the world
                With luck and wishes and no thanks!

J.B.:   That isn't fair. We're thankful, both of us.

Sarah: *cuddling Rebecca*
                Both! And both the same! Just look at you!
                A child shows gratitude the way a woman
                Shows she likes a pretty dress —
                Puts it on and takes it off again —
                That's the way a child gives thanks:
                She tries the world on. So do you.

J.B.:   God understands that language, doesn't He?
                He should. He made the colts.

Sarah: But you're not
              Colts! You talk. With tongues. Or ought to.

J.B.:   And we use them, don't we, baby?
              We love Monday, Tuesday, Wednesday..

Sarah: *rocking Rebecca on her knees*
              We love Monday, Tuesday, Wednesday.
              Where have Monday, Tuesday, gone?
              Under the grass tree,
              Under the green tree,
              One by one.

Jonathan: Say it again, Mother ... Mother!

Sarah: I never said it before. I don't
              Know ...

                        How would you think it would go?
              How does it go, Job? You said it.

J.B.:   I didn't. I said we loved the world:
              Monday, Tuesday, Wednesday, all of it.

Sarah: How would you think it would go, Jonathan?

The words fall into a little tune as she repeats them.

              I love Monday, Tuesday, Wednesday.
              Where have Monday, Tuesday, gone?
              Under the grass tree,
              Under the green tree,
              One by one.

Caught as we are in Heaven's quandary,
Is it they or we are gone
Under the grass tree,
Under the green tree?

I love Monday, Tuesday, Wednesday.
One by one.

Rebecca: *drowsily*   Say it again.

Sarah: Say it again?

Jonathan: You say it, Father.

J.B.:   To be, become, and end are beautiful.

Rebecca: That's not what she said at all.

J.B.:   Isn't it? Isn't it?

Sarah: *kissing her*   Not at all.

The light fades, leaving the two shadows on the canvas sky.

SCENE TWO

*The Platform. As the platform light comes on, the figures
fade from the canvas sky and Mr. Zuss and Nickles straighten
up, lifting their masks off, stretching, yawning.*

Mr. Zuss: Well, that's our pigeon.

Nickles: Lousy actor.

Mr. Zuss: Doesn't really act at all.

Nickles: Just eats.

Mr. Zuss: And talks.

Nickles: The love of life!
Poisoning their little minds
With love of life! At that age!

Mr. Zuss: No!
Some of that, I thought, was beautiful.

Nickles: Best thing you can teach your children
Next to never drawing breath
Is choking on it.

Mr. Zuss: Who said that?
Someone's spoiled philosophy, it sounds like:

112

Intellectual butter a long war
And too much talking have turned rancid.
I thought he made that small familiar
Feast a true thanksgiving ... only ...

Nickles: Only what?

Mr. Zuss: Something went wrong.

Nickles: That's what I've been telling you.

Mr. Zuss: He didn't
Act.

Nickles: He can't. He's not an actor.

Mr. Zuss: I wonder if he knows?

Nickles: Knows what?

Mr. Zuss: Knows that he's in it?

Nickles: Is he?

Mr. Zuss: Certainly.

Nickles: How can you tell?

Mr. Zuss: That's him. That's Job.
He has the wealth, the wife, the children,
Position in the world.

Nickles: The piety!

| Mr. Zuss: | He loves God, if that's what you're saying. |
| | A *perfect and an upright man.* |

Nickles:	Piety's hard enough to take
	Among the poor who *have* to practice it.
	A rich man's piety stinks. It's insufferable.

Mr. Zuss:	You're full of fatuous aphorisms, aren't you!
	A poor man's piety is hope of having:
	A rich man *has* his — and he's grateful.

Nickles:	Bought and paid for like a waiter's smirk!
	You know what talks when that man's talking?
	All that gravy on his plate —
	His cash — his pretty wife — his children!
	Lift the lot of them, he'd sing
	Another canticle to different music.

| Mr. Zuss: | That's what Satan says — but better. |

| Nickles: | It's obvious. No one needs to say it. |

| Mr. Zuss: | You don't like him. |

| Nickles: | I don't have to. |
| | You're the one who has to like him. |

| Mr. Zuss: | I thought you spoke of Job with sympathy. |

Nickles:	Job on his dung hill, yes. That's human.
	That makes sense. But this world-master,
	This pious, flatulent, successful man
	Who feasts on turkey and thanks God! —
	He sickens me!

Mr. Zuss: Of course he sickens you,
             He trusts the will of God and loves —

*Mr. Zuss is swollen with indignation and rhetoric. He swoops
his mask up from the rail with a magnificent gesture, holds it.*

             Loves a woman who must sometime, some-
                where,
             Later, sooner, leave him; fixes
             All his hopes on little children
             One night's fever or a running dog
             Could kill between the dark and day;
             Plants his work, his enterprise, his labor,
             Here where every planted thing
             Fails in its time but still he plants it...

Nickles: *nastily*
             God will teach him better won't He?
             God will show him what the world is like —
             What man's like — the ignoble creature,
             Victim of the spinning joke!

Mr. Zuss: Teach him better than he knows!
             God will show him God!

Nickles: *shrugging*   It's the same
             Thing. It hurts.

Mr. Zuss: *gathering momentum*   God will teach him!
             God will show him what God *is* —
             Enormous pattern of the steep of stars,
             Minute perfection of the frozen crystal,
             Inimitable architecture of the slow,

Cold, silent, ignorant sea-snail:
The unimaginable will of stone:
Infinite mind in midge of matter!

Nickles: Infinite mush! Wait till your pigeon
Pecks at the world the way the rest do —
Eager beak to naked bum!

Mr. Zuss: You ought to have your tongue torn out!

Nickles: All men should: to suffer silently.

Mr. Zuss: Get your mask back on! I tell you
Nothing this good man might suffer,
Nothing at all, would make him yelp
As you do. He'd praise God no matter.

Nickles: *whispering*
Why must he suffer then?

*The question catches Mr. Zuss with his mask halfway to his face.
He lowers it slowly, staring into it as though the answer might
be written inside.*

Mr. Zuss: *too loud*   To praise!

Nickles: *softly*
He praises now. Like a canary.

Mr. Zuss lifts his mask again.

Mr. Zuss: Well, will you put it on or won't you?

Nickles: Shall I tell you why?
        violently   To learn!
              Every human creature born
              Is born into the bright delusion
              Beauty and loving-kindness care for him.
              Suffering teaches! Suffering's good for us!
              Imagine men and women dying
              Still believing that the cuddling arms
              Enclosed them! They would find the worms
              Peculiar nurses, wouldn't they? Wouldn't they?

He breaks off; picks his mask up; goes on in a kind of jigging chant half to himself.

              What once was cuddled must learn to kiss
              The cold worm's mouth. That's all the mystery.
              That's the whole muddle. Well, we learn it.
              God is merciful and we learn it . . .
              We learn to wish we'd never lived!

Mr. Zuss: This man will not.

Nickles: Won't he? Won't he?
              Shall I tell you how it ends?
              Shall I prophesy? I see our
              Smug world-master on his dung heap,
              Naked, miserable, and alone,
              Pissing the stars. Ridiculous gesture! —
              Nevertheless a gesture — meaning
              All there is on earth to mean:
              Man's last word . . . and worthy of him!

| Mr. Zuss: | This man will not. He trusts God. |
| | No matter how it ends, he trusts Him. |

| Nickles: | Even when God tests him? — tortures him? |

| Mr. Zuss: | Would God permit the test unless |
| | He knew the outcome of the testing? |

| Nickles: | Then why test him if God knows? |

| Mr. Zuss: | So Job can see. |

| Nickles: | See what? |

| Mr. Zuss: | See God. |

| Nickles: | A fine sight from an ash heap, certainly! |

Mr. Zuss:	Isn't there anything you understand?
	It's from the ash heap God is seen
	Always! Always from the ashes.
	Every saint and martyr knew that.

| Nickles: | And so he suffers to see God: |
| | Sees God because he suffers. Beautiful! |

| Mr. Zuss: | Put on your mask. I'd rather look at . . . |

| Nickles: | I should think you would! A human |
| | Face would shame the mouth that said that! |

They put their masks on fiercely, standing face to face. The platform light fades out. The spotlight catches them, throwing

*the two masked shadows out and up. The voices are magnified
and hollow, the gestures formal, as at the end of the Prologue.*

Godmask: Hast thou considered my servant Job
                That there is none like him on the earth,
                A perfect and an upright man, one
                That feareth God and escheweth evil?

Satanmask: *sardonic*
                Doth Job fear God for naught?

The God-shadow turns away in a gesture of anger.

Satanmask: *deprecatingly*
                Hast thou not made an hedge about him
                And about his house
                And about all that he hath on every side?
                Thou hast blessed the work of his hands
                And his substance is increased.

The voice drops.

                But put forth thine hand now and touch
                All that he hath . . .

The voice becomes a hissing whisper.

                        and he will
                Curse thee to thy face!

Godmask: *in a furious, great voice, arm thrown out in a gesture
            of contemptuous commitment*
            Behold!
            All that he hath is in thy power!

The Satan-shadow bows mockingly; raises its two arms, advancing until the shadows become one shadow. The light fades. Suddenly, out of the darkness the Distant Voice of the Prologue.

The Distant Voice:
> Only ...

Silence.

Godmask:
> Only
> Upon himself
> Put not forth thy hand!

Darkness. The crash of a drum; a single stroke. Silence.

Note: *The play is conceived and written without breaks, but if recesses in the action are desired one might well be made at this point.*

SCENE THREE

The Table. As the lights come on the two leaning shadows, one thrown upon the other, are visible on the canvas sky. They fade as the scene brightens. The table has been pushed to one side as though against a window in a living room. Sarah stands before it arranging flowers in a bowl. J.B. is straddling a chair, watching.

Sarah: Look, Job! Look! Across the street.
Two soldiers.

J.B.:   What about them?

Sarah: Only they
Stare so.

J.B.:   Stare at what?

Sarah: The house.
I think they're drunk ... A little.

J.B. rises, stands beside her, his arm around her waist.

J.B.:   Plastered!

Sarah: One of them anyway. He wobbles.

J.B.:   That's no wobble. That's a waltz step.

Sarah:	They're crossing over.
J.B.:	They sure are.
Sarah:	What do you think they ...
J.B.:	Listen!
Sarah:	Yes ... What do you think they want, two soldiers?
J.B.:	No idea. Johnson will tend to them.
Sarah:	I've never seen such staring eyes.
J.B.:	Glazed. Just glazed.
Sarah:	They keep on ringing. I know what it is, J.B., They have some kind of message for us. David has sent them with a message — Something about his regiment. They're coming Every day now, ship by ship. I hear them in the harbor coming. He couldn't write and so he sent them.
J.B.:	Pretty drunk for messengers, those soldiers.
Sarah:	What does it matter. They're just boys. They've just got home. It doesn't matter.
J.B.:	Johnson's a judge of drunks. He'll handle them.
Sarah:	He mustn't send them off. Don't let him!

There is a commotion outside the canvas door. A voice, off.

Voice: Two young...gentlemen to see you.
                Friends, they say, of Mr. David.

Sarah: Oh, I knew! I knew! I knew!

Voice (off):   That's telling him, Puss-foot!

Voice (off):   Puss-face!

The two Messengers enter, dressed as soldiers. The First is flushed and loud; the Second, very drunk, pale as bone.

J.B.:   Come in, gentlemen. Come in. Come in.
                David's friends are always welcome.
                This is David's mother.

Sarah: Won't you sit
                Down?

First Messenger: What did I tell you, Punk!
                Any friends of David's.

Second Messenger: Any at
                All...

First M.:   I told you that boy meant it.
                What did I say when I see the joint?
                That's the number, Punk, I told you.
                Old Ten Twenty: that's the number.

He turns to Sarah.

Twenty if you're men, he told us —
Ten for horses' whatses. What the
Hell, he always said: we're friends.

Second M.:   Any at all he always . . .

First M.:   Pardon the
Language, lady.

Second M.:   Any a' . . .

Sarah: There!
Sit down.

First M.:   It's just, we saw the number.

Sarah: And David asked you to drop in.

First M.:   Any friend of his, he told us.
Any time.

Second M.:   And we were cold:
A cold, hard march . . .

First M.:   What the
Hell's the matter with *you!* You drunk?

Sarah: Sit by the fire, both of you. Where was he?

First M.:   Where was who?

Sarah: David.

First M.:   When?

J.B.:   When he told you.

First M.:   In the mess.
Any friend of his, he told us.
Any time at all. Why?
You think we're lying to you?

J.B.:   Certainly
Not.

First M.:   You think we never knew him?

Sarah: Of course. Of course you do.

First M.:   We knew him.

Second M.:   Fumbling among the faces ... knew him ...
Night ... our fingers numb ...

First M.:   Will you shut
Up or will I clout you, Big Mouth!

To Sarah.

That's why we come: because we knew him.
To tell you how we knew him.

Sarah: Thank you.

Silence.

Second M.: How it was with him . . .

First M.: Listen, Punk!

Second M.: How, by night, by chance, darkling . . .
By the dark of chance . . .

First M.: He's drunk.

Second M.: How, the war done, the guns silent . . .
No one knows who gave the order.

First M.: *raising his voice*
Like I say, because he said to.
Any friend of his he said to.
Just to tell you we knew David:
Maybe drink to David maybe . . .

Sarah: Yes! Oh yes! Let's drink to David!
J.B.!

J.B.: Bourbon? Scotch?

First M.: Now you're
Cooking! Take your pants off, Punk:
We're in.

Sarah: That's right. Put your feet up.
Oh, they're not too dirty. David's are
Dirtier. I'm sure of that.

First M.: David's feet! I'll say they are.
Look! What's going on here! David's
Feet!

Sarah: I meant — with all that marching.

First M.: I don't get it. Look, it's true
They didn't have the right length lumber:
We did the best we could...

J.B. starts to his feet.

J.B.: What in
God's name are you saying, soldier?

Sarah: *rising*

What does he mean, the lumber?

Silence.

First M.: You don't
Know? Ain't that the army for you!

To the Second Messenger.

They don't know. They never told them.

Sarah: Told us what?

First M.: We better go.

Sarah: No! Please! Please! No!

First M.:   Come on, we're getting out, you lunkhead.

J.B.:   Not until you've told me. Sarah!
        Perhaps you'd better, Sarah . . .

Sarah: Please,
        I want to hear it.

First M :   Jesus! . . . Jesus! . . .

*There is a long silence. The Second Messenger turns slowly to
J.B., his face drunken white, his eyes blank.*

Second M.:   *I only am escaped alone to tell thee* . . .

*The focus of light opens to include the Platform where Mr. Zuss
and Nickles stand staring down, their masks in their hands. Mr.
Zuss's face is expressionless. Nickles wears a twisted grin. The
Second Messenger's head falls forward onto his knees.*

Second M.:   . . . My tongue loosened by drink . . .

                                        my thought
        Darkened as by wind the water . . .

        That day is lost where it befell . . .

Sarah: *she is holding herself by the straining of her clenched
       hands*
        What is it we were never told?

J.B.:   It isn't
        True you little drunken liar!
        It can't be true! It isn't possible!

128

Silence. The passion ebbs from J.B.'s voice.

   We had a letter from him.

Silence. Then, uncertainly

         After the
  End of it we had a letter. . . .

Nickles jerks a crooked leg over the rail, starts awkwardly down the ladder, watching intently, peering back up at Mr. Zuss, watching.

Second M.: What shall I say to you . . . ?

         What I saw . . . ?

  What I believe I saw . . . ?

        Or what
  I must have seen . . .

      and have forgotten?

Sarah: *a cry* David is our son, our son, our son.

Nickles: *prompting her from his ladder in a harsh half-whisper*
    That's the tune. He's *ours*. Go on with it:
    Can't be happening to *us!* Can't be!
    God won't let it happen, not to
    Our kind, God won't!

He leers up at Mr. Zuss.

J.B.: *turning Sarah away from the Second Messenger into his arms*   Sarah! Sarah!
         David's all right. He has to be. He is.
         I know he is. The war is over.
         It never could have happened — never —
         Never in this world.

Nickles: *the whisper harsher*   Couldn't it?
         Ask him! Couldn't it? Suppose it did though:
         What would the world be made of then?

Second M.:   I only am escaped alone, companions
         Fallen, fallen, fallen . . .

                          the earth
         Smell remembers that there was a man.

Sarah: Job! He's dead! God has taken him!

The focus of light narrows, is extinguished.

SCENE FOUR

Darkness. Silence. Then the crash of a drum. Silence again.
Then two cigarettes are lighted, one high above the stage, one
lower. Then gradually the lights come on, making four circles
across the front of the stage like the circles of sidewalk brightness
under street lamps. Where the cigarettes were lighted Mr. Zuss
and Nickles are now visible on the platform rail and the ladder,
squatting there like two tramps on the stairs of a stoop, turning
their heads together one way and then the other, watching, not
speaking. After a time the First Messenger comes strolling in
from their right, a news camera slung from his neck. The Second
follows with a notebook. They wear battered felt hats with their
khaki shirts and trousers. They are followed at a little distance
by a stylishly dressed girl.

Girl: I don't like it.

First Messenger: You'll do fine.

Girl: I wish I was home in bed with a good
                Boy or something. I don't like it.

First M.:   You'll do fine.

Girl: I won't do fine:
            I'm frightened.

First M.:   All you do, you go up to them,
            Get them talking, keep them looking.

Girl:	Go up to them yourselves, why don't you?
First M.:	Sure, and get the brush-off. Girl like You can keep them talking; keep them Looking, that is. Pretty girl.
Girl:	I don't like it.
Second M.:	You'll get used to it.
Girl:	Not where I work. Not Society. Society page they never die. Girl gets asked. Girl gets married. Girl gets photographed in night club. Girl gets older. Girl gets off. Never catch them dead on Society.
Second M.:	Like the robins.
First M.:	Yeah, like robins.
Girl:	Why the robins?
Second M.:	Never see one Dead.
First M.:	Nor sparrows neither.
Second M.:	Either.
First M.:	Never hardly. Must be millions.
Second M.:	Hardly ever see one dead.

Girl: What happens to them?

Second M.:   They get over it.

Girl: Over what?

Second M.:   Over being there.

Girl: All I know is I don't like it.
Keep them talking till a flash bulb
Smacks them naked in the face —
It's horrible!

First M.:   It's genius! Listen, lady!
How do I get the. photograph without'
Answer me that. How do I get the
Look a mother's face has maybe
Once in a lifetime: just before
Her mouth knows, when her eyes are knowing?

Girl: I can't do it.

First M.:   *She* can't do it!
All you got to do is walk.
Wiggle your can. Keep them looking.
Then he tells them. Then I take them.
Then you beat it. Then that's that.
Except the drink we're going to buy you
Payday evening if you're good —
And if you're not there's lots of liars.

Second M.:   You don't have to tell them: I do.

Girl: Why do *you?*

Second M.:   Because I have to.
              I'm the one that has to tell them.

Girl: Why?

Second M.: *shrugging*
                    Oh . . .

Girl: Why?

Second M.:   There's always
              Someone has to tell them, isn't there?

Girl: Someone else can.

Second M.:   No. There's always . . .

He is groping from word to word.

              Someone chosen by the chance of seeing,
              By the accident of sight,
              By stumbling on the moment of it,
              Unprepared, unwarned, unready,
              Thinking of nothing, of his drink, his bed,
              His belly, and it happens, and he sees it . . .

He winces his eyes shut.

              Caught in that inextricable net

Of having witnessed, having seen ...

He alone!

Girl: *gently*   But you don't have to.

To the First Messenger.

Why does he have to?

Second M.:   It was I.
I only. I alone. The moment
Closed us together in its gaping grin
Of horrible incredulity. I saw their
Eyes see mine! We *saw* each other!

First M.:   He has to. He was there. He saw it.
Route Two. Under the viaduct.
Traveling seventy — seventy-five —
Kid was driving them was drunk,
Had to be drunk, just drove into it.
He was walking home. He saw it.
Saw it start to, saw it had to,
Saw it. J.B.'s son. His daughter.
Four in all and all just kids.
They shrieked like kids he said.

Second M.:   Then silent.
Blond in all that blood that daughter.

Girl: *her voice rising*
He can't tell them *that!*

First M.:   He has to.
           Someone has to. They don't know.
           They been out all evening somewhere.

Girl: *hysterically*
           They don't have to know!

First M.:   They have to.

Nickles and Mr. Zuss on their perches have seen something off to their right. They turn their heads together.

Girl: No!

First M.: *looking right, pulling his camera around*
                       That's them. They're coming. Quiet!

Girl: I can't do it.

First M.: *brutally*   You can do it.

J.B. and Sarah, arm in arm, walk slowly into the first circle of light. Nickles and Mr. Zuss lean forward, their masks dangling from their hands.

Second M.: *under his breath, staring at them as they come*
                       I only, I alone, to tell thee...
                       I who have understood nothing, have known
                       Nothing, have been answered nothing...

Girl: *crossing to meet them with an affected walk, the First Messenger screening himself behind her, the Second following*   Good
                       Evening! What a pleasant evening!

Back from the theatre so **soon?**
We're neighbors, don't you know? You've **met** my
Miffkin walking me each morning:
You know Muff, my purple poodle . . .

Isn't it a pleasant evening!

Second M.:   I'm from the press. There's been an accident . . .

He falters.

First M.:   Four kids in a car. They're dead.
Two were yours. Your son. Your daughter.
Cops have got them in a cab.
Any minute now they'll be here.

He raises his camera over the girl's shoulder.

Girl: *in her own voice, screaming*
Don't look! Cover your face!

Sarah: *with scarcely the breath to say it*
Mary . . . Jonathan . . .

*The flash. J.B. throws his elbow up as if to ward off a blow.
Sarah does not move.*

J.B.:   You bastards!
I'll beat your god damned brains out . . .

He lunges after them blinded by the flash as they scatter.

Where have you
Gone?

*Sarah moves like a sleepwalker through the circles of light,
one after the other, touches a chair, goes down on her knees
beside it, clinging to it.*

J.B.:   Answer me!

Silence.

J.B.:   Answer me!

Silence.

Sarah: *her voice dead*   It wasn't
          They that did it . . .

*J.B. comes slowly back out of the darkness, sees her, crosses
to her. There is a long silence, J.B. looking right and left along
the street.*

Sarah: Why did He do it to them?
          What had they done to Him — those chil-
          dren . . .
          What had they done to Him . . .

                              and we —
          What had *we* done? . . .

                              What had *we* done?

J.B.:   Don't, Sarah. Don't!

Nickles lights a cigarette, grins back over his shoulder to Mr.
Zuss in the handful of yellow glare.

J.B.:   It doesn't
         Help to think that.

Sarah: Nothing helps! . . .
         Nothing can help them now.

J.B.: *a clumsy gesture*   It . . . happened . . .

Sarah: *fiercely*
         Yes, and Who let it happen?

J.B.: *awkwardly*   Shall we . . .
         Take the good and not the evil?
         We have to take the chances, Sarah:
         Evil with good.
      then, in a desperate candor
                         It doesn't mean there
         Is no good!

Nickles: *in his cracked whisper*
                     Doesn't it? Doesn't it?

Mr. Zuss: *silencing Nickles with his hand, his whisper hardly*
         heard

         Go on! Go on! That path will lead you.

Sarah: *bitterly*
         When you were lucky it was God!

J.B.:   Sticks and stones and steel are chances.
                          There's no will in stone and steel . . .

His voice breaks.

                          It happens to us . . .

He drops on his knees beside her.

Sarah: No! . . .

                                                          Don't touch me!

She clings to the chair, motionless, not weeping.

The circles of light fade out.

SCENE FIVE

The dark diminishes until the white coats of Mr. Zuss and Nickles are visible on the platform. Mr. Zuss lifts a padded drumstick. Nickles balances on the rail and starts cautiously down the ladder.

Mr. Zuss: Ready?

Nickles: *cheerfully*   Got to be, don't they?

Mr. Zuss: I meant
                You.

Nickles: They've got no choice. Disaster —
                Death — mankind are always ready —
                Ready for anything that hurts.

Mr. Zuss: And you?

Nickles: I too! I too!

Mr. Zuss: Provided
                Someone else will bleed the blood
                And wipe the blinded eye?

Nickles: I watch
                Your world go round!

Mr. Zuss: It must be wearing.

Nickles: Oh, it has its compensations.
                Even a perfect and an upright man
                Learns if you keep turning long enough.

First he thought it wasn't happening —
Couldn't be happening — not to him —
Not with you in the stratosphere tooting the
Blue trombone for the moon to dance.
Then he thought it chanced by chance!
        a dry hiccup of laughter
Childish hypothesis of course
But still hypothesis — a start —
A pair of tongs to take the toad by —
Recognition that it *is* a toad:
Not quite comfort but still comfortable,
Eases the hook in the gills a little:
He'll learn.

Mr. Zuss: *preoccupied*   Learn what?

Nickles: Your — purpose for him!

Mr. Zuss: Keep your tongue in your teeth, will you?

He notices Nickles' descent on the ladder for the first time.

            Here! Wait a minute! Wait a
            Minute! Where are you off to?

Nickles: Bit of a
            Walk in the earth for my health — or some-
                body's.
        bitterly
            Up and down in the earth, you know —
            Back and forth in it . . .

Mr. Zuss: Leave him alone!

Nickles: He needs a helping hand: you've seen that —
             A nudge from an old professional.

Mr. Zuss: Leave him a
             Lone! He can't act and you know it.

Nickles: He doesn't have to act. He suffers.
             It's an old role — played like a mouth-organ.
             Any idiot on earth
             Given breath enough can breathe it —
             Given tears enough can weep.
             All he needs is help to see.

Mr. Zuss: See what?

Nickles: That bloody drum-stick striking;
             See Who lets it strike the drum!

*Mr. Zuss, whose lifted arm has been slowly falling, raises it
abruptly.*

Mr. Zuss: Wait!

He starts to strike the drum, stops the stroke in mid-air.

             Wait for me. I'm coming.
             Down!
                    Wait!
                          Wait I tell you!

The stroke of the drum. The light fades out.

Out of the dark two circles of light, one on the platform, one on the table. Behind the table are the two Messengers. The First, wearing a police sergeant's cap, sits on a chair. The Second, wearing a patrolman's cap, stands beside him. J.B., a raincoat over rumpled clothes, stands facing them. Above, on the platform, as on the landing of a stair, Sarah stands pulling a dressing gown around her shoulders. Nickles and Mr. Zuss, their masks in their hands, straddle a couple of chairs beyond the circle of light which centers on the table.

First M.:   Sorry to question you like this.
              We got to get the story.

J.B.: *impatiently*   Go on.

First M.:   Turning your house into a ...

J.B.:   No. Go on.
              It doesn't matter.

Sarah: *toneless*   Nothing matters but to
              Know.

First M.:   How many children?

Silence.

J.B.:   Two.

First M.: *writing*
              Girls?

Sarah: We had two boys.

144

First M.: *writing*   Girls.
          Names?

J.B.:   Ruth. Rebecca.

Sarah: Ruth is the
          Oldest . . . now.

First M.:   And you last saw her?

J.B.:   Ruth?

Sarah: *her voice rising*
          It's Rebecca is missing!

J.B.: *silencing her*   He
          Knows!

Sarah: *harshly*   No, it's God that knows!

There is an awkward silence. When Sarah speaks again her voice is dead.

          She's the littlest one. She's gone.

First M.:   How long ago?

Sarah: Oh . . . hours!

First M.:   It's three in the morning now.

J.B.:   Since seven.

First M.: *writing*
        And you reported it?

J.B.:   Yes.

First M.:   When?

J.B.:   One o'clock. A quarter after.
        We looked for her everywhere, of course.
        Then we thought — I thought — if somebody . . .

        Maybe the telephone would ring.

First M.:   And you'd do better on your own?

J.B.: *reluctantly*
        Yes.

Sarah: *with rising violence*
               Yes! Yes! Yes!
        We believe in our luck in this house!
        We've earned the right to! We believe in it . . .
    bitterly   All but the bad!

Nickles: *rocking back on his chair*
                  That's playing it!
        That's playing it!

He begins to sing in his cracked whisper, beating a jazzed rhythm on the back of his mask as though it were a banjo.

        If God is Will
        And Will is well

Then what is ill?
God still?
Dew tell!

Mr. Zuss does not seem to hear. He is listening intently to the scene at the table.

First M.:   And nobody telephoned?

J.B.:   Nobody telephoned.

First M.: *writing*   Dressed? How was she
Dressed?

J.B.: *turning for the first time to look up at Sarah*
                    White?

Sarah: White! You saw her
Glimmering in the twilight.

First M.: *writing*   White.

Sarah: All but her
Shoes.

The First Messenger looks up at the Second.

First M.:   Her shoes were what?

Sarah: Red.

The First Messenger looks up again. The Second turns his face away.

First M.:   Rebecca have a red umbrella?

Sarah: Parasol.

First M.:   Little toy umbrella.

Sarah: *startled*
                Parasol. Yes, she might have had one.

First M.:   You mean she owned one?

Sarah: Yes. It belonged to a
                Big doll we bought her once.
                Scarlet silk. It opens and closes.
                She kept it when the doll gave out.
                She used to take it to bed with her even —
                Open and close it.

The First Messenger looks up for the third time at the Second, whose face, still turned away, is like stone.

J.B.: *a step forward*   You've found the parasol!

Second M.: *not looking at him; a voice without expression or tone*   .
                What will it tell you? Will it tell you why?

J.B.: *to First M.*
                I asked you: have you found the parasol?

First M.:   He's the one. Ask him. He'll tell you.

Second M.: *with difficulty, like a man speaking out of physical pain*

Can the tooth among the stones make answer? . . .

Can the seven bones reply? . . .

Out in the desert in the tombs
Are potter's figures: two of warriors,
Two of worthies, two of camels,
Two of monsters, two of horses.
Ask them why. They will not answer you . . .

He brushes his hand heavily across his face.

Death is a bone that stammers . . .

                                  a tooth
Among the flints that has forgotten.

J.B.: *violently*
        Ask him! Has he found the parasol!

First M.:   We don't know. He found an umbrella —
              Doll's umbrella — red.

Sarah: Oh, where?

J.B.:   Nothing else? Just the umbrella?

First M.: *to Second*
        Tell them, will you!

*The Second Messenger does not move or speak. The First
shrugs, looks down at his pencil, rattles it off in a matter-of-fact
monotone.*

                              Just past midnight
                Pounding his beat by the back of the lumberyard
                Somebody runs and he yells and they stumble —
                Big kid — nineteen maybe —
                Hopped to the eyes and scared — scared
                Bloodless he could barely breathe.
                Constable yanks him up by the britches:
                "All right! Take me to it!"
                Just a shot in the dark, he was so
                Goddam scared there had to be something...

                Well ...

                      He took him to it ...

                                          back of the
                Lumber trucks beside the track.

J.B.:   Go on.

First M.:   She had a toy umbrella.
                That was all she had — but shoes:
                Red shoes and a toy umbrella.
                It was tight in her fist when he found her — still.

J.B.:   Let me see it! The umbrella!

First M.:   Constable will show it to you.

*The Second Messenger takes something wound in newspaper
out of his pocket. He does not look at it or them. The First
Messenger half opens it, lays it on the table.*

Sarah: Oh, my baby! Oh, my baby!

The First Messenger gets out of his chair, stands a moment awkwardly, goes out. The Second follows. J.B. stands motionless over the table. Sarah hugs her dressing gown around her, rocking herself slowly, her head bowed.

Nickles: *leaning forward toward J.B., a wheedling whisper*
                Now's the time to say it, mister.

Mr. Zuss: Leave him alone!

J.B.: *touching the parasol*   The Lord giveth . . .

His voice breaks.

                                                the
                Lord taketh away!

Mr. Zuss: *rising, whispering*   Go on!
                Go on! Finish it! Finish it!

Nickles: What should he
                Finish when he's said it all?

Mr. Zuss: Go on!

Nickles: To what? To where? He's got there, hasn't he?
                Now he's said it, now he knows.
                He knows Who gives, he knows Who takes now.

J.B. stands silent over the parasol.

                                                        151

Mr. Zuss:	Why won't he play the part he's playing?
Nickles:	Because he isn't.
Mr. Zuss:	Isn't what?
Nickles:	Isn't playing. He's not playing. He isn't in the play at all. He's where we all are — in our suffering. Only . . .

Nickles turns savagely on Mr. Zuss.

. . . Now he knows its Name!

Nickles points dramatically toward the canvas sky. Mr. Zuss's head tilts back following the gesture. He freezes into immobility.

Mr. Zuss:	Look! Look up!
Nickles:	That's your direction.
Mr. Zuss:	Look, I say! The staring stars!
Nickles:	Or only lights not meant . . .

Nickles twists his crooked neck, looks sidewise upward. The canvas sky has disappeared into a profound darkness. There seem to be stars beyond it.

Nickles:	You're mad. You've lost your mind. You're maundering . . .

They rise together, their heads back, peering into the darkness overhead.

Nickles: . . . maundering.

Mr. Zuss: Let's get back where we belong.

Nickles: Go on!

Mr. Zuss: No; you.

Nickles: All right . . . together.

They take each other's arm as the light fades.

SCENE SIX

Darkness and silence as before. The drum — a great crash and a long roll fading out. A gray light which has no visible source drifts across the stage where tables and chairs are scattered and overturned. Mr. Zuss and Nickles are huddled together on their platform peering down. J.B., his clothes torn and white with dust, faces what was once the door. The two Messengers, wearing steel helmets and brassards, stand there, carrying Sarah between them.

First Messenger:
> She said she lived around here somewhere.
> This is all there is.

J.B.:   Sarah!

First M.:   Where do you want her?

J.B.:   Sarah! Sarah!

First M.:   On the floor? You got a floor.
> You're lucky if you got a floor.

They lay her carefully down. J.B. takes his torn coat off, rolls it into a pillow, kneels to put it under her head.

J.B.:   Where was she?

First M.:   Underneath a wall.
        indicating Second Messenger
                    He heard her underneath a wall
                    Calling.
        to Second Messenger
                    Tell him what you heard her . . .

Second M.: *imitating*
                    Ruth! . . . Ruth!

First M.:   Nobody answered:
                    Nobody could have.

J.B. does not look up or speak. The First Messenger starts toward the door, kicking a fallen chair out of his way.

                    You been down there?
                    Whole block's gone. Bank block. All of it.
                    J.B.'s bank. You know. Just gone.
                    Nothing left to show it ever.
                    Just the hole.

Sarah stirs, opens her eyes. J.B. leans over her. She turns away.

                    J.B.'s millions!
                    That's a laugh now — J.B.'s millions!
                    All he's got is just the hole.
                    Plant went too — all of it — everything.
                    Ask him! Just the hole. He'll tell you.

Sarah: *faintly, her voice following the rhythm of the Second
        Messenger*
                    Ruth! . . . Ruth!

First M.:   He can tell you.
          He can tell you what he saw.

Sarah: *tonelessly like a voice counting*
          David ... Jonathan ... Mary ... Ruth ...
          I cannot say the last.

J.B.: *his hands on hers*   Rebecca.

Sarah: David ... Jonathan ... Mary ... Ruth ...

J.B.: *looking up over his shoulder, to the Second Messenger*
          You didn't find ... there wasn't ...

First M.:   Tell him.
          Tell him what you heard.

Second M.:   I heard
          Two words. I don't know what they mean.
          I have brought them to you like a pair of pebbles
          Picked up in a path or a pair of
          Beads that might belong to somebody.

J.B.:   There wasn't ... anyone beside?

Second M.: *almost a whisper*
          I only am escaped alone to tell thee.

Sarah: David ... Jonathan ... Mary ... Ruth ...

J.B.:   Sarah!

Silence.

Listen to me!

Silence.

Sarah!
Even desperate we can't despair —
Let go each other's fingers — sink
Numb in that dumb silence — drown there
Sole in our cold selves...

We cannot!...

God is there too, in the desperation.
I do not know why God should strike
But God is what is stricken also:
Life is what despairs in death
And, desperate, is life still...

Sarah!
Do not let my hand go, Sarah!

Say it after me:

The Lord
Giveth ... Say it.

Sarah: *mechanically*   The Lord giveth.

J.B.:   The Lord taketh away...

Sarah: *flinging his hand from hers, shrieking*
Takes!
Kills! Kills! Kills! Kills!

Silence.

J.B.:   Blessed be the name of the Lord.

The light fades.

SCENE SEVEN

Darkness. Silence. Then, out of the dark, Mr. Zuss's voice. It has recovered its confidence and timbre.

Mr. Zuss: Well, my friend...

The platform comes into light, Mr. Zuss and Nickles are still where they were, leaning over, elbows on the rail. They straighten up, stretching.

                                    ...you see the position.
              You see how it all comes out in the end.
              Your fears were quite unfounded, weren't they?

Nickles: *sourly*
              My fears for you?

Mr. Zuss: For me?... For me!
              Why should you fear for me?

Nickles: I can't
              Think!

Mr. Zuss: No, for him.

Nickles: That ham!

Mr. Zuss: Ham?

Nickles: Ham!

Mr. Zuss: *pleasantly* And you've been telling me
      Over and over that he isn't in it —
      Isn't acting even: only
      Living — breathing . . .

Nickles: Man can muff his
      Life as badly as his lines and louder.
      In it or out of it he's ham.
      He wouldn't understand if twenty
      Thousand suffocating creatures
      Shrieked and tore their tongues out at him
      Choking in a bombed-out town. He'd be
      Thankful!

Mr. Zuss: *stiffly* I think he understands it
      Perfectly! I think that great
      Yea-saying to the world was wonderful —
      That wounded and deliberate Amen —
      That — affirmation!

Nickles: Affirmation!
      Ever watch the worms affirming?
      Ever hear a hog's Amen
      Just when the knife first hurt? Death is
      Good for you! It makes you glisten!
      Get the large economy container,
      Five for the price of one!

          You think it's
      Wonderful . . .

He wheels on Mr. Zuss in a sudden fury.

I think it stinks!
One daughter raped and murdered by an idiot,
Another crushed by stones, a son
Destroyed by some fool officer's stupidity,
Two children smeared across a road
At midnight by a drunken child —
And all with God's consent! — foreknowl-
edge! —
And he blesses God!

Nickles points dramatically at the white, calm, unconcerned mask in Mr. Zuss's hands.

It isn't decent!
It isn't moral even! It's disgusting!
His weeping wife in her despair
And he beside her on his trembling ham-bones
Praising God! . . . It's nauseating!

Mr. Zuss: You don't lose gracefully, do you?

Nickles: *snarling*   I don't
Lose.

Mr. Zuss: You have.

Nickles: That's not the end of it.

Mr. Zuss: No, but that's the *way* it ends.

Nickles: Could have ended.

Mr. Zuss: What do you mean?

Nickles:	Would have, if God had been content
	With this poor crawling victory. He isn't.
	Still He must pursue, still follow —
	Hunt His creature through his branching veins
	With agony until no peace is left him —
	All one blazing day of pain:
	Corner him, compel the answer.
	He cannot rest until He wrings
	The proof of pain, the ultimate certainty.
	God always asks the proof of pain.
Mr. Zuss:	And Job, in his affliction, gives it.
Nickles:	No! God overreaches at the end —
	Pursues too far — follows too fearfully.
	He seals him in his sack of skin
	And scalds his skin to crust to squeeze
	The answer out, but Job evades Him.
Mr. Zuss:	Who can evade the will of God!
	It waits at every door we open.
	What does Dante say? His will...
Nickles:	Don't chant that chill equation at me!
Mr. Zuss:	His will: our peace.
Nickles:	Will was never peace, no matter
	Whose will, whose peace.
	Will is rule: surrender is surrender.
	You *make* your peace: you don't give in to it.
	Job will make his own cold peace
	When God pursues him in the web too far —

Implacable, eternal Spider.
A man can always cease: it's something —
A judgment anyway: reject
The whole creation with a stale pink pill.

Mr. Zuss: World is Will. Job can't reject it.

Nickles: God has forgotten what a man can do
Once his body hurts him — once
Pain has penned him in where only
Pain has room to breathe. He learns!
He learns to spit his broken teeth out —
Spit the dirty world out — spit!

Mr. Zuss: And that's the end of everything — to *spit?*

Nickles: Better than that other end
Of pain, of physical agony, of suffering
God prepares for all His creatures.

Mr. Zuss: *Is* it better? *Is* it better?
Job has suffered and praised God.
Would Job be better off asleep
Among the clods of earth in ignorance?

Nickles: Yes, when he suffers in his body:
Yes, when his suffering is *him.*

Mr. Zuss: His suffering will praise.

Nickles: It will not.

Mr. Zuss: Well,
We still have time to see.

Nickles: **Put on your**
                Mask! You'll see!

The light has faded but the faces of the actors are still visible.

Mr. Zuss: *raising his mask*   Put on your own!

Nickles leans over to find it, searching the floor of the platform with his hands. A long silence. From the silence at length:

The Distant Voice:
                Hast thou considered my servant Job
                That there is none like him on the earth,
                A perfect and an upright man, one
                That feareth God and escheweth evil?

Nickles: Wait a minute! I can't find . . .

The Distant Voice: *louder*
                And still he holdeth fast his integrity . . .

Nickles: Wait a minute, can't you? What the . . .

The Distant Voice: *almost a whisper*
                Although thou movedst me against him
                To destroy him . . .

Nickles rises, his mask in his two hands. He wheels on Mr. Zuss only to see that Mr. Zuss also has his mask in his hands and stands staring up into the canvas sky.

The Distant Voice is barely audible.

                        without cause . . .

Silence. The two old actors stand side by side, holding their masks, their heads moving slowly together as they search the dark.

Nickles: Who said that?

Silence.

Mr. Zuss: They want us to go on.

Nickles: Why don't you?

Mr. Zuss: He was asking *you.*

Nickles: Who was?

Mr. Zuss: He was.

Nickles: Prompter probably. Prompter somewhere.
              Your lines he was reading weren't they?

Mr. Zuss: Yes but...

Nickles: *shouting*   Anybody there?

Silence.

Mr. Zuss: They want us to go on. I told you.

Nickles: Yes. They want us to go on ...
              I don't like it.

Mr. Zuss: We began it.

They put their masks on slowly. The lights fade out. The huge shadows appear on the canvas sky, facing each other.

Godmask: ...And still he holdeth fast his integrity
            Although thou movedst me against him
            To destroy him...

His voice breaks.

                               without cause.

Satanmask: Skin for skin, yea, all that a man
            Hath will he give for his life.
            But put forth thine hand now and touch
            His bone and his flesh
            And he will curse thee to thy face.

The God-shadow raises its arm again in the formal gesture of contemptuous commitment.

Godmask: Behold he is in thine hand...

The God-shadow turns away. Silence.

                               but...
        Save his life!

The two shadows lean together over the earth.

        Note: A second break in the action may be
        made here if it is thought desirable.

SCENE EIGHT

There is no light but the glow on the canvas sky, which holds the looming, leaning shadows. They fade as a match is struck. It flares in Sarah's hand, showing her face, and glimmers out against the wick of a dirty lantern. As the light of the lantern rises, J.B. is seen lying on the broken propped-up table, naked but for a few rags of clothing. Sarah looks at him in the new light, shudders, lets her head drop into her hands. There is a long silence and then a movement in the darkness of the open door where four women and a young girl stand, their arms filled with blankets and newspapers. They come forward slowly into the light.

Nickles: *unseen, his cracked, cackling voice drifting down from the darkness of the platform overhead*

        Never fails! Never fails!
        Count on you to make a mess of it!
        Every blessed blundering time
        You hit at one man you blast thousands.
        Think of that Flood of yours — a massacre!
        Now you've fumbled it again:
        Tumbled a whole city down
        To blister one man's skin with agony.

Nickles' white coat appears at the foot of the ladder. The women, in the circle of the lantern, are walking slowly around J.B. and Sarah, staring at them as though they were figures in a show window.

167

Nickles: Look at your works! Those shivering women
              Sheltering under any crumbling
              Heap to keep the sky out! Weeping!

Mrs. Adams: That's him.

Jolly Adams: Who's him?

Mrs. Adams: Grammar, Jolly.

Mrs. Lesure: Who did she say it was?

Mrs. Murphy: Him she said it was.
              Poor soul!

Mrs. Lesure: Look at them sores on him!

Mrs. Adams: Don't look, child. You'll remember them.

Jolly Adams: *proudly*
              Every sore I seen I remember.

Mrs. Botticelli:
              Who did she say she said it was?

Mrs. Murphy: Him.

Mrs. Adams: That's his wife.

Mrs. Lesure: She's pretty.

Mrs. Botticelli: Ain't she.
              Looks like somebody we've seen.

Mrs. Adams: *snooting her*
    I don't believe you would have seen her:
    Picture possibly — her picture
    Posed in the penthouse.

Mrs. Botticelli: Puce with pants?

Mrs. Adams: No, the negligee.

Mrs. Botticelli: The net?

Mrs. Adams: The simple silk.

Mrs. Botticelli: Oh la! With sequins?

Mrs. Murphy:
    Here's a place to park your poodle —
    Nice cool floor.

Mrs. Lesure: Shove over, dearie.

The women settle themselves on their newspapers off at the edge of the circle of light. Nickles has perched himself on a chair at the side. Silence.

J.B.: *a whisper*
    God, let me die!

Nickles leers up into the dark toward the unseen platform.

Sarah: *her voice dead*   You think He'd help you
    Even to that?

Silence. Sarah looks up, turning her face away from J.B. She speaks without passion, almost mechanically.

Sarah: God is our enemy

J.B.:   No...No...No...Don't
              Say that Sarah!

Sarah's head turns toward him slowly as though dragged against her will. She stares and cannot look away.

                          God has something
              Hidden from our hearts to show.

Nickles: She knows! She's looking at it!

J.B.:   Try to
              Sleep.

Sarah: *bitterly*   He should have kept it hidden.

J.B.:   Sleep now.

Sarah: You don't have to see it:
              I do.

J.B.:   Yes, I know.

Nickles: *a cackle*   He knows!
              He's back behind it and he knows!
              If he could see what she can see
              There's something else he might be knowing.

J.B.:   Once I knew a charm for sleeping —

              Not as forgetfulness but gift,
              Not as sleep but second sight,

170

>   Come and from my eyelids lift
>   The dead of night.

Sarah: The dead . . .
                                        of night . . .

She drops her head to her knees, whispering.

>   Come and from my eyelids lift
>   The dead of night.

Silence.

J.B.:   Out of sleep
>   Something of our own comes back to us:
>   A drowned man's garment from the sea.

*Sarah turns the lantern down. Silence. Then the voices of
the women, low.*

Mrs. Botticelli:
>   Poor thing!

Mrs. Murphy: Poor thing!
>   Not a chick nor a child between them.

Mrs. Adams: First their daughters. Then their sons.

Mrs. Murphy: First son first. Blew him to pieces.
>   More mischance it was than war.
>   Asleep on their feet in the frost they walked
>   into it.

Mrs. Adams: Two at the viaduct: that makes three.

Jolly Adams: *a child's chant*
                 Jolly saw the picture! the picture!

Mrs. Adams: Jolly Adams, you keep quiet.

Jolly Adams: Wanna know? The whole of the viaduct . . .

Mrs. Adams: Never again will you look at them! Never!

Mrs. Lesure: Them magazines! They're awful! Which?

Mrs. Murphy: And after that the little one.

Mrs. Botticelli: Who in the
             World are they talking about, the little one?
             What are they talking?

Mrs. Lesure: I don't know.
             Somebody dogged by death it must be.

Mrs. Botticelli:
             Him it must be.

Mrs. Lesure: Who's him?

Mrs. Adams: You know who.

Mrs. Murphy: You remember the . . .

Mrs. Adams: Hush! The child!

Mrs. Murphy: Back of the lumberyard.

Mrs. Lesure: Oh! Him!

Mrs. Murphy: Who did you think it was —
Penthouse and negligees, daughters and dying?

Mrs. Botticelli:
Him? That's him? That millionaire?

Mrs. Lesure: Millionaires he buys like cabbages.

Mrs. Murphy: He couldn't buy cabbages now by the look of
him:
The rags he's got on.

Mrs. Botticelli: Look at them sores!

Mrs. Murphy: All that's left him now is her.

Mrs. Botticelli:
Still that's something — a good woman.

Mrs. Murphy: What good is a woman to him with that hide
on him? —
Or he to her if you think of it.

Mrs. Adams: Don't!

Mrs. Lesure: Can you blame her?

Mrs. Murphy: I don't blame her
All I say is she's no comfort.
She won't cuddle.

Mrs. Adams: Really, Mrs. . . .

Mrs. Murphy: Murphy call me. What's got into you? . . .
Nothing recently I'd hazard.

Mrs. Adams: You're not so young yourself, my woman.

Mrs. Murphy: Who's your woman? I was Murphy's.

Mrs. Lesure: None of us are maids entirely.

Mrs. Murphy: Maids in mothballs some might be.

Mrs. Adams: Who might?

Mrs. Murphy: You might.

Mrs. Adams: You! you're . . . historical!

Mrs. Murphy: I never slept a night in history!

Mrs. Botticelli:
            I have. Oh, my mind goes back.

Mrs. Adams: None of that! We have a child here!

Silence.

            How far back?

Mrs. Botticelli: I often wonder.
            Farther than the first but . . . where?

Mrs. Murphy: What do you care? It's lovely country.

Silence.

> Roll a little nearer, dearie,
> Me back side's froze.

Mrs. Lesure: You smell of roses

Mrs. Murphy: Neither do you but you're warm.

Mrs. Botticelli: Well,
Good night, ladies. Good night, ladies

*Silence. Out of the silence, felt rather than heard at first, a
sound of sobbing, a muffled, monotonous sound like the heavy
beat of a heart.*

J.B.: If you could only sleep a little
Now they're quiet, now they're still.

Sarah: *her voice broken*
I try. But oh I close my eyes and ...
Eyes are open there to meet me!

Silence. Then Sarah's voice in an agony of bitterness.

My poor babies! Oh, my babies!

*J.B. pulls himself painfully up, sits huddled on his table in
the feeble light of the lamp, his rags about him.*

J.B.: *gently*   Go to sleep.

Sarah: Go! Go where?
              If there were darkness I'd go there.
              If there were night I'd lay me down in it.
              God has shut the night against me.
              God has set the dark alight
              With horror blazing blind as day
              When I go toward it . . .
                              close my eyes.

J.B.:   I know. I know those waking eyes.
              His will is everywhere against us —
              Even in our sleep, our dreams . . .

Nickles: *a snort of laughter up toward the dark of the platform*
              Your will, his peace!
              Doesn't seem to grasp that, does he?
              Give him another needling twinge
              Between the withers and the works —
              He'll understand you better.

J.B.:   If I
              Knew . . . If I knew why!

Nickles: If he knew
              Why he wouldn't be there. He'd be
              Strangling, drowning, suffocating,
              Diving for a sidewalk somewhere . . .

J.B.:   What I *can't* bear is the blindness —
              Meaninglessness — the numb blow
              Fallen in the stumbling night.

Sarah: *starting violently to her feet*
              Has death no meaning? Pain no meaning?

She points at his body.

> Even these suppurating sores —
> Have they no meaning for you?

Nickles: Ah!

J.B.: *from his heart's pain*
> God will not punish without cause.

Nickles doubles up in a spasm of soundless laughter.

J.B.:   God is just.

Sarah: *hysterically*   God is just!
> If God is just our slaughtered children
> Stank with sin, were rotten with it!

She controls herself with difficulty, turns toward him, reaches her arms out, lets them fall.

> Oh, my dear! my dear! my dear!
> Does God demand deception of us? —
> Purchase His innocence by ours?
> Must we be guilty for Him? — bear
> The burden of the world's malevolence
> For Him who made the world?

J.B.:   He
> Knows the guilt is mine. He must know:
> Has He not punished it? He knows its
> Name, its time, its face, its circumstance,
> The figure of its day, the door,
> The opening of the door, the room, the mo-
>   ment . . .

177

Sarah: *fiercely*

> And you? Do you? You do not know it.
> Your punishment is all you know.

She moves toward the door, stops, turns.

> I will not stay here if you lie —
> Connive in your destruction, cringe to it:
> Not if you betray my children ...
>
> I will not stay to listen ...
>
>   They are
> Dead and they were innocent: I will not
> Let you sacrifice their deaths
> To make injustice justice and God good!

J.B.: *covering his face with his hands*

> My heart beats. I cannot answer it.

Sarah:

> If you buy quiet with their innocence —
> Theirs or yours ...

> *softly*   I will not love you.

J.B.:

> I have no choice but to be guilty.

Sarah: *her voice rising*

> We have the choice to live or die,
> All of us ...
>
>   curse God and die ...

Silence.

J.B.:
> God is God or we are nothing —
> Mayflies that leave their husks behind —
> Our tiny lives ridiculous — a suffering
> Not even sad that Someone Somewhere
> Laughs at as we laugh at apes.
> We have no choice but to be guilty. ·
> God is unthinkable if we are innocent.

Sarah turns, runs soundlessly out of the circle of light, out of the door. The women stir. Mrs. Murphy comes up on her elbow.

Mrs. Murphy: What did I say? I said she'd walk out on him.

Mrs. Lesure: She did.

Mrs. Botticelli: Did she?

Mrs. Murphy: His hide was too much for her.

Mrs. Botticelli:
> His hide or his heart.

Mrs. Murphy: The hide comes between.

Mrs. Botticelli:
> The heart is the stranger.

Mrs. Murphy: Oh, strange!
> It's always strange the heart is: only
> It's the skin we ever know.

J.B.: *raising his head*

>Sarah, why do you not speak to me? . . .
>Sarah!

Silence.

Mrs. Adams: Now he knows.

Mrs. Murphy: And he's alone now.

J.B.'s head falls forward onto his knees. Silence. Out of the silence his voice in an agony of prayer.

J.B.: Show me my guilt, O God!

Nickles:
>   *His*
>Guilt! His! You heard that didn't you?
>He wants to feel the feel of guilt —
>That putrid poultice of the soul
>That draws the poison in, not out —
>Inverted catheter! You going to show him?

Silence. Nickles rises, moves toward the ladder.

>Well? You going to show him . . . Jahveh?

Silence. He crosses to the ladder's foot.

>Where are those cold comforters of yours
>Who justify the ways of God to
>Job by making Job responsible? —
>Those three upholders of the world —
>Defenders of the universe — where are they?

Silence. He starts up the ladder. Stops. The jeering tone is gone. His voice is bitter.

Must be almost time for comfort! . . .

Nickles vanishes into the darkness above. The light fades.

SCENE NINE

Darkness.

J.B.'s Voice: If I had perished from the womb, not having
                 Been . . .

*A light without source rises slowly like the light at evening
which enlarges everything. The canvas walls dissolve into distance, the canvas sky into endlessness. The platform has been
pushed away to the side until only the ladder is visible. The
women and the child are huddled together like sleeping figures
on a vast plain. J.B. is alone in an enormous loneliness. Out of
that seeming distance the Three Comforters come shuffling
forward dressed in worn-out clothing. Zophar, a fat, red-faced
man wears the wreck of a clerical collar. Eliphaz, lean and
dark, wears an intern's jacket which once was white. Bildad is
a squat, thick man in a ragged wind-breaker. The women do
not see them, but Jolly Adams sits suddenly up clapping her
hands to her mouth. J.B., his head on his arms, sees nothing.*

J.B.:   Death cannot heal me . . .
                                                   Death
                 Will leave my having been behind it
                 Like a bear's foot festering in a trap . . .

Jolly Adams: *her voice rising word by word to a scream*
                 Look! Look! Look! Look!
                 Mother! Mother!

The women pull themselves up. The Three Comforters shuffle
on, squat in the rubbish around J.B.: Zophar lighting the stub
of a fat, ragged cigar; Eliphaz lighting a broken pipe; Bildad
lighting a crumpled cigarette.

Mrs. Murphy: Agh, the scavengers!

Mrs. Botticelli:
          Three old pokey crows they look like.

Mrs. Murphy:
          They are, too. It's the smell of the suffering.
          See that leather-backed old bucket? —
          Kind of character you hear from
          Sundays in a public park
          Pounding the hell out of everything . . . *you*
            know.

Mrs. Botticelli:
          I know. Wall Street. Bakers. Bankers.

Mrs. Lesure: All the answers in a book.

Mrs. Botticelli:
          Russkys got them all — the answers.

Mrs. Murphy:
          Characters like that, they smell the
          Human smell of heartsick misery
          Farther than a kite smells carrion.

Mrs. Lesure: Who's the collar?

183

Mrs. Murphy: Some spoiled priest.

Mrs. Botticelli:
                They can smell it farther even.

Mrs. Lesure: Not as far as dead-beat doctors:
               They're the nosies.

Mrs. Murphy: Let them nose!
          a tremendous yawn
               Ohhh, I'm halfway over . .
                                        drownding
               Down and down . . .
                              I hear the seagulls
               Singing soundings in the sea . . .

*She lets herself fall back on her newspapers. The others follow
one by one.*

Jolly Adams: I don't hear them.

Mrs. Botticelli: Pound your ears.

Mrs. Lesure: Slip your moorings . . . Oh, I'm numb.

Mrs. Murphy: Come alongside, dear.

Mrs. Lesure: I'm coming.

Mrs. Botticelli:
                That doctor one, he makes me creep.

Mrs. Murphy: Keep your thumb on your thoughts or he'll
diddle them.

Mrs. Botticelli:
Let him pry: he'll lose an eyeball.

Mrs. Lesure: He's a peeper. Watch your sleep.

Mrs. Murphy: Who was she, all gore, all story,
Dabbled in a deep blood sea,
And what she washed in, that was she?

Mrs. Lesure: *from her dream*
Some queen of Scotland . . .

Mrs. Murphy: Queen of Scones . . .

*A long silence. The Three Comforters squat smoking and
waiting. At length J.B. pulls himself painfully up to kneel on
his table, his face raised.*

J.B.: *a whisper*
God! My God! My God! What have I
Done?

Silence.

Bildad: *removing his cigarette*
Fair question, Big Boy.
Anyone answer you yet? No answer?

Zophar: *removing his cigar*
That was answered long ago —
Long ago.

185

Eliphaz: *knocking out his pipe*
                    In dreams are answers.
              How do your dreams go, Big Boy? Tell!

J.B.: *peering*
              Is someone there? Where? I cannot
              See you in this little light
              My eyes too fail me ...

Silence.

                                        Who is there?

Silence.

              I know how ludicrous I must look,
              Covered with rags, my skin pustulant ...

Silence.

              I know ...

Silence.

              I know how others see me.

A *long silence.*

              Why have you come?

Bildad: *a coarse laugh*   For comfort, Big Boy.
              Didn't you ring?

Zophar: *a fat laugh*   That's it: for comfort!

Eliphaz: *a thin laugh*
　　　　　All the comfort you can find.

Bildad:　　All the kinds of.

Eliphaz:　　　　　　　　*All* the comforts.

Zophar:　　You called us and we came.

J.B.:　　　　　　　　　　　　I called
　　　　　God.

Bildad:　　　　Didn't you!

Eliphaz:　　　　　　　Didn't you just!

Zophar:　　Why should God reply to *you*
　　　　　From the blue depths of His Eternity?

Eliphaz:　　Blind depths of His Unconsciousness?

Bildad:　　Blank depths of His Necessity?

Zophar:　　God is far above in Mystery.

Eliphaz:　　God is far below in Mindlessness.

Bildad:　　God is far within in History —
　　　　　Why should God have time for you?

J.B.:　　　The hand of God has touched me. Look at me!
　　　　　Every hope I ever had,
　　　　　Every task I put my mind to,
　　　　　Every work I've ever done

Annulled as though I had not done it.
My trace extinguished in the land,
My children dead, my father's name
Obliterated in the sunlight everywhere...

Love too has left me.

Bildad: Love!
      a great guffaw
              What's love to Him? One man's misery!

J.B.: *hardly daring*
              If I am innocent...?

Bildad: *snort of jeering laughter*   Innocent! Innocent!
              Nations shall perish in their innocence.
              Classes shall perish in their innocence.
              Young men in slaughtered cities
              Offering their silly throats
              Against the tanks in innocence shall perish.
              What's your innocence to theirs?
              God is History. If you offend Him
              Will not History dispense with you?
              History has no time for innocence.

J.B.:   God is just. We are not squeezed
              Naked through a ridiculous orifice
              Like bulls into a blazing ring
              To blunder there by blindfold laws
              We never learn or can, deceived by
              Stratagems and fooled by feints,
              For sport, for nothing, till we fall
              We're pricked so badly.

Bildad: *all park-bench orator*   Screw your justice!
          History is justice! — time
          Inexorably turned to truth! —
          Not for one man. For humanity.
          One man's life won't measure on it.
          One man's suffering won't count, no matter
          What his suffering; but All will.
          At the end there will be justice! —
          Justice for All! Justice for everyone!
   subsiding
          On the way — it doesn't matter.

J.B.:   Guilt matters. Guilt must always matter.
          Unless guilt matters the whole world is
          Meaningless. God too is nothing.

Bildad: *losing interest*
          You may be guiltier than Hell
          As History counts guilt and not
          One smudging thumbprint on your conscience.
          Guilt is a sociological accident:
          Wrong class — wrong century —
          You pay for your luck with your licks, that's all.

Eliphaz has been fidgeting. Now he breaks in like a professor in a seminar, poking a forefinger at the air.

Eliphaz: Come! Come! Come! Guilt is a
          Psychophenomenal situation —
          An illusion, a disease, a sickness:
          That filthy feeling at the fingers,
          Scent of dung beneath the nails . . .

Zophar: *outraged, flushed, head thrown back*

> Guilt is illusion? Guilt is reality! —
> The one reality there is!
> All mankind are guilty always!

Bildad: *jeering*

> The Fall of Man it felled us all!

J.B.'s voice breaks through the squabbling with something of its old authority.

J.B.:

> No doubt ye are the people
> And wisdom shall die with you! I am
> Bereaved, in pain, desperate, and you mock me!
> There was a time when men found pity
> Finding each other in the night:
> Misery to walk with misery —
> Brother in whose brother-guilt
> Guilt could be conceived and recognized.
> We have forgotten pity.

Eliphaz:

> No.
> We have surmounted guilt. It's quite,
> Quite different, isn't it? You see the difference.
> Science knows now that the sentient spirit
> Floats like the chambered nautilus on a sea
> That drifts it under skies that drive:
> Beneath, the sea of the subconscious;
> Above, the winds that wind the world.
> Caught between that sky, that sea,
> Self has no will, cannot be guilty.
> The sea drifts. The sky drives.
> The tiny, shining bladder of the soul

Washes with wind and wave or shudders
Shattered between them.

Zophar: Blasphemy!

Bildad: Bullshit!

Eliphaz: *oblivious*
There is no guilt, my man. We all are
Victims of our guilt, not guilty.
We kill the king in ignorance: the voice
Reveals: we blind ourselves. At our
Beginning, in the inmost room,
Each one of us, disgusting monster
Changed by the chilling moon to child,
Violates his mother. Are we guilty?
Our guilt is underneath the Sybil's
Stone: not known.

J.B.: *violently*   I'd rather suffer
Every unspeakable suffering God sends,
Knowing it was I that suffered,
I that earned the need to suffer,
I that acted, I that chose,
Than wash my hands with yours in that
Defiling innocence. Can we be men
And make an irresponsible ignorance
Responsible for everything? I will not
Listen to you!

J.B. *pulls his rags over his head.*

Eliphaz: *shrugging*   But you will. You will.

Zophar: Ah, my son, how well you said that!
How well you said it! Without guilt
What is a man? An animal, isn't he?
A wolf forgiven at his meat,
A beetle innocent in his copulation.
What divides us from the universe
Of blood and seed, conceives the soul in us,
Brings us to God, but guilt? The lion
Dies of death: we die of suffering.
The lion vanishes: our souls accept
Eternities of reparation.
But for our guilt we too would vanish,
Bundles of corrupting bones
Bagged in a hairless hide and rotting.
Happy the man whom God correcteth!
He tastes his guilt. His hope begins.
He is in league with the stones in certainty.

*J.B. pulls his rags from his head, drags himself around toward
the voice.*

J.B.:   *Teach me and I will hold my tongue.
Show me my transgression.*

Zophar: *gently*   No.
No, my son. You show *me.*

He hunches forward dropping his voice.

Search your inmost heart! Question it!
Guilt is a deceptive secret,
The labor often of years, a work

Conceived in infancy, brought to birth
In unpredictable forms years after:
At twelve the palpable elder brother;
At seventeen, perhaps, the servant
Seen by the lamp by accident...

J.B.: *urgently, the words forced from him*   My
Sin! Teach me my sin! My wickedness!
Surely iniquity that suffers
Judgment like mine cannot be secret.
Mine is no childish fault, no nastiness
Concealed behind a bathroom door,
No sin a prurient virtue practices
Licking the silence from its lips
Like sugar afterwards. Mine is flagrant,
Worthy of death, of many deaths,
Of shame, loss, hurt, indignities
Such as these! Such as these!
Speak of the sin I must have sinned
To suffer what you see me suffer.

Zophar: Do we need to name our sins
To know the need to be forgiven?
Repent, my son! Repent!

J.B.: *an agony of earnestness*   I sit here
Such as you see me. In my soul
I suffer what you guess I suffer.
Tell me the wickedness that justifies it.
Shall I repent of sins I have not
Sinned to understand it? Till I
Die I will not violate my integrity.

Zophar: *a fat chuckle*

Your integrity! Your integrity!
What integrity have you? —
A man, a miserable, mortal, sinful,
Venal man like any other.
You squat there challenging the universe
To tell you what your crime is called,
Thinking, because your life was virtuous,
It can't be called. It can. Your sin is
Simple. You were born a man!

J.B.: What is my fault? What have I done?

Zophar: *thundering*

What is your fault? Man's heart is evil!
What have you done? Man's will is evil.
Your fault, your sin, are heart and will:
The worm at heart, the wilful will
Corrupted with its foul imagining.

J.B. crouches lower in his rags. Silence.

J.B.: Yours is the cruelest comfort of them all,
Making the Creator of the Universe
The miscreator of mankind —
A party to the crimes He punishes...

Making my sin...

a horror...

a deformity...

Zophar: *collapsing into his own voice*

If it were otherwise we could not bear it...

194

Without the fault, without the Fall,
We're madmen: all of us are madmen...

He sits staring at his hands, then repeats the phrase:

Without the Fall
   We're madmen all.
We watch the stars
   That creep and crawl...

Bildad: Like dying flies
                         Across the wall
                         Of night...

Eliphaz: and shriek...
                         And that is all.

Zophar: Without the Fall...

A long silence. Out of the silence at last J.B.'s voice, barely audible.

J.B.:   God, my God, my God, answer me!

Silence.

His voice rises.

I cry out of wrong but I am not heard...
I cry aloud but there is no judgment.

Silence.

   violently
          Though He slay me, yet will I trust in Him...

Silence.

His voice drops.

But I will maintain my own ways before Him ...

Silence.

The ancient human cry.

Oh, that I knew where I might find Him! —
That I might come even to His seat!
I would order my cause before Him
And fill my mouth with arguments.

There is a rushing sound in the air.

Behold,
I go forward but He is not there,
Backward, but I cannot perceive Him ...

Out of the rushing sound, the Distant Voice; J.B. cowers as he hears it, his rags over his head.

The Distant Voice:
Who is this that darkeneth counsel
By words without knowledge? ...

Where wast thou
When I laid the foundations of the earth ...

When the morning stars sang together
And all the sons of God shouted for
Joy?

Hast *thou* commanded the morning?

Hast *thou* entered into the springs of the sea
Or hast *thou* walked in the search of the depth?

Have the gates of death been opened unto *thee*?

Where is the way where light dwelleth?
And as for darkness, where is the place thereof?

Hast thou entered into the treasures of the snow?

By what way is the light parted
Which scattereth the east wind upon the earth?

Can'st thou bind the sweet influences of the
    Pleiades?

Hast thou given the horse strength?
Hast thou clothed his neck with thunder?

He saith among the trumpets, Ha, ha;
He smelleth the battle afar off,
The thunder of the captains and the shouting.

Doth the eagle mount up at thy command?

Her eyes behold afar off.
Her young ones also suck up blood:
And where the slain are, there is she...

The rushing sound dies away. The Three Comforters stir un-
easily, peering up into the darkness. One by one they rise.

Bildad:	The wind's gone round.
Zophar:	It's cold.
Bildad:	I told you.
Eliphaz:	I hear the silence like a sound.
Zophar:	Wait for me!
Bildad:	The wind's gone round.

They go out as they came. Silence. J.B. sits motionless, his head covered. The rushing sound returns like the second, stronger gust of a great storm. The Voice rises above it.

The Distant Voice:
> Shall he that contendeth with the Almighty instruct
> Him? . . .

The rushing sound dies away again. The women sit up, huddle together.

Jolly Adams: *screaming*
> Mother! Mother! what was
> That?

Mrs. Adams: The wind, child. Only the wind.
Only the wind.

Jolly Adams: I heard a word.

Mrs. Adams: You heard the thunder in the wind.

Jolly Adams: *drowsy*
Under the wind there was a word...

Mrs. Adams picks her up. The women gather their newspapers and blankets and stumble out into the darkness through the door. For the third time the rushing sound returns.

The Distant Voice:
He that reproveth God, let him answer it!

J.B.:
Behold, I am vile; what shall I answer thee?
I will lay mine hand upon my mouth.

The Distant Voice:
Gird up thy loins like a man:
I will demand of thee, and declare thou unto me.

J.B. pulls himself painfully to his knees.

Wilt thou disannul my judgment?

J.B. does not answer.

Wilt thou condemn
Me that thou mayest be righteous?

Hast thou an arm like God? Or canst thou
Thunder with a voice like Him?

Deck thyself now with majesty and excellency
And array thyself with glory and beauty...

Then will I also confess unto thee
That thine own right hand can save thee.

J.B. raises his bowed head.

J.B.: *gently*   I know that thou canst do everything . . .

The rushing sound dies away.

> And that no thought can be withholden from
> thee.
> Who is he that hideth counsel without knowl-
> edge?
> Therefore have I uttered that I understood not:
> Things too wonderful for me, which I knew not.
>
> Hear, I beseech thee, and I will speak: . . .

Silence.

> I have heard of thee by the hearing of the
> ear . . .
> But now . . .

His face is drawn in agony.

> mine eye seeth thee!

He bows his head. His hands wring each other.

> Wherefore
> I abhor myself . . . and repent . . .

The light fades.

SCENE TEN

The Platform. As the lights come on the two actors turn violently away from each other, tearing their masks off. Nickles, with a gesture of disgust, skims his into a corner.

Nickles: Well, that's that!

Mr. Zuss: That's . . . that!

Silence. After a time Nickles looks cautiously around at Mr. Zuss.

Nickles: What's the matter with you?

Mr. Zuss: Nothing.

Nickles: You don't look pleased.

Mr. Zuss: Should I?

Nickles: Well,
           You were right weren't you?

Mr. Zuss: *too loud*   Of course I was right.

Nickles: *too soft*
           Anyway, you were magnificent.

Mr. Zuss: Thank you.

He looks at the mask in his hands: puts it down as though it had stung him. Silence. Mr. Zuss pretends to be busy with a shoelace.

Mr. Zuss: Why did you say that?

Nickles: What did I say?

Mr. Zuss: Why did you say it like that?

Nickles: Like what?

Mr. Zuss: *imitating*
                "Anyway!" ...
                                "*Anyway,* you were magnificent!"

Nickles: You know. "Anyway." Regardless.

Mr. Zuss: Regardless of
                What?

Nickles: Now, wait a minute! Wait a
                Minute! You were magnificent. I said so.

Mr. Zuss: Go on. Finish it.

Nickles: Finish what?

Mr. Zuss: Regardless of ... ?

Nickles: ... being right, of course.

What's got into you, my friend? What's eat-
 ing you?
Being magnificent and being right
Don't go together in this universe.
It's being wrong — a desperate stubbornness
Fighting the inextinguishable stars —
Excites imagination. You were
Right. And knew it. And were admirable.
Notwithstanding!

snickering   anyway!
a snarl   regardless!

Mr. Zuss: I knew you noticed.

Nickles: Of course I noticed.
              What lover of the art could fail to!

Something in Mr. Zuss's expression stops him.

                                        Noticed
              What?

Mr. Zuss: That tone! That look he gave me!

Nickles: He misconceived the part entirely.

Mr. Zuss: Misconceived the world! Buggered it!

Nickles: Giving in like that! Whimpering!

Mr. Zuss: Giving in! You call that arrogant,
             Smiling, supercilious humility
             Giving in to God?

Nickles: Arrogant!
                His suppurating flesh — his children —
                Let's not talk about those children —
                Everything he ever had!
                And all he asks is answers of the universe:
                All he asks is reasons why —
                Why? Why? And God replies to him:
                God comes whirling in the wind replying —
                What? That God knows more than he does.
                That God's more powerful than he! —
                Throwing the whole creation at him!
                Throwing the Glory and the Power!
                What's the Power to a broken man
                Trampled beneath it like a toad already?
                What's the Glory to a skin that stinks!
                And this ham actor! — what does *he* do?
                How does he play Job to that?
        attitude
                "Thank you!" "I'm a worm!" "Take two!"

                Plays the way a sheep would play it —
                Pious, contemptible, goddam sheep
                Without the spunk to spit on Christmas!

Mr. Zuss has watched Nickles' mounting rage in silence, staring at him. Nickles breaks off, shuffles, looks at Mr. Zuss, crosses to the ladder, swings a leg across the rail.

                Well . . .

He swings the other over.

                        you said he would . . .

204

He starts down.

You're right.

Another rung.

I'm wrong.

Another.

You win.

Another.

God always wins.

He peers down into the dark under the platform.

Where did I put that ... popcorn?

Mr. Zuss: Win!
Planets and Pleiades and eagles —
Screaming horses — scales of light —
The wonder and the mystery of the universe —
The unimaginable might of things —
Immeasurable knowledge in the waters some-
    where
Wandering their ways — the searchless power
Burning on the hearth of stars —
Beauty beyond the feel of fingers —
Marvel beyond the maze of mind —
The whole creation! And God showed him!

God stood stooping there to show him!
Last Orion! Least sea shell! ...
And what did Job do?

Mr. Zuss has worked himself up into a dramatic fury equaling Nickles'.

Job ... just ... sat!

Silence.

Sat there!

Silence.

Dumb!

Silence.

Until it ended!
Then! ... you heard him!

Mr. Zuss chokes.

Then, he *calmed* me!
Gentled me the way a farmhand
Gentles a bulging, bugling bull!
Forgave me! ...
for the world! ...

for everything!

Nickles: *poking around in the shadow under the platform*
          Nonsense! He repented, didn't he —
          The perfect and the upright man!
          He repented!

Mr. Zuss: That's just it!
          He repented. It was *him* —
          Not the fear of God but *him!*

Nickles: Fear? Of course he feared. Why wouldn't he?
          God with all those stars and stallions!
          He with little children's bones!

Mr. Zuss: *pursuing his mounting indignation*
          ...As though Job's suffering were justified
          Not by the Will of God but Job's
          Acceptance of God's Will...

Nickles: Well,
          What did you hope for? Hallelujahs?

Mr. Zuss: *not hearing*
          ...In spite of everything he'd suffered!
          In spite of all he'd lost and loved
          He understood and he forgave it!...

Nickles: *a contemptuous snort as he straightens to face Mr.*
          Zuss on the platform
          What other victory could God win?
          The choice is swallowing this swill of world
          Or vomiting in the trough. Job swallowed it,
          That's your triumph! — that he swallowed it.

207

Mr. Zuss: ...He'd heard of God and now he saw Him!
Who's the judge in judgment there?
Who plays the hero, God or him?
Is God to be *forgiven*?

Nickles: Isn't he?
Job was innocent, you may remember...

Silence.

     a nasty singsong
The perfect and the upright man!

Mr. Zuss: *deflated*
Don't start that again! I'm sick of it.

Nickles: *You* are!

Mr. Zuss: *I* am. Sick to death.
swinging his leg over the rail and starting down the ladder
I'd rather sell balloons to children...
Lights!...

He shouts.

                 Turn those lights on, can't you?
Want to see me break my neck?

The platform lights go out. Total darkness.

Louder.   Lights! Lights! That's not the end of it.

Nickles: *in the darkness*
Why isn't that the end? It's over.

Job has chosen how to choose.
You've made your bow? You want another?

The dangling light bulbs come feebly on. By their light J.B.
can still be seen kneeling on his broken table. Mr. Zuss and
Nickles crawl under the platform after their traps. Their voices
come from the shadow, punctuated by grunts and wheezes.

Mr. Zuss: You know as well as I there's more . . .

              There's always one more scene no matter
              Who plays Job or how he plays it . . .

              God restores him at the end.

Nickles: *a snort*
              God restores us all. That's normal.
              That's God's mercy to mankind . . .

              We never asked Him to be born . . .

              We never chose the lives we die of . . .

              They beat our rumps to make us breathe . .

              But God, if we have suffered patiently,
              Borne it in silence, stood the stench,
              Rewards us . . .

                            gives our dirty selves back.

Mr. Zuss emerges in his white jacket, adjusting his cap.

Mr. Zuss: Souls back!

Nickles: Selves back! Dirty selves
              We've known too well and never wanted.

Mr. Zuss: That's not this play.

*Nickles backs out with his jacket and cap and tray; puts them
on.*

Nickles: Hell it isn't.

Mr. Zuss tightens his balloon belt.

Mr. Zuss: God restores him *here*. On earth.

Nickles: *balancing his tray*
              So Job gets his in cash. That's generous.
              What percentage off for cash?

Mr. Zuss: Gets all he ever had and more —
              Much more.

Nickles: *cheerfully ironic*
                           Sure. His wife. His children!

Mr. Zuss: *embarrassed*
              He gets his wife back, and the children ...
              Follow in nature's course.

*Nickles, who has stooped to pick up a bag of popcorn, straightens
slowly, stares at Mr. Zuss.*

Nickles: *harshly*   You're lying.

Mr. Zuss: I'm not lying.

Nickles: I say you're lying.

Mr. Zuss: Why should I lie. It's in the Book.

Nickles: *jeering*
                    Wife back! Balls! He wouldn't touch her.
                    He wouldn't take her with a glove!
                    After all that filth and blood and
                    Fury to begin again! . . .
                    This fetid earth! That frightened Heaven
                    Terrified to trust the soul
                    It made with Its own hands, but testing it,
                    Tasting it, by trial, by torture,
                    Over and over till the last, least town
                    On all this reeling, reeking earth
                    Stinks with a spiritual agony
                    That stains the stones with excrement and
                        shows
                    In shadow on each greasy curtain!
                    After life like his to take
                    The seed up of the sad creation
                    Planting the hopeful world again —
                    He can't! . . . he won't! . . . he wouldn't touch
                        her!

Mr. Zuss: He does though.

Nickles: *raging*   Live his life again? —
                    Not even the most ignorant, obstinate,

Stupid or degraded man
This filthy planet ever farrowed,
Offered the opportunity to live
His bodily life twice over, would accept it —
Least of all Job, poor, trampled bastard!

Mr. Zuss has finished fooling with his balloons. He straightens up and marches off without a glance at Nickles.

It can't be borne twice over! Can't be!

Mr. Zuss: It is though. Time and again it is —
Every blessed generation...

His voice drifts back as he disappears.

Time and again...

Time and again...

Nickles starts to follow, looks back, sees J.B. kneeling in his rubble, hesitates, crosses, squats behind him, his vendor's cap pushed back on his head, his tray on his knees.

Nickles: J.B.!

J.B.: Let me alone.

Nickles: It's me.

J.B. shrugs.

I'm not the Father. I'm the — Friend.

J.B.:	I have no friend.
Nickles:	Oh come off it. You don't have to act with me.

J.B. *is silent.*

	O.K. Carry on. All I wanted was to help. Professional counsel you might call it ...

J.B. *is silent.*

	Of course you know how all this ends? ...

J.B. *is silent.*

	I wondered how you'd play the end.
J.B.:	Who knows what the end is, ever?
Nickles:	I do. You do.
J.B.:	Then don't tell me.
Nickles:	What's the worst thing you can think of?
J.B.:	I have asked for death. Begged for it. Prayed for it.
Nickles:	Then the worst thing can't be death.
J.B.:	Ah!

Nickles: You know now.

J.B.:   No. You tell me.

Nickles: Why should I tell you when you know?

J.B.:   Then don't. I'm sick of mysteries. Sick of
                  them.

Nickles: He gives it back to you.

J.B.:   What back?

Nickles: All of it.
                  Everything He ever took:
                  Wife, health, children, everything.

J.B.:   I have no wife.

Nickles: She comes back to you.

J.B.:   I have no children.

Nickles: *a nasty laugh*   You'll have better ones.

J.B.:   My skin is . . .

He breaks off, staring at the skin of his naked arms.

Nickles: Oh come on! I know the
                  Look of grease paint!

J.B.:   . . . whole! It's healed!

214

Nickles: *heavily ironic*
> You see? You see what I mean? What He plans
> for you?

J.B., *staring at his arms, is silent.*

Nickles: *leaning forward, urgently*
> Tell me how you play the end.
> Any man was screwed as Job was! ...

J.B. *does not answer.*

> I'll tell you how you play it. Listen!
> Think of all the mucked-up millions
> Since this buggered world began
> Said, No!, said, Thank you!, took a rope's end,
> Took a window for a door,
> Swallowed something, gagged on something ...

J.B. *lifts his head: he is listening but not to Nickles.*

> None of them knew the truth as Job does.
> None of them had his cause to know.

J.B.:
> Listen! Do you hear? There's someone ...

Nickles: *violently*
> Job won't take it! Job won't touch it!
> Job will fling it in God's face
> With half his guts to make it spatter!
> He'd rather suffocate in dung —
> Choke in ordure —

J.B.: *rising*   There is someone —
            Someone waiting at the door.

Nickles: *pulling his cap down, rising slowly*
                          I know.

The dangling lights dim out.

SCENE ELEVEN

A light comes from the canvas door. It increases as though day were beginning somewhere. Nickles has gone.

J.B.:   Who is it?

He crosses toward the door walking with his old ease. Stops.

Is there someone there?

There is no answer. He goes on. Reaches the door.

Sarah!

The light increases. She is sitting on the sill, a broken twig in her hand.

Sarah: Look, Job: the forsythia,
The first few leaves . . .

not leaves though . . .

petals . . .

J.B.: *roughly* Get up!

Sarah: Where shall I go?

J.B.:   Where you went!
              Wherever!

She does not answer.

More gently.   Where?

Sarah: Among the ashes.
              All there is now of the town is ashes.
              Mountains of ashes. Shattered glass.
              Glittering cliffs of glass all shattered
              Steeper than a cat could climb
              If there were cats still . . .
                                   And the pigeons —
              They wheel and settle and whirl off
              Wheeling and almost settling . . .
                                   And the silence —
              There is no sound there now — no wind
                 sound —
              Nothing that could sound the wind —
              Could make it sing — no door — no door-
                 way . . .

              Only this.

She looks at the twig in her hands.

                          Among the ashes!
              I found it growing in the ashes,
              Gold as though it did not know . . .

Her voice rises hysterically.

I broke the branch to strip the leaves off —
Petals again! . . .

She cradles it in her arms.

But they so clung to it!

J.B.:   Curse God and die, you said to me.

Sarah: Yes.

She looks up at him for the first time, then down again.

You wanted justice, didn't you?
There isn't any. There's the world . . .

She begins to rock on the doorsill, the little branch in her arms.

Cry for justice and the stars
Will stare until your eyes sting. Weep,
Enormous winds will thrash the water.
Cry in sleep for your lost children,
Snow will fall . . .
            snow will fall . . .

J.B.:   Why did you leave me alone?

Sarah: I loved you.
           I couldn't help you any more.
           You wanted justice and there was none —
           Only love.

J.B.:   He does not love. He
             Is.

Sarah: But we do. That's the wonder.

J.B.:   Yet you left me.

Sarah: Yes, I left you.
                 I thought there was a way away...

                 Water under bridges opens
                 Closing and the companion stars
                 Still float there afterwards. I thought the door
                 Opened into closing water.

J.B.:   Sarah!

He drops on his knees beside her in the doorway, his arms around her.

Sarah: Oh, I never could!
                 I never could! Even the forsythia...

She is half laughing, half crying.

                 Even the forsythia beside the
                 Stair could stop me.

They cling to each other. Then she rises, drawing him up, peering at the darkness inside the door.

J.B.:   It's too dark to see.

She turns, pulls his head down between her hands and kisses him.

Sarah: Then blow on the coal of the heart, my
                    darling.

J.B.:   The coal of the heart ...

Sarah: It's all the light now.

Sarah comes forward into the dim room, J.B. behind her. She lifts a fallen chair, sets it straight.

> Blow on the coal of the heart.
> The candles in churches are out.
> The lights have gone out in the sky.
> Blow on the coal of the heart
> And we'll see by and by ...

J.B. has joined her, lifting and straightening the chairs.

> We'll see where we are.
> The wit won't burn and the wet soul smoulders.
> Blow on the coal of the heart and we'll know ...
> We'll know ...

The light increases, plain white daylight from the door, as they work.

CURTAIN

ROBERT FROST

A MASQUE OF REASON

A FAIR *oasis in the purest desert.*
A man sits leaning back against a palm.
His wife lies by him looking at the sky.

MAN   You're not asleep?

WIFE   No, I can hear you. Why?

MAN   I said the incense tree's on fire again.

WIFE   You mean the Burning Bush?

MAN   The Christmas Tree.

WIFE   I shouldn't be surprised.

MAN   The strangest light!

WIFE   There's a strange light on everything today.

MAN   The myrrh tree gives it. Smell the rosin burning?
     The ornaments the Greek artificers
     Made for the Emperor Alexius,
     The Star of Bethlehem, the pomegranates,
     The birds, seem all on fire with Paradise.
     And hark, the gold enameled nightingales
     Are singing. Yes, and look, the Tree is troubled.
     Someone's caught in the branches.

WIFE   So there is.
     He can't get out.

MAN   He's loose! He's out!

WIFE   It's God.
     I'd know Him by Blake's picture anywhere.
     Now what's He doing?

MAN   Pitching throne, I guess.
     Here by our atoll.

WIFE   Something Byzantine.
     (The throne's a plywood flat, prefabricated,
     That God pulls lightly upright on its hinges
     And stands beside, supporting it in place.)

Perhaps for an Olympic Tournament,
Or Court of Love.

MAN   More likely Royal Court—
Or Court of Law, and this is Judgment Day.
I trust it is. Here's where I lay aside
My varying opinion of myself
And come to rest in an official verdict.
Suffer yourself to be admired, my love,
As Waller says.

WIFE   Or not admired. Go over
And speak to Him before the others come.
Tell Him He may remember you: you're Job.

GOD   Oh, I remember well: you're Job, my Patient.
How are you now? I trust you're quite recovered,
And feel no ill effects from what I gave you.

JOB   Gave me in truth: I like the frank admission.
I am a name for being put upon.
But, yes, I'm fine, except for now and then
A reminiscent twinge of rheumatism.
The let-up's heavenly. You perhaps will tell us
If that is all there is to be of Heaven,
Escape from so great pains of life on earth
It gives a sense of let-up calculated
To last a fellow to Eternity.

GOD   Yes, by and by. But first a larger matter.
I've had you on my mind a thousand years
To thank you someday for the way you helped me
Establish once for all the principle
There's no connection man can reason out
Between his just deserts and what he gets.
Virtue may fail and wickedness succeed.
'Twas a great demonstration we put on.
I should have spoken sooner had I found
The word I wanted. You would have supposed
One who in the beginning *was* the Word
Would be in a position to command it.
I have to wait for words like anyone.
Too long I've owed you this apology
For the apparently unmeaning sorrow
You were afflicted with in those old days.
But it was of the essence of the trial

You shouldn't understand it at the time.
It had to seem unmeaning to have meaning.
And it came out all right. I have no doubt
You realize by now the part you played
To stultify the Deuteronomist
And change the tenor of religious thought.
My thanks are to you for releasing me
From moral bondage to the human race.
The only free will there at first was man's,
Who could do good or evil as he chose.
I had no choice but I must follow him
With forfeits and rewards he understood—
Unless I liked to suffer loss of worship.
I had to prosper good and punish evil.
You changed all that. You set me free to reign.
You are the Emancipator of your God,
And as such I promote you to a saint.

JOB   You hear him, Thyatira: we're a saint.
Salvation in our case is retroactive.
We're saved, we're saved, whatever else it means.

JOB'S WIFE   Well, after all these years!

JOB   This is my wife.

JOB'S WIFE   If You're the deity I assume You are—
(I'd know You by Blake's picture anywhere)—

GOD   The best, I'm told, I ever have had taken.

JOB'S WIFE   —I have a protest I would lodge with You.
I want to ask You if it stands to reason
That women prophets should be burned as witches
Whereas men prophets are received with honor.

JOB   Except in their own country, Thyatira.

GOD   You're not a witch?

JOB'S WIFE   No.

GOD   Have you ever been one?

JOB   Sometimes she thinks she has and gets herself
Worked up about it. But she really hasn't—
Not in the sense of having to my knowledge
Predicted anything that came to pass.

JOB'S WIFE   The witch of Endor was a friend of mine.

GOD   You wouldn't say she fared so very badly.
I noticed when she called up Samuel

His spirit had to come. Apparently
A witch was stronger than a prophet there.

JOB'S WIFE   But she was burned for witchcraft.

GOD   That is not
Of record in my Note Book.

JOB'S WIFE   Well, she was.
And I should like to know the reason why.

GOD   There you go asking for the very thing
We've just agreed I didn't have to give.
  *(The throne collapses. But He picks it up
  And this time locks it up and leaves it.)*
Where has she been the last half hour or so?
She wants to know why there is still injustice.
I answer flatly: That's the way it is,
And bid my will avouch it like Macbeth.
We may as well go back to the beginning
And look for justice in the case of Segub.

JOB   Oh, Lord, let's not go *back* to anything.

GOD   Because your wife's past won't bear looking into?
In our great moment what did you do, Madam?
What did you try to make your husband say?

JOB'S WIFE   No, let's not live things over. I don't care.
I stood by Job. I may have turned on You.
Job scratched his boils and tried to think what he
Had done or not done to or for the poor.
The test is always how we treat the poor.
It's time the poor were treated by the state
In some way not so penal as the poorhouse.
That's one thing more to put on Your agenda.
Job hadn't done a thing, poor innocent.
I told him not to scratch: it made it worse.
If I said once I said a thousand times,
Don't scratch! And when, as rotten as his skin,
His tents blew all to pieces, I picked up
Enough to build him every night a pup tent
Around him so it wouldn't touch and hurt him.
I did my wifely duty. I should tremble!
All You can seem to do is lose Your temper
When reason-hungry mortals ask for reasons.
Of course, in the abstract high singular

There isn't any universal reason;
And no one but a man would think there was.
You don't catch women trying to be Plato.
Still there must be lots of unsystematic
Stray scraps of palliative reason
It wouldn't hurt You to vouchsafe the faithful.
You thought it was agreed You needn't give them.
You thought to suit Yourself. I've not agreed
To anything with anyone.

JOB   There, there,
You go to sleep. God must await events
As well as words.

JOB'S WIFE   I'm serious. God's had
Aeons of time and still it's mostly women
Get burned for prophecy, men almost never.

JOB   God needs time just as much as you or I
To get things done. Reformers fail to see that.
She'll go to sleep. Nothing keeps her awake
But physical activity, I find.
Try to read to her and she drops right off.

GOD   She's beautiful.

JOB   Yes, she was just remarking
She now felt younger by a thousand years
Than the day she was born.

GOD   That's about right,
I should have said. You got your age reversed
When time was found to be a space dimension
That could, like any space, be turned around in?

JOB   Yes, both of us: we saw to that at once.
But, God, I have a question to raise.
(My wife gets in ahead of me with hers.)
I need some help about this reason problem
Before I am too late to be got right
As to what reasons I agree to waive.
I'm apt to string along with Thyatira.
God knows—or rather, You know (God forgive me)
I waived the reason for my ordeal—but—
I have a question even there to ask—
In confidence. There's no one here but her,
And she's a woman: she's not interested
In general ideas and principles.

GOD What are her interests, Job?

JOB   Witch-women's rights.
    Humor her there or she will be confirmed
    In her suspicion You're no feminist.
    You have it in for women, she believes.
    Kipling invokes You as Lord God of Hosts.
    She'd like to know how You would take a prayer
    That started off Lord God of Hostesses.

GOD I'm charmed with her.

JOB   Yes, I could see You were.
    But to my question. I am much impressed
    With what You say we have established.
    Between us, You and I.

GOD   I make you see?
    It would be too bad if Columbus-like
    You failed to see the worth of your achievement.

JOB You call it mine.

GOD   We groped it out together.
    Any originality it showed
    I give you credit for. My forte is truth,
    Or metaphysics, long the world's reproach
    For standing still in one place true forever;
    While science goes self-superseding on.
    Look at how far we've left the current science
    Of Genesis behind. The wisdom there though,
    Is just as good as when I uttered it.
    Still, novelty has doubtless an attraction.

JOB So it's important who first thinks of things?

GOD I'm a great stickler for the author's name.
    By proper names I find I do my thinking.

JOB's WIFE God, who invented earth?

JOB   What, still awake?

GOD Any originality it showed
    Was of the Devil. He invented Hell,
    False premises that are the original
    Of all originality, the sin
     That felled the angels, Wolsey should have said.
    As for the earth, we groped that out together,
    Much as your husband Job and I together
    Found out the discipline man needed most

Was to learn his submission to unreason;
And that for man's own sake as well as mine,
So he won't find it hard to take his orders
From his inferiors in intelligence
In peace and war—especially in war.

JOB   So he won't find it hard to take his war.

GOD   You have the idea. There's not much I can tell you.

JOB   All very splendid. I am flattered proud
To have been in on anything with You.
'Twas a great demonstration if You say so.
Though incidentally I sometimes wonder
Why it had to be at my expense.

GOD   It had to be at somebody's expense.
Society can never think things out:
It has to see them acted out by actors,
Devoted actors at a sacrifice—
The ablest actors I can lay my hands on.
Is that your answer?

JOB   No, for I have yet
To ask my question. We disparage reason.
But all the time it's what we're most concerned with.
There's will as motor and there's will as brakes.
Reason is, I suppose, the steering gear.
The will as brakes can't stop the will as motor
For very long. We're plainly made to go.
We're going anyway and may as well
Have some say as to where we're headed for;
Just as we will be talking anyway
And may as well throw in a little sense.
Let's do so now. Because I let You off
From telling me Your reason, don't assume
I thought You had none. Somewhere back
I knew You had one. But this isn't it
You're giving me. You say we groped this out.
But if You will forgive me the irreverence,
It sounds to me as if You thought it out,
And took Your time to it. It seems to me
An afterthought, a long long afterthought.
I'd give more for one least beforehand reason
Than all the justifying ex-post-facto
Excuses trumped up by You for theologists.

The front of being answerable to no one
I'm with You in maintaining to the public.
But Lord, we showed them that. The audience
Has all gone home to bed. The play's played out.
Come, after all these years—to satisfy me.
I'm curious. And I'm a grown-up .man:
I'm not a child for You to put me off
And tantalize me with another "Oh, because."
You'd be the last to want me to believe
All Your effects were merely lucky blunders.
That would be unbelief and atheism.
The artist in me cries out for design.
Such devilish ingenuity of torture
Did seem unlike You, and I tried to think
The reason might have been some other person's.
But there is nothing You are not behind.
I did not ask then, but it seems as if
Now after all these years You might indulge me.
Why did You hurt me so? I am reduced
To asking flatly for a reason—outright.

GOD   I'd tell you, Job—

JOB   All right, don't tell me then
If you don't want to. I don't want to know.
But what is all this secrecy about?
I fail to see what fun, what satisfaction
A God can find in laughing at how badly
Men fumble at the possibilities
When left to guess forever for themselves.
The chances are when there's so much pretense
Of metaphysical profundity
The obscurity's a fraud to cover nothing.
I've come to think no so-called hidden value's
Worth going after. Get down into things
It will be found there's no more given there
Than on the surface. If there ever was,
The crypt was long since rifled by the Greeks.
We don't know where we are, or who we are.
We don't know one another; don't know You;
Don't know what time it is. We don't know, don't we?
Who says we don't? Who got up these misgivings?
Oh, we know well enough to go ahead with.

I mean we seem to know enough to act on.
It comes down to a doubt about the wisdom
Of having children—after having had them,
So there is nothing we can do about it
But warn the children they perhaps should have none.
You could end this by simply coming out
And saying plainly and unequivocally
Whether there's any part of man immortal.
Yet You don't speak. Let fools bemuse themselves
By being baffled for the sake of being.
I'm sick of the whole artificial puzzle.

JOB'S WIFE   You won't get any answers out of God.

GOD   My kingdom, what an outbreak!

JOB'S WIFE   Job is right.
Your kingdom, yes, Your kingdom come on earth.
Pray tell me what does that mean. Anything?
Perhaps that earth is going to crack someday
Like a big egg and hatch a heaven out
Of all the dead and buried from their graves.
One simple little statement from the throne
Would put an end to such fantastic nonsense;
And, too, take care of twenty of the four
And twenty freedoms on the party docket.
Or is it only four? My extra twenty
Are freedoms from the need of asking questions.
(I hope You know the game called twenty questions.)
For instance, is there such a thing as Progress?
Job says there's no such thing as Earth's becoming
An easier place for man to save his soul in.
Except as a hard place to save his soul in,
A trial ground where he can try himself
And find out whether he is any good,
It would be meaningless. It might as well
Be Heaven at once and have it over with.

GOD   Two pitching on like this tend to confuse me.
One at a time, please. I will answer Job first.
I'm going to tell Job why I tortured him
And trust it won't be adding to the torture.
I was just showing off to the Devil, Job,
As is set forth in chapters One and Two.

231

(Job takes a few steps pacing.) Do you mind?
(God eyes him anxiously.)

JOB   No. No, I mustn't.
'Twas human of You. I expected more
Than I could understand and what I get
Is almost less than I can understand.
But I don't mind. Let's leave it as it stood.
The point was it was none of my concern.
I stick to that. But talk about confusion!
How is that for a mix-up, Thyatira?
Yet I suppose what seems to us confusion
Is not confusion, but the form of forms,
The serpent's tail stuck down the serpent's throat,
Which is the symbol of eternity
And also of the way all things come round,
Or of how rays return upon themselves,
To quote the greatest Western poem yet.
Though I hold rays deteriorate to nothing,
First white, then red, then ultra red, then out.

GOD   Job, you must understand my provocation.
The tempter comes to me and I am tempted.
I'd had about enough of his derision
Of what I valued most in human nature.
He thinks he's smart. He thinks he can convince me
It is no different with my followers
From what it is with his. Both serve for pay.
Disinterestedness never did exist
And if it did, it wouldn't be a virtue.
Neither would fairness. You have heard the doctrine.
It's on the increase. He could count on no one:
That was his look out. I could count on you.
I wanted him forced to acknowledge so much.
I gave you over to him, but with safeguards.
I took care of you. And before you died
I trust I made it clear I took your side
Against your comforters in their contention
You must be wicked to deserve such pain.
That's Browning and sheer Chapel Non-conformism.

JOB   God, please, enough for now. I'm in no mood
For more excuses.

GOD   What I meant to say:

232

Your comforters were wrong.

JOB   Oh, that committee!

GOD   I saw you had no fondness for committees.
        Next time you find yourself pressed on to one
        For the revision of the Book of Prayer
        Put that in if it isn't in already:
        Deliver us from committees. 'Twill remind me.
        I would do anything for you in reason.

JOB   Yes, yes.

GOD   You don't seem satisfied.

JOB   I am.

GOD   You're pensive.

JOB   Oh, I'm thinking of the Devil.
        You must remember he was in on this.
        We can't leave him out.

GOD   No. No, we don't need to.
        We're too well off.

JOB   Someday we three should have
        A good old get-together celebration.

GOD   Why not right now?

JOB   We can't without the Devil.

GOD   The Devil's never very far away.
        He too is pretty circumambient.
        He has but to appear. He'll come for me,
        Precipitated from the desert air.
        Show yourself, son. I'll get back on my throne
        For this I think. I find it always best
        To be upon my dignity with him.
                (The Devil enters like a sapphire wasp
                That flickers mica wings. He lifts a hand
                To brush away a disrespectful smile.
                Job's wife sits up.)

JOB'S WIFE   Well, if we aren't all here,
        Including me, the only Dramatis
        Personae needed to enact the problem.

JOB   We've waked her up.

JOB'S WIFE   I haven't been asleep.
        I've heard what you were saying—every word.

JOB   What did we say?

JOB'S WIFE You said the Devil's in it.

JOB She always claims she hasn't been asleep.
And what else did we say?

JOB'S WIFE Well, what led up—
Something about— (*The three men laugh.*)
—The Devil's being God's best inspiration.

JOB Good, pretty good.

JOB'S WIFE Wait till I get my Kodak.
Would you two please draw in a little closer?
No—no, that's not a smile. That's a grin.
Satan, what ails you? Where's the famous tongue,
Thou onetime Prince of Conversationists?
This is polite society you're in
Where good and bad are mingled everywhichway,
And ears are lent to any sophistry
Just as if nothing mattered but our manners.
You look as if you either hoped or feared
You were more guilty of mischief than you are.
Nothing has been brought out that for my part
I'm not prepared for or that Job himself
Won't find a formula for taking care of.

SATAN Like the one Milton founded to fool himself
About his blindness.

JOB'S WIFE Oh, he speaks! He *can* speak!
That strain again! Give me excess of it!
As dulcet as a pagan temple gong!
He's twitting us. Oh, by the way, you haven't
By any chance a Lady Apple on you?
I saw a boxful in the Christmas market.
How I should prize one personally from you.

GOD Don't *you* twit. He's unhappy. Church neglect
And figurative use have pretty well
Reduced him to a shadow of himself.

JOB'S WIFE *That* explains why he's so diaphanous
And easy to see through. But where's he off to?
I thought there were to be festivities
Of some kind. We could have charades.

GOD He has his business he must be about.
Job mentioned him and so I brought him in
More to give his reality its due
Than anything.

JOB'S WIFE   He's very real to me
    And always will be. Please don't go. Stay, stay
    But to the evensong and having played
    Together we will go with you along.
    There are who won't have enough of you
    If you go now. Look how he takes no steps!
    He isn't really going, yet he's leaving.

JOB   *(Who has been standing dazed with new ideas)*
    He's on that tendency that like the Gulf Stream,
    Only of sand not water, runs through here.
    It has a rate distinctly different
    From the surrounding desert; just today
    I stumbled over it and got tripped up.

JOB'S WIFE   Oh, yes, that tendency! Oh, do come off it.
    Don't let it carry you away. I hate
    A tendency. The minute you get on one
    It seems to start right off accelerating.
    Here, take my hand.
                        (He takes it and alights
                In three quick steps as off an escalator.
                The tendency, a long, long narrow strip
                Of middle-aisle church carpet, sisal hemp,
                Is worked by hands invisible off stage.)
    I want you in my group beside the throne—
    Must have you. There, that's just the right arrangement.
    Now someone can light up the Burning Bush
    And turn the gold enameled artificial birds on.
    I recognize them. Greek artificers
    Devised them for Alexius Comnenus.
    They won't show in the picture. That's too bad.
    Neither will I show. That's too bad moreover.
    Now if you three have settled anything
    You'd as well smile as frown on the occasion.
            (Here endeth chapter forty-three of Job.)

A GUIDE TO JOB'S ENCOUNTER

by

JUNE K. SINGER

NOTE TO THE READER

This *Guide to Job's Encounter* is intended to be used as an accompaniment to the text, *Job's Encounter* and to the Biblical Book of Job. It contains plans for twenty-four, or possibly twenty-five individual study sessions of approximately 45 minutes each. Sufficient material has been supplied so that it will not always be possible to cover all the questions, discussions and projects that are suggested. The discussion leader should not feel that it is necessary to cover all the material herein contained. It is far better to permit the material to stimulate discussion following the student's own reactions to his readings, than it is to insist on close adherence to the material at hand. There are, however, times when elaboration on the text is enriching to the concepts being formed, and these should not be overlooked.

The *Guide* materials are basically of three kinds: first, expository material which comments on and elucidates the text; second, specific questions which may be asked; third, possible answers or parts of answers that may be anticipated. One word of caution: this *Guide* is not a "catechism," with set questions demanding set answers. The questions are only aids for the student who may add to them or eliminate from them according to his or her interests and abilities. Undoubtedly, each leader will develop his own questions in his reading of the text and of the Book of Job, and he should freely add his own contributions to the material at hand. As valuable as the contribution of the leader, will be the questions that come from the participants, who should be encouraged to read with an eye to the problems of the book, and to express those problems in the group as they occur. Only by a free exchange among members of the group can an educational experience take place.

The point must be made that the "answers" given in this *Guide* are not really answers at all, but just the response of one individual to the infinite possibilities aroused by the reading of the Book of Job and *Job's Encounter*. Other answers may be equally valid, or more valid. Therefore the wise reader will look upon the material here provided as a source of stimulation and not as a repository of definitive answers. The purpose of the *Guide* is to stimulate him to devote his attention to a thoughtful consideration of the vital issues posed by that magnificent testament of man's striving for understanding, the Book of Job.

SESSION I

The leader's major aim, during the first session, should be to stimulate interest in reading the Bible and, specifically, in reading the Book of Job. Since the participants will usually come to the first meeting of the group without advance preparation, the leader will do well to begin by discussing with them the general methods by which the discussions will be conducted, and then he should present in his own words the material contained in the Introduction and the first chapter, "Reading the Bible," in the text, *Job's Encounter*.

The leader who follows this *Guide* closely will ask the group to read an assigned portion of *Job's Encounter* in preparation for each meeting, and in addition, to read some chapters in the Book of Job for each of the next seven sessions. For those who wish to gain an overall view of the Book of Job at the outset, it is recommended that the entire Book be read before the next meeting, but this need not be required.

The Bible is the most widely read book in the world, and it means many different things to different people. Everyone who reads the Bible does not approach it in the same way—we are influenced by our parents' attitudes, the attitude of the religious group to which we belong, the attitude of the larger society in which we live, and perhaps to a greater degree than all of these by our own personal temperament—whether we seek support for our own ethics, intellectual stimulation, or a relationship with our cultural and ethnic forebears. The Bible serves people in many ways.

In discussing the various uses of the Bible, the leader may ask the group for their ideas on uses to which the Bible has been put. The following are taken from the text of *Job's Encounter,* and these may be offered when no ideas from the group are forthcoming. Whenever possible a good leader will try to elicit material and examples from the members of the group. He will, however, always be prepared with some material to fill in the gaps in the students' information. The following uses of the Bible may be listed as they are presented, together with countless additional ones which may be brought up. The group could also be asked to give examples of how the Bible might be used in each way:

1. The Bible as a maximum authority for a satisfactory religious life.

   examples: Religious fundamentalists who are taught to regard every word in the Bible as literally true. Segregationists who use it as a text to justify their views: "Cursed be Canaan; a slave of slaves shall he be" (Gen 9:25). *Kashruth* laws in Orthodox Judaism, as well as laws pertaining to the strict observance of the Sabbath, etc.

2. The Bible as a source of spiritual and social goals.

   examples: The work of medical missionaries in emphasizing doing according to the precepts of the Bible rather than spreading the literal Word. Religious social action groups.

3. The Bible as a guide to history.

   examples: Archaeologists, anthropologists, sociologists seeking historical information and material treasures.

4. The Bible as literature.

   examples: Study in the schools as literature, study in comparative religions; related to this also is the study of the Bible as source of inspiration for painters, sculptors and composers of music.

5. The Bible as evidence of God's covenant with Israel.

   examples: Possible basis of Jews' sense of special social responsibility to another, the tradition of "The Chosen People" among Jews, claims of certain people of the right of the Jews to possess the land of Israel, basis of some exclusivistic tendencies on the part of some Jews, possible basis of anti-Semitism among some non-Jews.

239

6. The Bible as an expression of people and their experiences.

examples: Stories about Biblical characters have survived through millennia because the problems of these people are typical and recurring problems for all mankind. Such was the life of Job, and many others who also faced universal situations, like Adam (Why did I have to lose the happy paradise of my early days and go forth into the world to work for my daily bread?), Eve (The serpent tempted me—in the face of temptation what is the responsibility of the individual?), Jacob (By what right do I enjoy the inheritance I obtained by deceit and trickery?), Ruth (Can a non-Jewish woman be accepted fully by her Jewish husband and his family, or in the sight of God?)

Many more examples can and should be given, and these will prepare the way for the introduction of the central problem in Job. To understand Job we will have to follow his experiences and his thoughts, and we will have to consider them in relation to ourselves—how such experiences might affect us, and how we might respond personally to some of the issues raised in the Book of Job. But to do this it is necessary to read the Book of Job and the companion volume of explanatory and related material, *Job's Encounter*.

After we have read the Book of Job and gotten our own impressions, we shall try to discover what Biblical critics have learned about it. The Biblical critics are scholars who examine the Bible to learn as much as possible about the authors of the books, the times in which they were written, and whatever additional data can help to shed light on the meanings of these books. *Job's Encounter* reviews for us the work of Biblical critics, and brings to us the best thinking of scholars and writers, philosophers and statesmen who have dealt in one way or another with the universal concerns that have made the Book of Job one of mankind's immortal works.

The Book of Job deals with "the passionate outpourings of human hopes and fears and questions, and in our individual responses to what we read there, is evidence of the chain of feeling that binds all mankind together," says the author of *Job's Encounter*. Our knowledge that our ancestors suffered, and that they did not understand why they suffered "is a link in this chain of human memory which connects modern man to his forebear . . ."

Today many people have tried to answer the question of why some people suffer without apparent reason, while some who seem to deserve a bitter fate go through life apparently without pain or sorrow. Perhaps you have observed some ways in which some people have tried to deal with this eternal problem of mankind. How have some people sought to reconcile what they see about them with their own ideas of justice?

Possible examples that might come from the discussion:

1. The Christian fundamentalist view that in the life after death, the good will be rewarded and the evil will be punished.

2. The view, more common in the East, that physical suffering can be subordinated to a point where spiritual exaltation can take its place.

3. An absolute denial of the existence of evil, as in the doctrine of Christian Science, as well as an early (4th century) Church doctrine in which evil is defined as an "absence of good."

4. The idea of a state of non-feeling as a goal, where pleasure as well as pain cease to exist for the individual.

5. Asceticism, in which self-denial becomes a virtue.

We are not concerned with evaluating the various ways in which man throughout the ages has tried to deal with this question. It is important for us at this time only to recognize that it *has* concerned mankind all over the earth and in all ages. We will begin, next time we meet, to consider and to try to understand the nature of one man's experience with this universal problem.

Assignment for Session 2:

Read text, pp. 16–26 and Book of Job, Chapters 1 and 2 (and further if you wish).

SESSION 2

The Book of Job, as you probably have discovered already, is divided into three sections: the prologue, the long poetic story section, and the epilogue. In your assignment for today, you have read the prologue, that is, the first two chapters.

What is a Prologue?

(A prologue sets the stage: it prepares the reader for what is going to happen. It is not necessarily essential to the drama itself, but is more in the nature of a preface or an introduction. However, it may provide us with information which helps us to gain a deeper appreciation of the personalities in the play and the surroundings and situations in which they find themselves.)

What does the Prologue tell us about the times in which Job lived?

(Kind of society: they were basically a herdsmen society, as noted from the size of Job's flocks. Yet they lived in houses, not tents, so apparently they were not wandering nomads. We learn of Job's economic condition, that he was very wealthy—he had many servants and each of his sons had his own house.

Kind of religion: during this period animal sacrifice was still being practiced, thus suggesting a very early date to this story's origin. Job is a man who believes that he can atone for any possible sins of his children by offering animal sacrifices to God. There is no suggestion made in this prologue that God does not desire animals for sacrifices—as is expressed later, for example, by Amos—see Amos 5:21–24.)

Do we find any specific indication that Job is a Hebrew?

(No, this is not stated either in the prologue nor elsewhere in the Book of Job.)

Relate what occurred when God called up his sons and Satan appeared among them?

(See Chapter 1:6–12, Job.)

Questions for discussion:

What is your understanding of the figure of Satan? How may modern man regard him?

(It may be brought out that when God is perceived as the principle of creativity, then Satan is often thought to be responsible for the destructive forces in the world; when God is Lord over the good and beautiful, then Satan dominates the evil and ugly; when God supports the hero, then Satan strengthens the antagonist. There

cannot be an altogether positive value [i.e., God] without a nega-
tive one, for an idea only assumes value by cause of its comparison
with or relationship to its opposite. Thus, if a God-principle exists
in the form of a Supreme Being who provides Job with all riches
and virtues, then Satan must strive to demonstrate what can be
the result of the withdrawal of these values.)

*What happened to Job as a result of Satan's challenge of
God?*

How did Job accept his fate?

*How does Satan explain Job's ability to hold fast to his in-
tegrity?*

(Job 2:4–5.)

What new trial does Satan now propose?

Why do you think God agrees to this?

What now happens to Job?

How does Job's wife react?

How does Job respond to his wife?

*What do Job's three friends do when they come to comfort
him?*

("They sat with him on the ground seven days and seven nights,
and no one spoke a word to him, for they saw that his suffering
was ver great." Here it may be interesting to comment on some of
the oldest customs of mourning in the Jewish faith, and their possible origins. Solomon B. Freehof in his book *Reform Jewish Practice*, states that when visitors come to pay their respects to the house
of mourning there should be very little conversation. The *Talmud*
says: the reward gained from visiting the house of bereavement is
earned by silence. The custom of quiet consolation is derived from
the fact that when Moses spoke to Aaron after the death of Aaron's
two sons, "Aaron was silent." Lev. 10:3. The period of seven days
of mourning, called *Shiv'ah* is based on a number of Biblical prece-
dents. Joseph mourned seven days for his father Jacob. Gen. 50:10:
"He made a mourning for his father seven days." The rabbis of
the *Talmud* derived the rule of seven days from certain Biblical
hints, as in Amos 8:10: "I will turn your feasts into mourning";
just as a feast is seven days, so shall the period of mourning be
seven days. Likewise do they find a reference to the *Shiv'ah* period
in Gen. 7:4: "For in seven days I will send rain upon the earth

forty days and forty nights." And they explain that the coming of the flood was delayed for seven days because those were the days of mourning for Methusaleh, who had just died.)

What was the purpose of animal sacrifices in the days of Job?

(According to Cruden's *Complete Concordance*, a sacrifice is an offering of any sort to a deity with the idea of procuring favor or avoiding disaster. The idea of sacrifice is found among every race at the earliest known period of its history as a well-established and thoroughly understood custom. The burnt offering was thought to appease an angry god when displeased and ready to bring disaster upon man. The first several chapters of Leviticus deal with the methods of offering sacrifices as communicated to the people of Israel through Moses, and the class may find it interesting to read a few passages from this section of the Bible, to learn what the priestly customs of sacrifice were.)

How did the prophets differ from the priests in their approach to the matter of sacrifices?

(Amos 5:21 ff. could be quoted here: "I hate, I despise your feasts, and I take no delight in your solemn assemblies. Even though you offer me your burnt offerings and your cereal offerings, I will not accept them, and the peace offerings of you fatted beasts I will not look upon. . . . But let justice roll down like waters, and righteousness like an everflowing stream." The priests were interested in adhering to the letter of the Levitical law, while the prophets later had begun to express the idea that God does not want burnt offerings, but desires the proper behavior of man to be his offering to God.)

Why could neither the priests nor the prophets have explained why God had permitted such terrible misfortunes to fall upon Job?

(One possible answer is that both priest and prophet were instructing the people how they could act in order to propitiate their God. While each group had its own idea of what God desired of man, they did agree that if man were to conduct himself in the prescribed manner he would be rewarded by God. Thus, if Job was a truly righteous man, and according to the picture of Job that we are given in the Prologue he was such a person, then there was no

244

relationship to be seen between his conduct and God's treatment of him.)

How does the introduction of Satan help to explain Job's misfortunes?

(When man's concept of God is one of total goodness and righteousness, the evil in the world must somehow be explained by a force or power other than that of God. Satan, then compensates for God, by taking the responsibility for that which is known as evil.)

Is this a satisfactory explanation to you? Why or why not?

(Here the group should be encouraged to give some thought to this question and to write, during the session, if possible, a paragraph stating their personal point of view. Such paragraphs should be kept by the leader, until the end of the course, and then the same question can be asked of the participants. It will be most interesting to spend a final session considering how the participants' concepts relating to the matter of the relationship of God and Satan, good and evil, punishment and reward, change or enlarge during the course of the study of Job and *Job's Encounter.*)

Job maintained his belief in God's justice. Job also maintained his belief that he had done no wrong. How can such apparently conflicting beliefs be held at the same time?

(Bring out the fact that man can do evil and not be aware of it. He must accept the possibility of unconscious acts. Is he to be held responsible for these? Also, question whether the acts of a supreme creative and guiding force can properly be judged by human standards.)

Assignment for Session 3:
Read text, pp. 26–38 and the Book of Job, Chapters 3–7.

SESSION 3

Job's desire to die, expressed in the poignant verses of Chapter 3, introduces the specifically Joban attitudes toward the mystery of death. References to death are plentiful, of course, in the Bible. In the Book of Genesis (25:7) we read: "These are the days of the years of Abraham's life, a hundred and seventy-five years. Abraham breathed his last and died in a good old age, an old man and full of years, and was gathered to his people."

This natural, and almost relaxed acceptance of the inevitability of death, is modified by an alternate attitude toward dying. We read, with reference to Jacob's sadness over Joseph's presumed tragedy: "Then Jacob rent his garments and put sackcloth upon his loins, and mourned for his son many days. All his sons and daughter rose up to comfort him; but he refused to be comforted, and said, 'No, I shall go down to Sheol to my son, mourning.'"

To "go down to Sheol, mourning..." was the kind of death Biblical figures sought to avoid. Sheol is a word whose precise meaning is not known. It seems to denote the place where those who died congregated after their death. Sheol appears to be underneath the earth: "Ask a sign of the Lord your God; let it be deep as Sheol or high as heaven," (Isaiah 7:11).

Rarely in the Bible does death become frightful and a fearful threat to man. Only occasionally are petitions offered to God to save man from his fate, as in Psalm 86: "Incline thy ear, O Lord, and answer me, for I am poor and needy. Preserve my life, for I am godly; save thy servant who trusts in thee." But in the wisdom literature of the Bible we find man resigned to his fate that there is no other prospect for him than the dreary shades in Sheol. However, this made life on earth all the more precious and sweet. Thus we read in Ecclesiastes: "A good name is better than precious ointment; and the day of death, than the day of birth." (Eccl: 7:1).

What is the nature of Job's lament as he cries out in grief and sorrow?

(See pages 26–29 of *Job's Encounter*.)

Does he complain that God should not have permitted his suffering?

How does he react to his bitter fate?

How do you understand Job's attitude toward death?

Job's friends, Eliphaz, Bildad, and Zophar, offer him comfort. In what manner does Eliphaz explain what has happened to Job?

(Eliphaz presents to Job words which came to him "Amid thoughts

246

from visions of the night when deep sleep falls upon men." These words came as in a dream.)

What do you suppose was thought to be the significance of ideas that appeared in dreams, in the days when the Bible was being written?

(In general it may be said that the dream was thought to be a kind of communication from God to man. Often there was a prophetic aspect to the dream. The dreams which Joseph interpreted for the Pharoah's chief butler and chief baker, and later for the Pharoah himself, are especially interesting in this respect. See Genesis 40:9–20; 41:1–36. The importance of correct interpretation of dreams was so great, you will recall, that Pharoah brought Joseph up from the dungeon and set him in command second only to himself, over all the land of Egypt, because he had explained a dream. Another great interpreter of dreams in the Bible was Daniel, and not only was he able to tell the meaning of Nebuchadnezzar's dream to him, but he was able to relate the dream himself from beginning to end. This was because "the mystery was revealed to Daniel in a vision of the night. Then Daniel blessed the God of heaven. Daniel said: 'Blessed be the name of God for ever and ever, to whom belong wisdom and might . . . he reveals deep and mysterious things . . . and hast now made known to me what we asked of thee, for thou hast made known to us the king's matter.' " To read the episode in its entirety, see Daniel, Chapter 2.)

Eliphaz' conclusion is that Job must turn to God, and acknowledge his own error, and that then at last he shall find peace once more. How does Job respond to this advice?

(He rejects Eliphaz' advice and refuses to admit that he has been guilty of any wrong which would occasion such dreadful retribution.)

In his longing for death, is there any indication that Job is considering suicide?

(No, and actually suicide is extremely rare in the Bible. The best known are the stories of Samson and Saul. It will be remembered how Samson avenged himself upon the Philistines who took him captive and gouged out his eyes—by pulling down the pillars of the great house upon the Philistines, killing the lords and all the people

247

who were in it: "So the dead whom he slew at his death were more than those whom he had slain during his life." For the complete story, see Judges 16:23–31. Saul had seen his own sons killed and had been sorely wounded in battle. He asked his armor-bearer to kill him, lest he be found by the enemy and they kill him and make sport of him. When the armor-bearer refused to do this, Saul fell upon his own sword. See I Samuel, 31:1–13.)

From what you know about Job and the times in which he lived, how would you explain Job's attitude toward death and suicide in particular?

Do you believe that such a view is held valid by most religious people today?

(After receiving responses on this matter, it may be interesting to point out that in the *Talmud* suicide was considered to be a crime and none of the regular mourning rituals were to be followed in the case of a suicide. However the Central Conference of American Rabbis in the *Yearbook,* Vol. XXXIII, states: ". . . according to Jewish law one is considered a suicide only when there is absolute certainty that he premeditated and committed the act with a clear mind not troubled by some great fear or worry which might have beset him for the moment and caused him temporarily to lose his mind. In the absence of such certain evidence he is given the benefit of the doubt . . . whenever possible we should try to spare the surviving relatives the disgrace which would come to them by having their relative declared a suicide." In this spirit it is the general custom among Reform Jewish congregations to bury suicides in their family plots.)

Does Eliphaz believe Job can, by his own actions, influence God to behave in a certain way? What does Eliphaz suggest?

How would you compare the kind of God Eliphaz has in mind with the kind of God to whom we are introduced in the Prologue?

(Note that Eliphaz' God concept is of a Being of Absolute Justice, while in the prologue as God and Satan determine Job's fate, the question of justice does not even enter. Here God appears as a whimsical deity, making wagers with men's lives. Here again the question may be raised as to whether the prologue is truly in harmony with the major sections of the Book of Job, Chapters 3–41 inclusive.)

How does Job's idea of God compare with Eliphaz? How does it differ from that of Eliphaz?

Group project:

Discuss the question: How would you speak to a friend whose life had suddenly and unexpectedly turned into tragedy like that of Job? If time permits, the participants might be asked to write a letter of consolation in which they expresses their own personal religious viewpoint or the viewpoint of Judaism as they understand it.

Assignment for Session 4:

Read text, pp. 38–50, and Job, Chapters 8–14.

SESSION 4

Last time we read the agonized lament of Job in which he questions God, saying: "What is man that thou dost make so much of him, and that thou dost set thy mind upon him, dost visit him every morning, and test him every moment? How long wilt thou not look away from me, nor let me alone till I swallow my spittle? If I sin, what do I do to thee, thou watcher of men? Why has thou made me thy mark? Why have I become a burden to thee?" (see text, pages 37–38) Job's comforters have listened to his words and they, too, must have felt the questions rising in their own throats. Yet they are believers in a moral order of cause and effect where God is the Supreme Judge, rewarding good with his gracious gifts and evil with fearful punishment. They reprove Job for his questioning attitude and, as they urge Job to renew his faith in the justice of God, they renew their own faith.

Bildad, the second of the comforters, reaffirms his confidence in the justice of God, insisting that there must be cause for the misfortunes that have come to Job. We begin to sense from Bildad's words to Job: ". . . if you are pure and upright then he (God) will rouse himself up for you," that Bildad doubts Job's righteousness.

Recalling the picture we have been given of Job, can we find any possible ways in which Job might have sinned?

(We might call attention to the way in which Job set up daily sacrificial offerings for his sons, but not for himself, thus assuming that others might be guilty of sin, but never he, himself. Is this certainty of his own righteousness, plus his presumption in questioning God, a certain sign of self-righteousness that lacks the virtue of personal humility?)

What authority does Bildad use to support his belief in the concept of righteousness rewarded and evil-doing punished?

(He turns to tradition, saying: "Inquire . . . of bygone ages, and consider what the fathers have found; for we are but of yesterday and know nothing, for our days on earth are a shadow. Will they not teach you, and tell you, and utter words out of their understanding?" 8:8–10.)

How is this looking to tradition carried forward from the past as a basis for determining good or evil behavior still carried on today?

How does the young child first learn to discriminate good from evil? At home, at school, in the greater community, for example?

For adults, who sets the standards?

How does Bildad rationalize the good life Job has led in relation to what has befallen him?

(He takes the approach that, since God is just, Job will yet receive happiness, since he deserves it.)

How far is Job willing to accept Bildad's assurance of God's Divine Justice?

(Job recognizes that there must be a relationship between man's actions and God's deeds. But Job does not believe that man can expect God's justice to be based on human standards of justice.)

Why is this idea an important development of Job, beyond the point of view expressed by the comforters?

(When we recognize that God operates by other laws than man is capable of comprehending, the whole man-God relationship begins to change. God becomes less a force which man can influence by his own actions, and more a vessel for the will of God. Instead of trying, then, to behave in a way that will force God to be good to man, man must begin to search the universe and his own soul as well for clues and bits of understandings to discover what it is that God wants from us.)

Job takes the first step in this direction, by acknowledging his own weakness before God when he tries to contend with him. He feels that he has no possibility to affect God's actions through his supplication. What, then, is his mood after hearing Bildad out? What does he want from God?

(Job again says that he hates his life and asks only for a little peace before his death.)

Do you believe this is really what Job wants at this point?

(It would appear that Job seeks an understanding of God's ways, from the very openness of his questions. Had he sought forgiveness he would have spoken of his own sense of guilt or knowledge of sin. But Job admits no sin.)

Zophar, hearing Job's despairing request to end his life, becomes incensed, and tells Job that God exacts of him less than he deserves. Zophar says of God: "For he knows worthless men; when he sees iniquity, will he not consider it?" 11:11.

Why does Zophar suggest that Job may be one of the worthless men?

How does Zophar suggest that Job find the way to reunite with God and to regain God's favor?

(See text, pp. 45–46.)

Job now turns to his three friends and rebukes them for their pretensions of wisdom. He compares the wordy arguments of his friends with the understandings of God's less complicated creatures who do not speak: "But ask the beasts and they will teach you; the birds of the air, and they will tell you; or the plants of the earth, and they will teach you; and the fish of the sea will declare to you. Who among all these does not know that the hand of the Lord has done this?" 12:7–9.

How would you say Job's concept of wisdom differs from the three comforters' concept of wisdom?

(The comforters pretend to be wise, to know and understand God's ways, and man's. They believe that wisdom resides in man—but Job appreciates the beasts, the birds, the plants, the fish, who do not confuse their puny abilities to draw nourishment from their environment and to reproduce themselves, with wisdom—but they honor God as the source of wisdom.)

When Job has told his friends that he is not inferior to them, he then begins to address God in defense of his ways. In a beautiful passage (Chapter 14 may be read here) he compares man to a tree.

How does Job look upon his life's meaning for man?

(He finds no hope of immortality.)

Question for discussion: *How can modern man find any hope in this statement of Job's?*

At the conclusion of this session it may be appropriate to discuss some of the letters of consolation that were written at the close of the previous session.

Assignment for Session 5:
Read text, pp. 50–60, Job, Chapters 15–21.

SESSION 5

In our last two sessions we were introduced to Job's comforters, Eliphaz, Bildad and Zophar. From their words of consolation, if they may be so designated, we have arrived at some idea of the thinking of these three men. It may be of interest to learn more about them than we are given in the Book of Job, particularly concerning Eliphaz, who has been the subject of consideration by Talmudists as well as by modern Biblical scholars.

Eliphaz, known also as the "Temanite," is supposed to have come from Teman, which was an important city in Edom. Teman is referred to by Amos (1:12) when he speaks of the punishment God is about to visit upon Edom. Obadiah (1:8) also refers to Teman, as he states: "Will I not on that day, says the Lord, destroy the wise men out of Edom, and understanding out of Mount Esau?" Jeremiah (49:19–21) also refers to Teman: "What shepherd can stand before me? Therefore hear the plan which the Lord has made against Edom and the pur-

252

poses which he has formed against the inhabitants of Teman:
Even the little ones of the flock shall be dragged away; surely
their fold shall be appalled at their fate."

It would appear that Eliphaz is a kind of representative of
the wisdom of the Edomites, which was well known in anti-
quity. It has been suggested that the name "Eliphaz" for the
spokesman of Edomite wisdom may have been suggested to the
author of the Book of Job by the tradition which gave the name
Eliphaz to Esau's son, the father of Teman: (Gen 36:9–11)
"These are the descendants of Esau, the father of the Edomites,
in the hill country of Seir. These are the names of Esau's sons:
Eliphaz, the son of Adah the wife of Esau, Reuel the son of
Basemath the wife of Esau. The sons of Eliphaz were Teman,
Omar, Zepho, Gatam, and Kenaz."

The long history of Edom can be traced through the Bible
from its beginning as the portion of land given to Esau by his
father, Isaac. At first the Edomites lived in a mountainous and
rocky country, and were hunters, like their progenitor. Gradually the Edomites became a powerful tribal entity, first ruled
by tribal chieftains but later, as their number increased, they
organized into a kingdom. By the time Saul, the first king of
Israel, began his reign, the Edomites had already had eight
monarchs. The Book of Numbers (20:14ff) describes the warlike
attitude of the Edomites toward the Israelites who were making
their way with Moses toward the Land of Canaan. In Deuteron-
omy (2:1–8) we learn of the armed truce that existed between
the Israelites and the Edomites, which apparently existed until
the time of Saul, when he defeated the Edomites in battle. (See
I Samuel 14:47.) David again defeated the Edomites and following this Edom was under the control of the Israelites. After
the split of the United Kingdom of Israel into Israel and Judah,
Edom began to grow stronger until, during the reign of Jehoram
(851–844 B.C.) the Edomites were able to proclaim their own
king and win their independence.

In the time of Nebuchadnezzar, the Edomites took part in
the bloody fighting and in the sacking of Jerusalem (586 B.C.).
The Babylonian conquerers permitted the Edomites to settle in
southern Palestine, where they prospered for more than four
centuries. Conquered briefly by Judas Maccabeus in 163 B.C.,
and again by John Hyrcanus in 125 B.C., they were at last incorporated into the Jewish national collective. The country of
the Edomites was known as Idumea by the Greeks and later by

the Romans. The Idumean Antipater began the reigning dynasty which ruled over Jerusalem until its final destruction by the Romans in 70 A.D. Herod was one of the kings of the Idumean dynasty.

The Talmudists used the term "Edom" to refer to the Roman empire and they applied to Rome all of the Biblical passages which dealth with Edom or with Esau.

The comment can be made with some justification, therefore, that the designation of Eliphaz as a Temanite, a resident of Edom, is a somewhat prejudicial introduction. It is interesting to note that Eliphaz' statements to Job do not depart from a certain Edomite approach to morality which is by no means separate from some Judaic approaches. Eliphaz has one ongoing thought: the righteous cannot perish; the wicked alone suffer and, moreover, they suffer in relationship to their sins. This is stated by Eliphaz in Job (4:7–9): "Think now, who that was innocent ever perished? Or where were the upright cut off? As I have seen, those who plow iniquity and sow trouble reap the same."

The legend is told that when Job refused the advice of Eliphaz, that Eliphaz called upon his associates to abandon Job to his fate and go their way. But Bildad reminded him that some allowances ought to be made for someone who suffered so much. Bildad wanted to test Job's sanity so he asked him how it came about that God, whom he trusted so completely, could inflict such dire agony. Job replied that man cannot comprehend Divine Nature, "but," he continued, to prove he was of right mind, "listen to the question which I shall put to you. Solid food and liquid combine inside man and they separate again when they leave his body. Who effects the separation?" And when Bildad admitted that he was unable to answer the question, Job went on: "If you cannot understand the changes in your own body, how can you hope to understand the movements of the planets?"

And it is further told that Zophar, after Job had finished speaking to Bildad, was convinced that his suffering had no effect on his mind, asked him whether he would permit himself to be treated by the physicians of his three friends. Job refused the offer, saying, "My healing and my restoration come from God, the Creator of all physicians."

Let us now consider the dialogue between Job and his friends as we find it in the Book of Job:

*When Eliphaz says to Job, "Your own mouth condemns you
. . . your own lips testify against you," what do you suppose
he means by this?*

(One possibility is that Job's arrogance is bringing him deeper and
deeper into sin.)

Is it, in your opinion, arrogance to question the ways of God?

(This is an important question because it revolves about the matter
of how much one is willing to accept authority without question,
and how one could conceivably question while maintaining at the
same time the appropriate respect for and cognizance of the authority. The problem of what motivates the questioning should be
discussed here, too: Is the questioning of God by man done in order
better to understand his ways, or rather, to justify man's own behavior?)

*Describe Job's mood as he responds to Eliphaz and contem-
plates his own death.*

(See 16:6 ff.)

*If their places had been reversed, and Eliphaz had been suf-
fering, how do you think he would have reacted? What would
have been his prayer?*

*Were Job the comforter, what do you suppose he might have
said to Eliphaz?*

(The above dialogue could be assigned, if desired to two persons
to discuss outside the meeting and prepare to present briefly before
the group.)

*Bildad speaks to Job about the fate of the wicked man—re-
counting the miseries to which he is subjected. He suggests that
Job is such a man. Could you, in your own words, express the
reasoning of Bildad which leads him to the conclusion that Job
is wicked? And what would Bildad say is the nature of his wickedness?*

Job again begs his friends to end their tormenting of him.
He continues to speak of his sufferings.

*Of all the agonies he endures, from which do you think he
suffers most, and why?*

Does he ever doubt his belief in God's eternal reality?

How and when does Job believe that his position will at last be vindicated?

(See text, p. 55. Or possible reference to the day of Judgment, Job 19:25-26.)

Zophar describes in detail the suffering of the wicked man. If we read Chapter 20 carefully, we can understand what constituted the concept of wicked behavior in the days when the Book of Job was written.

What were some forms of wickedness of which Job was accused?

How does this description of Job seem to fit him?

(Compare this description with the description in the prologue which introduces us to Job.)

Would Zophar's description of wickedness find acceptance in modern American society? How would it be interpreted in the light of today's social values?

Job disagrees with Zophar's interpretation of the fate of the wicked. What has Job personally observed concerning this? What observations of your own would tend to make you agree with Job—with Zophar?

Job raises an interesting question concerning the fate of the wicked. He fails to see any difference between their fate and that of the righteous, saying: (21:23-26) "One dies in full prosperity, being wholly at ease and secure, his body full of fat and the marrow of his bones moist. Another dies in bitterness of soul, never having tasted of good. They lie down alike in the dust, and the worms cover them."

How would you reply to this question, which might as well be asked today?

Assignment for Session 6:

The third and last cycle of speeches. Read text, pp. 60-74, and Job, Chapters 22-31.

The Book of Job itself sets forth in dialogue form the words exchanged by Job and his three comforters. In this rather abstract discussion, there seems to be missing the undercurrent of human faith which has no intellectual element, but which depends on a simple trust in and love of God. This element occurs in legends which have grown up around the story of Job and which were told by the rabbis in Talmudic times. In Louis Ginsberg's *The Legends of the Jews,* a rich source of folklore relating to Bible characters, the following is related:

> While the three kings (comforters) were speaking with Job, his wife appeared clothed in rags, and she threw herself at the feet of her husband's friend, and spoke amid tears, "O Eliphaz, Bildad and Zophar, remember what I was in days gone by, and see how I am changed, coming before you now in rags and tatters." The sight of the unhappy woman touched them so deeply that they could do nothing but weep, and no word could they force from their mouths. Eliphaz, however, took his royal mantle of purple and laid it about the shoulders of the pitiful woman. Job's wife asked only one favor, that the three kings should order their soldiers to clear away the ruins of the building under which her children lay entombed so that she could give them a decent burial. The command was given to the soldiers, but Job put out his hand and said, "Do not put yourselves to trouble in vain. You will not find my children, for they are safely gathered up by their Lord and Creator." Again Job's friends were sure he was bereft of his senses. Job arose, however, and prayed to God, and at the end of his devotions, he bade his friends look eastward, and when they did so they beheld his children next to the Ruler of heaven, with crowns of glory on their heads. Job's wife prostrated herself and cried out, "Now I know that my memorial rests with the Lord." And she returned to Job's house, from which she had absented herself against his will. He had forbidden her to leave it, because he had feared that the three kings would take her with them.

In reading Job's lament and the first cycle of speeches, we were introduced to Job's understanding of God through the way in which he reacted to his personal suffering; and, further, through the words of the three comforters, we learned something of how the people among whom Job lived conceived of the nature of God. In the second cycle of speeches we obtained a deeper insight into the relationship of evil-doing and punishment, righteousness and reward. We see this from two differing viewpoints—that of the friends, who tend to identify their own ideas of justice with what they believe to be God's idea of justice; and Job's, who admits that he is only a man and frankly cannot understand God's idea of justice which is obviously not the same as that of most men, but on quite another level.

Now, in the third and last cycle of speeches, we see the interplay of all the different viewpoints in collision; how they sometimes affect one another, and how at other times each remains stubbornly encircled and out of contact with the other.

Eliphaz, again the first to speak, enumerates the sins he accuses Job of having committed.

What are these sins?

(See text, pp. 61–62.)

How would you evaluate Eliphaz' reasoning?

Do you agree with Eliphaz that Job was wicked in the eyes of God?

What has the author of the Prologue to say about this?

(See Chapter 1:1 and 1:8.)

How would Eliphaz have Job restore himself to the favor of God?

Do you agree that man can, by his own acts of will, win favor or lose favor with God?

How is this belief in the possibility of winning the favor of God by deliberate action sometimes expressed in modern-day terms?

(We have all often heard of incidents where someone in danger or at the point of death, promises to make some sacrifice to God if God will only spare him. Many shrines and churches have been built for this kind of reason. There are, too, certain charitable organizations which use this belief in man when they find it to motivate giving: the idea sometimes being proposed that one cannot be truly religious unless he gives to this or that cause. The Bible, too, is full of such references, *e.g.*, "Honor your father and your mother, that your days may be long in the land which the Lord your God gives you." Ex. 20:12. We might also refer to the story of Hannah, the barren woman, who prays to God for a son, promising that should she bear one she would give him up to the Lord. When her son Samuel is born, she keeps him only until he is weaned, then takes him to the temple of the Lord, to minister to the Lord in the presence of Eli the priest. [I Sam. 1.])

Job does not answer the charges of Eliphaz directly. Rather, he wants to place his case before God, that God and not man may judge him.

What is Job's belief concerning the kind of judgment God would make?

(Even though Job would like to speak directly with God that he may gain a better understanding of God's ways, this is at the time denied to him.)

How does Job comment upon a world in which man and God apparently have no opportunity to communicate with one another?

(See Job 24.)

Bildad reminds Job of the lowly place of man in the eyes of God, and warns Job that he is being presumptuous in expecting God to hear his cause. "How then can man be righteous before God?" (25:4)

Can Job, in his integrity, accept this warning of Bildad? How does he reply to his comforter?

(See pp. 65-66, text.)

Do you agree with the statement of Biblical scholars (text, bottom of p. 66) that the section on divine wisdom (text, p. 68) is out of harmony with what we have been taught of "normative" or "basic" Judaism?

What point of view do you think was held by the writers or editors who might have had this section inserted in the manuscript?

In Chapter 29, Job reviews his life as it was before tragedy overtook him.

How does this recitation compare with the accusations of Eliphaz (text, p. 61)?

What has become of the people whom Job had befriended in days gone by?

(See Chapter 30, or text, pp. 71–72.)

In Chapter 31, Job summarizes his entire life and his personal philosophy, and thus he ends his case. And this time the three "comforters" are silent.

Why do you believe they have nothing more to say?

(Possible answers might be: Job cannot be helped by them, and they recognize this. Job was righteous in his own eyes. They saw nothing to be gained by further talk. They were ready to wait and to leave the decision to God's judgment. They would see what would now happen.)

And now, into this apparently deadlocked situation, a new figure enters. He is a young man, with all the recklessness and fire of youth. In our next meeting we will learn how his completely different approach brings Job to the very brink of the mighty climax of his life.

Assignment for Session 7:
Text, pp. 74–83, Book of Job, Chapters 32–37.

SESSION 7

In the first thirty-one chapters of the Book of Job we have read how Job was removed from his enviable position of a rich man, perhaps even a king, enjoying the favors of God, to a pitiable wreck of humanity divested of every material asset, of his own health, and of the love and concern of his fellow man. We have heard him cry out in his suffering and express the wish that he had never been born, or, having been born, that he might now be left to die in peace. Three comforters, Eliphaz, Bildad and Zophar have tried in their own ways to console him. Beyond that, they have made suggestions as to what Job might do in order to influence God to restore him to his former position and wealth. Job has answered them all, refusing to acknowledge to God or to man that he has done evil, and also refusing to curse God. At last he has ended his plea in an eloquent final speech in which he implores God to hear him and to deal with him.

Now we are told that a fourth man has been standing by listening to the discourse among Job and the three comforters, and that this man, Elihu, has been greatly angered by what he has heard. Elihu is said to have been a cousin to Bildad and Zophar, whose fathers were all reported to be sons of Buz, who was a brother of Job and a nephew of Abraham. But other traditional commentary on the Book of Job states that Elihu was animated by Satan to speak scurrilous words against Job, upbraiding him for his unshakable confidence in God.

Perhaps we, too, as we have read the words of the comforters and the lamentations of Job, felt that we would have found ourselves angry and possibly also wearied with all the talk.

Had you been standing by as Elihu was, listening to the discussions, what might you have said to Job at this point?

Would you have been sympathetic? Why, or why not?

(Elihu, we are told, was anything but sympathetic to Job.)

Why was he angry with Job?

(See text, p. 74.)

Elihu was also angry with the friends of Job. What kind of answer to Job does Elihu seek that he has been unable to find in the words of Eliphaz, Bildad or Zophar?

Why had Elihu waited so long to speak?

Elihu says, "It is not the old that are wise, nor the aged that understand what is right." (32:9) What then, according to Elihu, is the source of understanding in a man?

("It is the spirit in a man, the breath of the Almighty, that makes him understand." 32:8)

As we study the words of Elihu further, let us consider whether he speaks with greater wisdom than his elders, the comforters, as he insists he does.

One of Job's complaints has been that God did not answer his words. Elihu criticizes Job for wanting to argue with God, and moreover he insists that God does speak to man, and not only in one way, but in two.

What are the two ways in which, according to Elihu, God speaks to man?

(1. "In a dream, in a vision of the night, when deep sleep falls upon man, while they slumber upon their beds, then he opens the ears of men . . ." 33:15–16. 2. "Man is also chastened with pain upon his bed . . . "33:19.)

What does Elihu conceive to be the meaning of dreams?

(They seem to him to be warnings from God so that man can stop and consider his evil ways and turn aside from them so that he will not subject himself to God's awe-ful punishment.)

Is there any other place in the Book of Job where a dream was used in the sense of warning?

(Recall the dream of Eliphaz, text, pages 31–32.)

What were some of the ways in which dreams were understood in ancient times?

(They were thought to be voices from God, or from the gods. They were regarded as oracles to indicate to people how they should behave in a particular, doubtful situation.

They were often considered judgments of God. A German folk-tale may here be used to illustrate this concept of the dream: In a small town one morning a corpse was found in the streets, having been robbed and murdered during the preceding night. It was determined that the act could only have been committed by one of two strangers who had come to town the day before, named Vigilio and Urbini. The two were jailed, and on the following day the judge asked Urbini if he had dreamed during the night. "Yes," said Urbini, "I dreamed I lay in the middle of the main street of the town and could not move, and just at dawn I knew all the carts would be coming to market and I feared they would run over me and crush me to death, and I woke sweating from fright." "So be it," said the judge, and Urbini was bound up with ropes and left at dawn in the middle of the street when all the carts were about to arrive; but on this particular morning no carts came. A landslide had occurred just outside the town limits, and had barricaded the entrance to the street. This was considered incontrovertible proof of the man's innocence, and Urbini was freed. The next night the judge asked Vigilio whether he had dreamed anything. "Oh, yes," laughed Vigilio, "but it was really nothing. I dreamed I put my hand in the mouth of the stone lion at the gate of the town hall." "Then you must be innocent, too," said the judge. "The lion bit me," remarked Vigilio. "The stone lion?" returned the judge, scratching his head. "That was the dream," replied the prisoner. "Then we shall take you to the town hall and you shall put your hand in the mouth of the stone lion, and if he does not bite you, then you are a free man." Laughing, Vigilio and the wardens went to where the lion stood and Vigilio placed his hand in the stone mouth. Suddenly he let out a shriek of pain —and those standing by saw that a scorpion ran out of the stone cavern of the lion's mouth while Vigilio dropped gasping to the ground. It was not necessary for the judge to pronounce sentence upon Vigilio, for the dream had already done so.)

How do man's painful experiences serve as messages from God?

(They cause him to consider his life and his suffering and to try to understand why he suffers. In sickness, frequently man is taken away from his imminent material problems and has time to lie in quiet reflection and experience consciousness in another dimension. When man errs and bring emotional difficulties upon himself, often losing the respect and affections of friends and dear ones, he is compelled to consider the meaning of his painful experience in the light of his relationship to the eternal values he has come to associate with his religious beliefs.)

How would Elihu have man respond to the two ways in which God speaks to him?

(Elihu says, in 33:26, "Then man prays to God and he accepts him, he comes into his presence with joy.")

Elihu gives Job an opportunity to reply, but Job does not. Can you imagine what might have been going on in the mind of a suffering old man like Job smarting under the criticism of the young Elihu?

(But Job's silence only taunts Elihu into even sharper words. He accuses Job of having said, "It profits a man nothing that he should take delight in God.")

Why is this idea so troublesome to Elihu?

(See pages 77–78, text.)

What seems to you to be the central point of disagreement between Elihu and Job?

(Elihu believes that "of a truth God will not do wickedly, and the Almighty will not pervert justice." 34:12. And, as we have seen, Job accepts what God has done to him, even though he does not understand his suffering in terms of justice.)

We have read (text, pp. 78–81) how Elihu goes on to say that Job does not know how to approach God. Elihu explains in the quotation on page 80 beginning "Where is God, my Maker..." how man should properly come before his God.

Do you agree with Elihu on this?
What should or should not be included in a prayer to God?
Elihu speaks of God as a teacher. What does he mean by this?

(God uses punishment as a way to let man know that he has sinned. See 36:8–12, 22–23. Elihu applies this to Job by justifying what has happened to Job as a kind of Divine instruction meant to make Job more sensitive to the wrongs he has committed. While Job had taken more gifts of God for granted in the past, now in his pain and anguish he had become more aware of himself and everything around him.)

Elihu concludes his advice to Job by reminding him to consider the wondrous works of God, which are beyond man's understanding. Elihu believes that man cannot question God. Indeed, he can do nothing but praise him.

And then, in a tremendously impressive description of the coming of God, Elihu sets the stage for the great climax, Job's encounter with God. It is as if the presence of God were made known by its blinding light as it was in the beginning, in the first act of creation, when God said, "Let there be light." We should read aloud the closing words of Elihu: "And now men cannot look on the light when it is bright in the skies, when the wind has passed and cleared them. Out of the north comes golden splendor; God is clothed with terrible majesty. The Almighty—we cannot find him; he is great in power and justice, and abundant righteousness he will not violate. Therefore men fear him; he does not regard any who are wise in their own conceit." 37:21–24.

Assignment for Session 8:

We will complete our reading of the Book of Job, Chapters 38–42, and the text, pp. 83–96.

SESSION 8

The comforters were silent, and Job had laid his cause before God. Even the fiery young Elihu had finished with his lengthy criticism of Job's attitude toward God, and he had expressed his own belief in the power of a God who cannot be questioned by finite man, but only worshipped by him in abject humility. The faith of Job in his God, and his idea of his personal relationship to that God, had been examined from the points of view of several men. Then, suddenly, out of the whirlwind, appears the voice which Job has asked to hear, the mysterious, unknowable voice of God. All the words of the comforters, who warned Job not to demand God's appearance are as naught, for God has listened to Job, arrogant as he may be, and has determined to show Himself to the questioning and suffering human being.

God answers Job, but not in the way Job expects. The Lord is not concerned with replying to the searching questions Job has put. He is rather concerned with the nature of the contact between man and his God, and for this He must ask Job to see himself as he truly is. For Job in reality could never challenge the Creator of the universe, to be able to perceive that Creator is goal enough for any human. And so God faces Job with these words: "Who is this that darkens counsel by words without knowledge? Gird up your loins like a man, I will question you, and you shall declare to me." (38:2–3)

He then begins with a description of the physical world which He has made, in one of the most awe-inspiring sections of the entire Bible. God does not attempt to justify Himself. Rather, He asks Job if he is able to understand the ways of God. One has the feeling, as one reads, of ranging over the earth and the heavens with God, observing everywhere the evidences of His ordering power and His creative nature, and at the same time being painfully aware of how far all this is beyond the possibility of man to comprehend.

Let us read aloud some of the verses that are filled with the description of the might and the glory of God, and try to imagine as we read the feelings of a man who suddenly becomes aware of what it means to know God, not to know *about* God, but to know God as the supreme creating and guiding force. (Selections from Job, Chapters 38, 39.)

How would a man feel who had experienced God in such an encounter, whether out of the whirlwind, or in the quiet recesses of his own meditations?

(The impact of this passage has been felt by almost everyone who has read it, and it may be of interest to us to turn to the illustrations for *Job's Encounter*, and look for a moment at one man's response to the lines "Where were you when I laid the foundation of the earth? Tell me if you have understanding. Who determined its measurements—surely you know! Or who stretched the line upon it? On what were its bases sunk, or who laid its cornerstone, when the morning stars sang together, and all the sons of God shouted for joy?" The series of illustrations from *The Book of Job* was the last complete work of the famed English poet, painter and engraver of the late eighteenth early nineteenth century, and it was the climax of his career as a symbolic artist. The pictures, like so many of Blake's are not primarily illustrations to a given text, but a map of the way to perception of the spiritual aspect within every man. This meaning is the inner meaning of life to every mystic. Blake was for the last time trying to reconcile all the great contradictions of the universe and justify the ways of God to men. S. Foster Damon, in his book *William Blake: His Philosophy and Symbols* describes Blake's personal response to this section of the Book of Job, and we will quote it here in order that you may compare it with your own response:

"The Job of the Bible is the innocent and just man suddenly struck down by overwhelming misfortunes. The author was endeavoring to refute the idea that catastrophe is the punishment of sin. Job is upright, yet he is ruined in a moment. But he is saved by faith; for God descends in a whirlwind, talks with him, and at the end leaves Job more prosperous than ever. The problem of evil, nevertheless, is left unsolved: the Deity says that Job cannot understand the Divine way, and is presumptuous in questioning it. Faith, and not knowledge, is the secret of salvation.

"Blake was not satisfied with such an evasion of the great world problem. He himself was not the ordinary type of mystic who feels truth in a vision, but can never express it. Blake had grasped a solution which satisfied him; so he deliberately outdid the author of the Book of Job by giving the answer which had been withheld.

"His answer was this: that Job, living in accordance with laws written by others, rather than by the instincts of his own heart, had left himself open to the inroads of Satan. He had relied upon a moral code for his happiness, not realizing that invulnerable happiness comes only from a sacrifice of self. The catastrophes poured upon him by Satan spring really from his own false notions of virtue; and as long as Job is self-satisfied, he will be afflicted by these unexpected turns of 'fate,' a fate which he himself invoked upon others, and which recoil upon himself eventually. But his troubles soon drive him to look inward, into his own soul. As soon as he does this, he not only recognizes and casts out the error of his life; he sees Divinity itself; and after such a vision, nothing more can trouble him.'

Damon goes on to say that the illustration for "When the morning stars sang together" shows that moment of mystical vision which is followed by an immediate perception of the truth lying hid in the universe. This picture, with the poem *The Tyger*, kept Blake's name alive in the years of obscurity which followed his death. Everyone who has seen it must have felt the splendor and passion of it, though few have really understood the meaning from which all this glory sprang.)

God has challenged Job to reply to the questions He has posed. Now Job is called upon as a faultfinder, who contends with the Almighty, and God says, "He who argues with God, let him answer it." This is Job's moment of opportunity, for which he has waited so long.

How does he respond to the challenge?

(See Job 40:3–5.)

What has happened to Job to make him respond in this way? Has Job had an intellectual experience? Does he really un-

derstand anything any better than he did before God spoke? Has he any really new information?

If not, then, what kind of experience was it for Job?

What did he realize?

How did the impact of the encounter with God affect him?

What changed in his relationship with God?

(His attitude toward God changed from one of contention to one of deep and profound awe.)

What remained the same?

(The facts. God in speaking to Job did not change anything. He merely explained what Job already knew. But He showed His work in its true measure, the magnitude of which had not been appreciated fully before. The act of *communication* between God and man was more important than the content which was communicated.)

When Job cannot, or rather, will not answer God, how does God accept Job's excuse that he is of small account and is unable to speak further to God?

(God expresses the idea in 40:7-9 that for a man to condemn God and justify himself he must be able to equate himself with the Almighty. He goes on to show what one would have to be capable of doing were he to address God on an equal basis, and to expect a reply from God.)

What do you suppose is the significance of the descriptions of the Behemoth (40:15-24) and the Leviathan (Chapter 41)?

("No one is so fierce that he dares to stir him [Leviathan, the crocodile] up. Who then is he that he can stand before me?" [41:10] "Can one take him [Behemoth] with hooks, or pierce his nose with a snare?" [40:21] If the ability of man is so feeble as not to be able to conquer this beast of God's creation, how then can man attempt to equate himself with God, or to call God to account for His actions?)

Now at last Job has felt the power and majesty of God in the very depths of his being. And now he can speak out. But his speech is quite different from what we would have expected from the man who complained so bitterly to his comforters.

What would you have expected Job to have said to God, had he been able to speak as soon as Elihu had finished castigating him?

(But Job did not speak. It was God who appeared and who spoke, and now Job, in his encounter with God, is moved to express himself in a very different way. Let us read his answer to God: [See text p. 95 or Job 42:2; 3b; 5–6]).

What do you suppose Job is trying to express when he tells God: "I had heard of thee by the hearing of the ear, but now my eye sees thee..."?

(The hearing of the ear suggests "hearsay," learning something through education, through the experiences of others, retold. But now Job has had a personal experience. He has encountered God and known Him through his own perception.)

And now, instead of challenging God to explain His actions in bringing hardship upon Job, Job despises himself and repents in dust and ashes. What does this mean?

(The meaning of "despise" here is probably "to regard as inferior." For now Job has seen himself in a new relationship to God, where God is the Creator and moving force in the world and in man, and man can only be less than God. And so he lowers himself and shows his humility in the expression "dust and ashes.")

The rest of the Book of Job is known as the Epilogue. The moving orations are completed, and God and Job have a new and deeper relationship, in which Job is a different man from what he was at the time of his original good fortune, and, indeed, also different from the man who argued with his comforters.

How does God acknowledge the change in Job?

(See Job 42:7–9.)

How does God recompense Job for the misery he has suffered?

(See Job 42:10–17.)

We have followed the fortunes of Job from beginning to end. Much has come clear, but the Book of Job leaves many questions unanswered. Perhaps this is the fascination of this Book. In our next session we will begin to deal with the questions. But surely, as you have read and as we have talked, questions have occurred to you that may not have been dealt with in the book *Job's Encounter* up to this point. I should like to ask you for our next meeting to bring to class, one or more written questions of your own concerning the Book of Job.

Assignment for Session 9:

Your own questions. Text, pp. 96–101.

SESSION 9

Last time we met we completed our reading of the Book of Job, and we saw how Job, after experiencing personally the meaning of God's greatness, was humbled before the realization of His power—and how, in his humility, he was restored to his former condition of wealth and security and good health. Yet, as we have read in our text, *Job's Encounter,* many questions were raised in the Book of Job which have not been answered for us. Perhaps some of you have reflected on some of these questions and would like to express your own reactions to them.

Particularly interesting is the question of Satan, introduced in the first two chapters of the Book of Job, and not referred to after that. We are left to decide why Satan had to be introduced at all, and why, once introduced, there was no clarification as to whether in the end God's point of view or Satan's prevailed.

In your opinion, who really won the wager?

(This question might be presented as a topic for a brief debate, with the participants divided into two groups, each of which could prepare from material in the Book of Job, evidence for his side of the argument.)

At this point it may be interesting to ask what the wager was all about. What aspect of Job's nature was Satan betting on to achieve dominancy when Job was tried and tested to the point where all his values, built up through his entire lifetime, were suddenly destroyed? And what aspect of his nature was God betting on? Can it really be said that man is either (1) basically self-centered, concerned only with his physical needs and instincts for survival, or (2) basically a growing, developing creature, adapting to new situations, able to see himself ever more in a relationship to the world about him and to those spiritual forces which activate that world as well as the individuals within it? Or is there an ever-existing struggle in which the wager is neither won nor lost, but where at times one side appears to have the advantage, at times the other?

The following additional questions raised in the text may be discussed:

Why did Job hold out so long against his friends' urging, only to capitulate at last by confessing his guilt and recognizing that his demand for justice from God was sheer arrogance on his part?

(Here the importance of the *personal encounter* with God as the factor which transformed Job from a man of pride to a man of humility should be considered. It might be helpful to cite other examples of this kind of transforming experience, *e.g.,* the struggle of Jacob with the angel, in which the transformation is symbolized by the giving of a new name, "Israel," meaning "he who strives with God." [Gen. 32:24–30.] The class may have additional examples to offer.)

What is the meaning of the deaths of the innocent sons and daughters of Job as well as the deaths of his servants?

(One possibility is that the sons, daughters, and servants of Job are meant as symbols of Job's *personal* striving after wealth and power and a continuation of his good name. When these are removed one begins to see the real Job, who is a lost and lonely man. The new family and the new wealth, coming as it does after Job's encounter with God, may then be understood as symbols of man's *spiritual* strivings toward a greater goal than his own personal ambition. This greater goal might be the achievement of a closer relationship with the creative force within himself as well as that within the universe; in another sense, with the God of the universe who is also the God indwelling within man.)

At this point the unanswered questions prepared by the group may be taken up in an open discussion:

Following this discussion, we may move on to the subject of Biblical criticism.

Bible scholars have long sought to uncover the deeper meanings of the Book of Job, indeed of the entire Bible, in many different ways. Recognizing that the Biblical books as we know them today are a conglomerate of the writings and the editorial efforts and the inexact copyings of many generations of scribes who assembled their raw material from ancient scrolls and from oral tradition, Bible critics attempt to discover the variations in authorship of the different books and of the passages within each book.

Israel, which has often been called "the People of the Book," might as fitly be called "the People of Biblical criticism." Criticism is used here in the modern sense to mean the same thing as the then popular term, *exegesis,* meant a few decades ago: interpretation and explanation of the text. This is the one science which was created and developed as a part of Judaism after the Hebrews had produced, during the first long period of their history, the Bible itself. During the thousand years following the collection of the different books of the Scripture, the intellectual activity of Judaism was directed almost exclusively to the critical treatment of the Bible and the systematic development of the law derived from it. When, through contact with Hellenic and Arabic learning, the Jewish intellect was led into new channels, Bible study still retained its interest; it was the first to feel the influence of the new thought. Biblical criticism in the Middle Ages took the forms of two new sciences—Hebrew philology, the study of the culture of the people through a critical examination of the language—and the philosophy of religion. During centuries of decadence which followed, the exposition of the Bible still remained the most popular and assiduously cultivated occupations of the Jewish mind. The epoch known as Mendelssohnian begins with a renaissance of Bible criticism. And modern Judaism is characterized by two reforms founded on the study and exposition of the Bible: the reinstatement of the Bible in its legitimate place in the instruction of the young, where it had long been secondary to the study of the *Talmud;* and the sermon in the synagogue, based as it so often is on the Biblical text. In the past several decades scientific developments have made it possible to date ancient manuscripts more exactly, and have added much information to advance the work of Biblical scholars.

What was the Talmudic approach to Biblical criticism, and how did it differ from that of our time?

(See text, pp. 100–101.)

Why do you suppose many Bible critics such as Spinoza and Simon had such difficult times at the hands of the religious authorities of their own times?

(A threat is nearly always posed to the established order by a new discovery or a new point of view. When the authority of the Bible was believed to rest in God's own words, it could not be questioned. The religious leader who merely taught and expounded and amplified the text was supported in his endeavor by incontrovertible authority. But when some men protested that the Bible was composed by men, some of whom often included their own views and their disagreements with the manuscripts and traditions with which they worked, these men threatened the *binding quality* of the Biblical injunctions upon men. If the Bible was subject to scholarly perusal, might it not as well later become subject to individual interpretation?)

Indeed, how did this in fact take place?

(The Reform movement within Judaism, with its insistence upon discerning the spirit of the law rather than clinging to ancient customs because of their basis in the authority of the Bible, is an outgrowth of the development of 19th-century Biblical criticism.)

Assignment for Session 10:
Chapter III, text: Problems in Job. pp. 102–111.

SESSION 10

Our text, *Job's Encounter,* has presented some modern views of Bible scholars concerning the composition of the Book of Job. As we consider them, let us be aware of the way in which these scholars work, using their knowledge of the Hebrew language, of the history of the Hebrew people from its earliest beginnings, and also of the eternal and relatively unchanging psychological aspects of man that make him handle his human relationships and his man to God relationships in certain universal and rather predictable ways.

What are some of the bases for the belief of many modern scholars that the Prologue (Chapters 1–2) and the Epilogue (Chapters 42:7–17) are derived from an old folktale that was well known before the central dialogue portion of the Book of Job was written?

(They note that the arrangement of the text of Prologue and Epilogue is quite different from that of the bulk of the work; also that Job's ideas and arguments found in the body of the book are set against the prevailing tradition.)

If, as stated in Job's Encounter (p. 103), scholars believe that the original story was told without the Satan episodes in Chapters 1:6–12; 2:1–7a, how do you suppose the meaning of the original story differs from what we understand to be the meaning of our version, complete with Satan?

(It is evident that even in very ancient times the concept of evil had to be accounted for. It was a problem in those days, too, and the writer who hooked up the poetry of the dialogues with the Satanic explanation of Job's suffering was dealing with this problem according to the understandings of his times. Now, from the point of view of twentieth-century Bible interpretation, we must re-examine the relationship of evil and Satan to one another. If we do not accept the existence of Satan literally, we must nevertheless accept the notion that the *idea* of Satan symbolizes a concept with which we all have to come to terms, that of the evil which exists in every man, and which often goes unrecognized except as he sees this evil in its reflected form in the world about him.)

What may have been the purpose of cloaking the real essence of the message of the Book of Job with the appealing trappings of an old folk tale?

(Possibly to capture the attention of the reader or listener with a well-loved and familiar story—so that this attention would be at its peak when the author was ready to express his more revolutionary ideas.)

It may be interesting, now that we are somewhat familiar with the approach of modern critics to the Book of Job, to look back for a moment into Rabbinic writings and learn what the Talmudists had to say about this always-controversial book. Because of the importance of the book, Talmudists occupied themselves frequently with its leading character. It is reported that one of the rabbis expressed himself in the presence of Samuel ben Nahmani that Job never existed and that the whole story was a fable. An opinion couched in similar words by Simeon ben Lakish was interpreted to mean that such a person as Job existed, but that the narratives in the drama are inventions. Apart from these utterances, all of the rabbis took for granted that Job existed, but they differed widely as to the epoch in which he lived, and as to his nationality, two points very closely connected. Every one of the Talmudists inferred Job's epoch and nationality from an analogy between two Biblical words or sentences. According to one, Job lived in the time of Abraham; according to another, in the time of Jacob, he having married Dinah, Jacob's daughter. One rabbi said that Job lived in the time of Jacob's sons; and another said that Job was born when Jacob and his children entered Egypt and that he died when the Israelites left that country. Putting this all together it would appear that Job lived 210 years.

Another statement made by the Talmudists was that when Satan came to accuse the Israelites of being idolaters, God set him against Job, whence Job's misfortunes. This opinion was supported by the statement that Job with Jethro and Balaam was consulted by Pharaoh as to the means of reducing the number of the children of Israel, and that Job was stricken with calamity because he had remained silent. There are many other statements made by the rabbis. In fact it almost appears as though every rabbi who dealt with the questions raised in the Book of Job had worked out his own individual answer.

What made possible this great variety of opinion among the religious teachers of Talmudic times?

(The Book of Job itself, as we have read in our text, contains many contradictions in spirit, that is, some parts do not seem to be in character with other sections. Since there was no actual proof as to which sections were genuine integral elements of the original Book, and which were added at a later date, or were errors of transcription, or were purposely inserted to change emphases, it was possible for these individual scholars or teachers to select a word or phrase or chapter as authentic and then to make deductions using the section as a reference point. Someone else would then come along and say, in my opinion another point is more basic, and from here we must make different deductions.)

In our times, as Robert Pfeiffer has pointed out, we cannot expect to find a Book of Job in complete harmony according to the literary standards with which we have become accustomed. We must try to understand the words of the writers of the Book of Job within their own contexts. With this in mind, how can we explain the inclusion of sections such as the long speech of Elihu, which does not seem to have any connection with what has gone before, nor with the following sections?

(If Elihu is an integral part of the tale, one wonders why he is not mentioned earlier in the book. He suddenly appears, as if from nowhere, makes his impassioned speech refuting what the three comforters have said to Job, and then disappears again, so that, in the last chapter, when God speaks to Eliphaz and his two friends, He does not even acknowledge that Elihu has been among the comforters. Elihu's ideas differ basically with those of the comforters, as well as with Job's. But the major point is not so much how he disagreed or on what specific points. Elihu's problem was that he did not approve of any questioning at all, either by Job or by the questioners, of God's justice. His is a much more orthodox point of view than any other character has seen fit to express, and apparently somewhere along in the composition of the Book of Job, it was felt necessary that this tenet of Orthodox Judaism be expressed.)

What is the danger of approaching the matter of Biblical criticism in a modern rational way, using our best philosophical methods of thinking?

(The writers of the Bible had never been exposed to modern ways of logic and organization of materials. They had different criteria for including or not including a section in the Bible. At times the sheer beauty of a passage was sufficient enough to warrant its insertion in a likely place, even though it had been found elsewhere. Or, when a modification of a section brought it into better harmony with the spirit of the times, an old manuscript would be altered without a qualm. It was because of this easy and flexible way of collecting Biblical materials, that it was necessary eventually to close the canon, that is, to declare that the Bible was complete and must remain in its present form with no further changes permitted. But even though there have been no changes for a long time, other than new translations, the Bible is nevertheless a repository of centuries of writings with layers of conflicting ideas superimposed upon and intermingled with one another. This does not detract from its meaning. On the other hand this is the reason for its richness and variety, for the fact that it deals with almost every problem that had plagued the spirit of man, and that it has some message of significance for every reader.)

Assignment for Session 11:
Chapter IV, text, pp. 112–118.

SESSION 11

The problems connected with dating and assigning authorship to the Book of Job have concerned Biblical scholars for generations. In our last meeting we discussed some of the opinions expressed by scholars as to when the events ·that are described in the Book of Job may have been presumed to have taken place. If there was disagreement in that area, such disagreement is small in comparison with the wide variation of opinion as to when the Book of Job was composed, and over who was responsible for the composition.

What is the earliest date that has been assigned to the composition of the Book of Job?

(The earliest date given is the time of Moses. Levi ben Lahma, a rabbinical writer of the Middle Ages is said to have held that not only did Job live during the time of Moses, but that Moses was the writer of the Book of Job. Another rabbi declared that the one servant of Pharaoh who feared the word of God was Job. A third rabbi, specifying the time more accurately, said Job lived in the time of the spies who were sent by Moses to explore the land of Canaan. According to these rabbis, Job was a Gentile, and others express the opinion that Job was a "pius Gentile" or "one of the prophets of the Gentiles.")

What is the latest date commonly assigned for the composition of the Book?

(The third century B.C.)

When do most contemporary scholars believe that this book was written?

(It is generally ascribed to the period of Jewish history known as the "Exilic Period"—from 586–538 B.C.)

Why is it perhaps unimportant to try to assign a specific time to the composition of the Book?

(There is so little agreement on the date that one cannot find satisfactory evidence for coming to a valid conclusion. Furthermore, the important matter is not so much when the Book was actually written, but rather, how old are the source materials. It is believed that the Book stems from very ancient folktales, at least in part, and that these cannot be designated as representative of a specific time. Indeed, the place is also obscure, as legends similar to that of the story of Job have appeared in the cultures of many nations.)

Project: **DEBATE**

There is much evidence to support the belief that the writer of the Book of Job was a Judean, and it would then follow that Job was designated as a Jewish hero. On the other hand, there is also good basis for the belief that Job may not have been Jewish. Therefore, it might prove interesting to organize members of the group into two teams who could debate the subject, "Resolved that the writer of the Book of Job was a Judean." Some of the material that will have to be dealt with to develop an argument for either view, are found in the text, pp. 113–114. The following questions should be considered here:

Where does the name of the God of Israel (Yahweh) *occur, and what is the significance of these occurrences?*

Could the God described in the Book of Job conceivably have been the God of another people, not necessarily the Jewish people? Why or why not?

What, if any, references are made to the Land of Israel?

What, if any, references are made to Jewish customs and ceremonies? More specifically, it would be important to discover whether, for example, animal sacrifice in the form of burnt offerings was practiced in other lands in the vicinity of the Land of Israel, and if so, by whom and in what manner?

What are the interests of the writer of the Book of Job with respect to social practices?

How would the opinions of Ernst Renan, P. Dhorme and Robert Pfeiffer buttress one or the other point of view?

Check Job 12:17–25, the passage which is assumed to refer to the Assyrian Exile in 722 B.C. or the Judean Exile in 597 B.C. Is it clear whether there is anything specifically Judaic or Israelitic about the kind of humbling of the mighty that is described here?

Note on the debate: Because the material for the debate can be found in the text and in the Book of Job, this could well be prepared within the regular class hour, and presented in the same hour. It need not be long or involved, but should serve primarily to point up the difficulty scholars have with coming to definite conclusions when they deal with Biblical materials in a critical way. It will be shown how a relatively small body of material could give rise to interpretations that differ greatly one from the other.

Further questions for class discussion:

We stated earlier that the exact dating of the Book of Job has not been considered very important. However, the assigning of authorship to a Judaic or a Gentile source has relatively great importance for the scholar. Why?

(The question of authorship is very much bound up with the philosophical character of the Book of Job. Authorship and meaning go hand in hand, and the meaning cannot be fully understood without having some idea as to whom this particular story had this particular meaning.)

How does the Book of Job's comment on retribution for sinfulness compare with the prophetic ideas on this subject?

(The prophets, with the possible exception of Ezekiel and Jeremiah, conceived of the religious community as a totality rather than as a collection of responsible individuals. Therefore, when there was sinfulness among Jews, retribution was almost always national in scope.)

With what earlier Biblical writings could the more individualistic concept of the God-man relationship, as seen in the Book of Job, be compared?

279

(The text gives the Garden of Eden and the Tower of Babel stories. To this might be added, the story of Cain and Abel, and the story of Noah and the Ark. The class should be able to summon forth several more examples.)

What other possible influences may have been at work upon the author of the Book of Job to produce this highly individual approach to the question of sin and punishment?

(Egyptian and Oriental writings of a more individualistic nature than that of the prophets of Israel and Judah.)

How do the religious ideas of Job progress during the course of the Book? Where is he at its beginning, where at its end?

(At the beginning, Job is a man who believes that by material sacrifices to God a man may win his favor. As the book progresses, Job realizes that this is not true, and that further, man may live in a way he believes to be in accord with the will of God and still fail to win his favor. So he is forced to accept God without understanding His ways, and also to consider behavior as a matter more of importance in the relationships between men, than in the God-man relationship.)

The earlier Biblical philosophers had a concept of a God who was the supreme ruler of the world. He was all powerful, His justice was perfect, He practiced deeds of righteousness in relationship to man. He was, furthermore, all-knowing and all-merciful. Concerning every characteristic enumerated as being an attribute to God in the eyes of the early Biblical writers, the Book of Job has something contrary to say. How does the author of the Book of Job demonstrate that God was not (1) all-powerful, (2) perfect in justice, (3) righteous in relation to man, (4) all-knowing, or (5) all-merciful?

How does the author make these rather startling concepts more acceptable to the ancient reader?

(We can now understand why it was felt necessary to begin the book with a familiar folktale which would capture the attention and gain the confidence of the reader.)

Assignment for Session 12:

For our next meeting we will read Chapter V in the text,

dealing with the literary quality of the Book of Job. Pages 119–132.

SESSION 12

Today it will be our task to concern ourselves with the Book of Job as a literary work. Before we do this, we might as well ask ourselves the question:

How is a literary work judged today? What makes one work of value, another not?

(Members of the class will have many suggestions. A few points that should not be overlooked include:

Descriptive quality: how well does the writing bring to life the experiences of the senses and show every possible aspect so that the writing is accurate, lively, and meaningful?

Communication between writer and reader: how well does the writer convey the sense of what he wants to express so that it reaches the reader with real impact?

Does it go beyond the commonplace in the sensitivity of expression and of perception?

Has it integrity of form—as a play, a poem, a novel, a short story, a descriptive essay, etc.? That is, does it use the form best suited to the message it seeks to convey?

Has it significance beyond its immediate plot or story or description; that is, does it deal with one or more of the basic problems of life in such a way as to make its conclusions or conjectures meaningful beyond the limits of the work itself?

Is the language and the style skillfully employed to achieve the purpose of the author as effectively as possible?)

We have perhaps listed many qualities that the modern reader, trained as he is by the modern literary critic, will look for. But were these the values sought in literature by our ancestors? Remember, when the story of the Book of Job was first committed to writing, most of the people who thrilled to its masterful drama could neither read nor write. The tale was an old and familiar one, told as a legend, at first, and later read to a hushed audience from a sacred scroll. How were such works of literature esteemed in ancient times; what purposes did they serve?

(Possibly, at first, they were thought of primarily as entertainment. Whenever people came together and shared a meal either around a desert campfire or at a ceremonial feast in the season of a pilgrimage, the recounting of tales made the event memorable. The education of the young, also, was carried on almost exclusively by word of mouth imparting of the tales of the group. The cultural heritage of a people was one of the bases of tribal belonging. Before the days of mass media, before even the introduction of the printing press, each group could be characterized to a large degree by its literary production. By studying these early writings we can learn a great deal about the lives of the people who wrote them, their customs, their problems, their values, their beliefs, their stage of development.)

Today we consider to be literature almost all the writings of the earliest peoples. Why is this so?

(Early people wrote down only the very best of their spoken words. Writing was hard work, and writing materials were scarce. Therefore time and effort were reserved to record what people felt was of greatest importance.)

Why do you suppose a modern playwright like Archibald MacLeish would take so old a theme as the Book of Job and make of it a play for modern Broadway?

(Perhaps he might have had in mind the same idea as the writer of the Biblical Prologue and Epilogue: to capture the attention of the reader or listener with a well-loved and familiar story so that his attention would be at its peak when the author was ready to express his own, revolutionary ideas. Or perhaps MacLeish, like many other writers who have used Biblical themes, recognized the applicability of the dilemmas of ancient man to the searchings of humanity of all ages, including our own.)

In our text the statement was made that some scholars have suggested that the Book of Job has had a very considerable influence on other great literary works. Three were mentioned, *The Divine Comedy, Paradise Lost,* and *Faust.* We may look briefly at bits of these works and see whether we, ourselves can discern this influence. (Another possibility is to assign to various students the responsibility of examining these works and bringing to the session whatever evidence they can find of the influence of the Book of Job in them.) The following samples indicate what any student may discover for himself:

Let us read the following lines from Canto XIX of Dante's *Divine Comedy:* "He who turned the compasses at the verge of the world, and distributed within it so much occult and manifest, could not imprint His Power on all the universe that His Word should not remain in infinite excess. . . . Therefore our vision, which must needs be one of the rays of the Mind with which all things are replete, cannot in its own nature be so potent as not to discern its origin far beyond that which is apparent to it. . . . Therefore the sight into the Eternal Justice which your world receives penetrates within as the eye into the sea; which, though from the shore it can see the bottom, on the main sees it not, and nevertheless it is there, but the depth conceals it . . . " Now compare with those lines, the following from Job 38:4-5; 8-10: "Where were you when I laid the foundation of the earth? Tell me, if you have understanding. Who determined its measurements—surely you know! . . . Or who shut in the sea with doors, when it burst forth from the womb; when I made clouds its garment, and thick darkness its swaddling band, and prescribed bounds for it, and set bars and doors. . . . "

And this same passage in Job has left its unmistakable imprint, many believe, in the following lines from Milton's *Paradise Lost,* Book V, lines 853–857:

> " . . . who saw
> When this creation was? rememberst thou
> Thy making, while the Maker gave thee being?
> We know no time when we were not as now;
> Know none before us. . . . "

Or compare Job 38:7 "When the morning stars sang together, and all the sons of God shouted for joy," with this from *Paradise Lost,* Book VII, lines 252–256:

> "Thus was the first Day Eev'n and Morn:
> Nor past uncelebrated, nor unsung
> By the Celestial Quires, when Orient Light
> exhaling first from Darkness they beheld:
> Birth-day of Heav'n and Earth; with joy and shout
> The hollow Universal Orb they fill'd."

Again compare Job 14:14: "If a man die, shall he live again?"

283

with *Paradise Lost* XI, line 550: "Live well, how long or short permit to Heaven..."

An even more striking literary comparison may be found in Goethe's *Faust*, in a dialogue between "The Lord" and "Mephistopheles," and it will not be necessary to quote from the Prologue of Job to find our parallel:

"THE LORD: Do you know Faust?

MEPHISTOPHELES: The Doctor?

THE LORD: Yes, my servant!

MEPHISTOPHELES: He!
Forsooth, he serves you most peculiarly.
Unearthly are the fool's drink and his food;
The ferment drives him forth afar.
Though half aware of his insensate mood,
He asks of heaven every fairest star
And of the earth each highest zest,
And all things near and all things far
Can not appease his deeply troubled breast.

THE LORD: Although he serves me now confusedly,
I soon shall lead him forth where all is clear.
The gardener knows, when verdant grows the tree,
That bloom and fruit will deck the coming year.

MEPHISTOPHELES: What will you wager? Him you yet shall lose,
If you will give me your permission
To lead him gently on the path I choose.

THE LORD: As long as on the earth he shall survive,
So long you'll meet no prohibition.
Man errs as long as he doth strive.

MEPHISTOPHELES: My thanks for that, for which the dead I've never got
Myself entangled of my own volition.
I like full, fresh cheeks best of all the lot.
I'm not at home when corpses seek my house;
I feel about it as a cat does with a mouse.

THE LORD: 'Tis well! So be it granted to you today!
Divert this spirit from its primal source
And if you can lay hold on him, you may
Conduct him downward on your course,
And stand abashed when you are forced to say:

284

A good man, though his striving be obscure,
Remains aware that there is one right way.

MEPHISTOPHELES: All right! But long it won't endure!
I have no fear about my bet, be sure!
When I attain my aim, do not protest,
But let me triumph with a swelling breast.
Dust shall he eat, and that with zest,
As did the famous snake, my near relation.

THE LORD: In that too you may play your part quite free:"[1]

Before leaving the subject of the literary quality of the Book of Job, we ought to ask what is the literary structure of the book?

(See text, pp. 120–121.)

The language of the Book of Job is unique in the Bible; its vocabulary contains many words not used elsewhere in Scripture. How do scholars explain this?

(See text, p. 125.)

What conclusions may we draw concerning the literary skill of the author(s) of the Book of Job by reading the section quoted in today's assignment?

(He was a man of great imagination, as shown, among other places, in his description of the nether-world in 3:13–19.

He was a believer in visions, from his vibrant recounting of Eliphaz' experience.

He was a masterful observer of natural phenomena.

He was well-informed about his own times.

He showed great understanding of how human beings behaved under every possible situation.

He was highly educated and sophisticated, as shown in his treatment of the theodicy where he explored every possible side of the issue.)

Assignment for Session 13:

Job's Revolutionary Philosophy, and The Philosophical Argument, text, pp. 133–164.

---

1 *Great Books of the Western World*, Vol. 47. Chicago, Ill., 1952, Encyclopaedia Britannica, Inc.

SESSION 13

Today we are going to try to understand something of the nature of Job's philosophy, which the writer of *Job's Encounter* describes as "revolutionary."

But first let us try to define "philosophy" so that we are all agreed on what we are talking about.

(Philosophy—literally from the Greek: "love of learning," or "love of wisdom." The philosopher is interested in all aspects of reality, and in the underlying causes and properties of reality. Philosophy is not necessarily a specific branch of knowledge, rather it is to be thought of as an approach to any branch of knowledge, be it mathematics, politics, fine arts, language study, even medicine and public relations.)

What does a philosopher attempt to do?

(Basically, the philosopher is not particularly interested in *doing* anything—his world is the world of theory—he seeks principles by which phenomena can be better understood.)

Let us try to name some well-known people whom we might call "philosopher" in various scientific fields.

(We might begin with the example of Charles Darwin, a philosopher in the field of biology. In his work *The Origin of Species by Means of Natural Selection* he abstracted certain ideas from his observations and deductions which, while they cannot be proved, nevertheless exist within his system and have become the bases of further researches by other scientists, in some cases leading to practical applications. The group will undoubtedly have many more examples to offer.)

What is meant by the statement, "A most interesting quality of philosophy is its subjectivity?"

(See text, p. 134.)

In what respect must subjectivity be taken even more into account when we are dealing with questions of theology?

(In the sciences we do have some objective facts upon which a phi-

286

losophy may be grounded. We have observations with which we can deal, directly perceived through our own sensory apparatus, or with the aid of mechanical contrivances as the spectroscope and the camera in astronomy, for example. But in the field of theology, we have no such evidence upon which the concepts we draw concerning God can be firmly based. While we believe we may have ample evidence of Gods existence all about us, we have no really objective proof of His existence, nor do we know for certain what His nature is, nor what sort of plan He has for the universe or for man's place in it. We only have our own experience and perhaps of some limited value, second-hand experiences of others, to work with. Out of this material, plus our own personal approach to life, we have to develop our concept of God. So it is with every theologian—the results of his thinking may have other influences incorporated within them, but most of all they are a personal expression, full of the element of subjectivity. It is, therefore, of vital importance that the student of ideological questions be aware that the expressions of others are largely a result of their own subjective approaches. What seems clear and acceptable to one individual, appears absurd to another. And there is no final way of judging it. Therefore, the various ideas deserve respect as individual expressions, and consideration, but one need not feel bound to accept an idea because it has been considered acceptable by someone whom one may respect.)

What is the point of departure for the philosophical discussion in the Book of Job; that is, what is the classical philosophical position regarding the relationship between God and man?

(This relationship, as expressed in the words of the comforters, who take the classical position of the day, sees man as a weak and helpless and dependent human creature who is able to do little more than extend frail hands and pitiful cries to the Almighty.)

Theologically speaking, can you describe the kind of God which Eliphaz, Bildad and Zophar have in mind when they address Job?

(See text, p. 139.)

In Eliphaz' mind, what is the nature of God's mercy?

(God's mercy is not of the overflowing kind. First, God's justice must be recognized, and man must realize that he has sinned, before the possibility of mercy is opened to him. Then, having realized, he must confess his sin in true humility, and he must accept the punishment that is meted out to him. Only when this has been done will it be possible to expect that the mercy of God will be forthcoming.)

The question may be asked as to whether this idea of mercy is in keeping with the concept of mercy held by members of the class.

Job was a man of his times, and yet he was more than that. In the course of the Book of Job we see in the man, Job, a development of thinking and experiencing that was beyond that of his contemporaries. We might, then, take time to make some interesting comparisons:

How is Job's concept of God in harmony with that of his friends?

(Job believes, as do his friends, that God is all-powerful. At no time does he question this. He sees it in the divine control of natural events and in the futility of man's attempts to defy the will of God.)

Where does Job's concept of God differ from that of his friends?

(The friends believe that God is just and merciful in His reward and punishment of human beings. God is aware of everything that man does, and He has no choice but to reward or punish man accordingly as He observes man's deeds. Job will not agree that there is a relationship, necessarily, between man's performance and God's response. Job comes to this point of view out of his own experience and, throughout his discussions with the three comforters he maintains his position that his misfortunes are undeserved. While admitting that he may have sinned in his youth, he contends that essentially he is a good and pious individual and that he does not deserve the kind of treatment he has received at the hand of God.)

What is the nature of Job's faultfinding with God? What are Job's accusations against God?

(See text, p. 140–143.)

What were Job's "revolutionary ideas" concerning man's evil-doing and God's punishment?

(Job suggested that there is really no relationship between the sin that man commits and the evil that befalls him. He asserts that what happens to man is a kind of meaningless fate. God is not concerned with the good or evil that an individual man occupies himself with. Good and evil are alike to God, and it is by chance that man has unhappy or satisfying experiences in his life. The terms, reward and punishment, so much a part of the theology of his contemporaries, seems no longer to exist in the viewpoint of the suffering Job. Such chance experiences of the good life or of misfortune do not seem in Job's thinking, to be a part of man-God relationship.)

What were the reactions of the friends of Job to these "revolutionary ideas"?

(Job's friends feared the effect on society if such ideas as Job's were to become popular. As in our times to a large extent people believe that laws and the penalties imposed for the infringement of these laws is what keeps people acting in a socially acceptable way. So did Job's friends believe that it was the fear of God and His punishment for infringement of His laws that maintained the workings of society. Were people to cease believing in divine punishment, there would be no way of stopping them from doing evil. Nor would goodness be sought as a goal of man, bringing with it the promise of the blessings of health and riches and happiness from the hand of God. A society which held firmly to a cause and effect concept of behavior and result would be greatly undermined by such ideas as Job expressed. Therefore, the friends of Job reacted by urging Job to reconsider and recant his words, to realize that he was bringing upon himself even greater suffering by his own attitude, and to humble himself before God. Last and most important, they required of him that he admit his sin, so that they, in their own minds, could justify the suffering that Job was forced to endure.)

How does the story of Adam and Eve deal with the similar problem of apparent lack of relationship between the sin and the punishment—as told in the expulsion from Eden?

(See text, p. 146–148.)

The story of the Tower of Babel, in Genesis, Chapter 11, raised some related questions concerning the nature of God. What were these questions?

(See text, p. 148–149.)

Did the prophet Amos really come to terms with the question of just reward and just punishment, as directly related to man's acts?

(Amos believed, as firmly as Eliphaz, Bildad and Zophar, in the basic justice of God, rewarding good with good and evil with misfortune. When God heaped heavy difficulties on the children of Israel, it was not because He was being unjust. It was, in Amos' approach, the children of Israel who had misunderstood God's requirements for them. Instead of bringing sacrifices and precious gifts they were to bring God the offerings of righteousness and justice toward their fellowmen. However, when man acted in the way prescribed by God and expressed by Amos, then swiftly just reward would follow.)

In what respect were the experiences of Jeremiah and Ezekiel, and the prophecies growing out of those experiences, closer in feeling to the expressions of Job than were the prophecies of Amos?

(While Amos thought of Israel's relationship to God as a collective relationship in which a nation behaves in a certain way, and the nation is punished or rewarded—Jeremiah and Ezekiel, like Job, perceived the individual nature of the relationship between man and his God. Although they, too, accepted the doctrine of retribution, there are passages which suggest that the actual experiences of their lives at times called this belief into question. See especially the quotations from Jeremiah 20:7–9, 14–15, 18.)

What other attempts have been made in the Bible to explain an apparent lack of relationship between evil-doing and punishment?

(Evil, rather than being always a result of man's misdeeds, was sometimes ascribed to the inciting of Satan. See I Chronicles 21:1, 7. Further, in the Book of Daniel 12:2–3, and in Isaiah 26:19, 21, the promise is made that in the eternal life to come after the life we know on earth, the Lord will come to judge man and to reward the righteous with eternal bliss and to punish the evil for their iniquity until the end of time.)

What explanation of this unsolved problem is treated in a unique manner by Job?

(It is Job, alone, who conceives of an indifferent God, unconcerned with the welfare of the suffering of man, as even nature is herself indifferent.)

What inescapable conclusion must Job draw from this line of reasoning, which he has pursued throughout the bulk of the Book?

(See text, page 163.)

As a final discussion the class could be asked whether this is the only possible conclusion to be drawn from the material presented in the Book or, what alternative conclusions members of the class may come to. The result of this discussion will show several different points of view. It will be apparent that ways of thinking, believing and worshipping God are dependent on much more than the evidence we have at hand from our own experience and from literature pertaining to religion. There is that hard-to-pin-down factor, the individual psychology of man, which determines the approach he will have to these weighty questions. In the next session, we will begin the study of the psychological insights of the Book of Job.

Assignment for Session 14:
Read text, Chapter VII, "Psychological Insights," pp. 165–189.

SESSION 14

In our last meeting we dealt with some of the philosophical and theological concepts found in the Book of Job. We cannot help having been impressed by the variety of possibilities for individual interpretation as each person studies this Biblical book and brings to bear on its words the personal experiences and insights peculiar to that reader and to him alone. Each of us has his own psychological make-up, and this distinguishes him from his fellow human beings quite as substantially as does his physical make-up. Indeed, whether he is tall or short, dark or light in complexion, of great physical endurance or a weakling, these factors are not nearly so important as his reactions to these facts, the way he perceives them and the way he acts upon them. What to one may be a disadvantage will be to another a source of inspiration to go on to greater accomplishment. All depends on the psychological approach he has. A man may be gifted with intellectual talent: does this make him feel superior to his fellow man and does he then become intolerant of those whose capacities are less, or does he welcome the privilege of using his gifts to better the lot of those who may not possess the capacities to improve their own situation to the same degree that he does? This depends on his psychological set, his attitude, that inborn way of reacting to a situation which characterizes a man as an individual.

The psychologist studies man with an eye toward those factors which make him behave as he does. The factors are intangible, to be sure; one cannot recognize them readily as one can see in his visage traces of his racial background. Yet anyone who has given a thought to the natural characteristics of people has quickly recognized such obvious qualities as those of the open, friendly, warm-hearted person who rejoices in the company of friends as contrasted with the more quiet, contemplative, reserved individual who looks forward at the end of the day to curling up with a good book, or spending hours in his workroom fitting together model ships, or listening to favorite records. No one would suggest that it is better to be the first type of person than to be the second. They are merely different, that's all. And, recognizing those differences as intrinsic, one would not suggest that the first type of person should become, say a draftsman, who works for hours in silence over painstaking details, any more than he would send the second type of person into a big department store as a shoe salesman. A man can only be what he is, and he experiences his world within the limitations of his own psychological make-up.

Accepting this, we can only deal with Job as Job, an unusual man, who was of his own time, yet had a somehow different spark in his personality which made it possible for him to take a different look at the same set of conditions, and come to a different result. We must consider the psychology of Job not from our own point of view, but as a psychologist would try to do, to somehow enter into the framework of Job himself, and try to follow Job's own responses to the problems which beset him.

To begin with, we must look at this man, Job, as he is presented to us at the beginning of the Book.

Is he indeed the perfect man, as the Bible states at the outset? Or did he actually behave in a self-serving manner, realizing that since God was a Being who rewarded good deeds with bountiful favors, it was to a man's advantage to act in the manner he believed to be pleasing to God?

What were Job's feelings, at the beginning of the Book, about the causal relationship between evil and punishment?

Would you say that this is an outworn idea, or are there evidences of its still being accepted in some measure by people today? Explain.

(See text, pp. 171–172.)

Why does the causalistic approach to man's problems seem so necessary to so many people today? How does it help them to achieve a feeling of security?

(See text, p. 172.)

How do these simple causalistic explanations for the things that happen to us sometimes fail to provide this comfortable feeling of security?

(See text, p. 173.)

What was Job's immediate reaction to the calamities that befell him, and how did his logical, inflexible, causal approach serve him?

(Job's beliefs were not adaptable to change. He could not understand what had happened to him or why it should have happened, but he continued to react in the old way, accepting the punishment of God as he had accepted God's blessing, mourning, suffering, but not questioning. See Job 1:20–21.)

Surely Job is a pious man, but could we say that he continues to be "the perfect man"?

293

(One wonders if Job's piety might not be an expression of his disbelief of the reality of what has happened to him. It is the behavior of a man in a state of shock, and when we understand it in this way, we are not surprised, nor do we ascribe inordinate goodness to his utterings. Perhaps his pious worshipping was unconsciously at least, an attempt on the part of Job to call attention to himself before God—to say, "Look what you have done to me, O God, and see how dutifully I have responded. Reward me, then with your gracious mercy, which is vouchsafed to the pious man."

What is your response to the reaction of Job's wife, who says, in 2:9, "Do you still hold fast your integrity? Curse God and die."?

What was Job's immediate emotional reaction to the arrival of his three friends?

(See text, pp. 174–176, in which is seen the change from a stubborn man who cannot come to terms with an impossible fate, to a man of self-pity, wallowing in his misery.)

What does Job's expression of his wish for death indicate about the psychological state in which he finds himself?

(He has been completely drained by his experience of all desire and ability to cope with his problems. In a sense he has given up, and perhaps this is necessary at this time. For in times of great stress many people find it necessary to retire from the world for a time, figuratively if not actually, in order to regain strength to be able to find a new approach to life. This is, for example, the function of the period of convalescence after a serious illness. There must be a partial experience of "death" before the individual can be born to live again. And before Job can be born to his new ideas, the old ones must die in him. This is perhaps the symbolic meaning of Job's wish to die. And symbolic this wish must be, for at no time in the Book does one have the feeling that Job really means to take his own life.)

How do Job's friends react to his orgy of self-pity?
(See text p. 176.)

Now we see that Job stiffens in the face of human injustice. He determines to maintain his personality as a righteous man, even despite the hard-to-bear injustice meted out to him by God. He does not understand either the laws of God or man, and yet he holds onto an inner, directing force which somehow keeps him going—his own personality, his integrity. And, with the principle of causality, which has been a guide for him all his life until now, falling about him, he begins to comprehend the world with a new and different principle and approach.

What is Job's new approach to the world, now that the principle of causality no longer serves him?

(The principle of randomness, which asserts that in the world there is no apparent relationship between what a man does and what happens to him. See text, p. 179.)

In the Book of Job, Job demands almost at the start of his trouble, an opportunity to seek redress from God. What is the nature of the process through which Job must go before he can, in truth, come to terms with God?

(See text, p. 183.)

The God of the Book of Job has been described in very human terms. The Prologue gives us an idea of what people of the day imagined God to be like. So do the speeches of Eliphaz, Bildad and Zophar. What are these "human" qualities of the God of the Book of Job?

(He is jealous of His ruling powers, just as man is jealous of his personal dignity and prestige. He becomes angry with man when man dares to challenge Him. He plots and plans and schemes, just as man does—not in accord with His best nature. He can be petty, oppressing the poor and the weak. God is seen in the image of man—and all this before God Himself appears to Job. We can here recognize the difference between an understanding of God based on the tradition of the times and the words of other men, and that understanding which comes to Job later, based on his own personal encounter. How differently God appears when at last Job can say "I had heard of thee by the hearing of the ear, but now my eye sees thee. . . ." 42:5.)

What does the author of the Book of Job seem to be saying about the human understandings of God and the limitations of those understandings?

(See text, p. 187.)

Assignment for Sessions 15–21 inclusive:

The next chapter of *Job's Encounter* is Chapter VIII, "The Impact of the Book of Job on Modern Thought." Because of the importance of this material in relating what we have learned from the Book of Job to the modern western intellectual tradition, we will use the next seven sessions to elaborate on the material in our text. The readings for each week in the text are very short, and we will ask members of the group to take it upon themselves to select a topic for supplementary reading, and to prepare a report to be given orally, of five to ten minutes in length. At this time we will make the assignments of reports for the next seven weeks, so that you may have ample opportunity to make your preparation. The subjects follow:

For Session 15:

1. Biographical sketch of Herman Melville, to include a consideration of what aspects of his life touched problems raised in the Book of Job.
2. Compare the early American Calvinistic idea of "Innate Depravity and Original Sin" with the theology expressed in the Book of Job.
3. Biographical sketch of Tolstoy, with emphasis on his social background and his unorthodox ideas, up to the completion of his writing of *War and Peace* in 1869.
4. Complete the biographical sketch of Tolstoy, including the further development of his religious ideas from 1869 to 1910. Compare Tolstoy's personal suffering in his later years with the trials of Job, and the ways in which each man was affected.

For Session 16:

1. Biographical sketch of Dostoevsky, showing how his own experiences prepared him to deal with "the problem which has tormented me all my life—the existence of God."
2. Read, in *The Brothers Karamazov*, Book VI—"The Russian Monk"—Biographical Notes at the end of Chapter 1. Report on the influence of the Book of Job on the life and thought of Father Zossima.
3. Biographical sketch of Machiavelli, stressing the attitude toward religion which was current among the ruling offi-

cials in Florence at the end of the 15th and beginning of the 16th centuries.

4. Report on the events in the life of Machiavelli immediately preceding his writing of *The Prince*. In what way did these events parallel to some degree the experience of Job?

5. Read *The Prince*—Chapter XXV—"What Fortune Can Effect in Human Affairs, and How to Withstand Her." Compare Machiavelli's approach to an understanding of the seemingly senseless relationship between man's acts and events that befall man, with the points of view expressed in the Book of Job.

For Session 17:

1. Biographical sketch of Thomas Hobbes, including Hobbes' ideas relating to causality in the workings of nature.

2. Report on Chapter XXXVI of *Leviathan* titled "Of the Word of God, and of the Prophets," in which Hobbes discusses the many occasions in the Bible in which God appeared to various prophets and other individuals. Compare these meetings with Job's encounter.

3. Read Pascal's *Pensées*, Section VII—"Morality and Doctrine." Here Pascal asserts "that man without faith cannot know the true good, nor justice." Read and report on the several paragraphs in which Pascal substantiates this view.

4. What is Jansenism? Can the Jansenist views be shown to have any relationship with the attitudes of Job's comforters?

For Session 18:

1. Biographical sketch of Montesquieu, showing how he was accepted as a "man of his own times," yet in his later years questioned the new, universal ideas of his philosopher contemporaries and so stepped beyond his own era.

2. Read in *The Spirit of Laws*, the first chapter of Book I—"Of Laws in General." Discuss Montesquieu's view, here expressed, of a God who acts in accordance with specific laws.

3. Biographical sketch of Voltaire, showing how he in his own time, like Job, was seen as a person possessing some "revolutionary ideas."

4. Read *Candide* and discuss how Voltaire treated the problem of the theodicy in this book.

For Session 19:

1. Biographical sketch of Jean-Jacques Rousseau, including his concept of the sources of good and evil in the world.

For Session 20:

1. Review Jefferson's philosophy and contrast his way of dealing with oppression to that of Job's comforters. Consider how Jefferson might counsel a man who appears to be a victim of divine injustice.
2. *Job's Encounter* refers to man's intimate contact, even contest, with God as narrated in Hasidic literature, as an essential aspect of Judaism carried forward from the days when Job first challenged God. Find examples of one or two such stories and bring to the class. (Suggested sources: Martin Buber—*In Search of Heaven* or *Chasidic Tales*; Louis Ginsberg, *Legends of the Jews*.
3. How did religion, once the concern of the state, become a private matter during the course of the American Revolution and the founding of the new nation?

For Session 21:

1. Biographical sketch of Sigmund Freud, describing his own religious background and training.
2. Summarize Freud's approach to religion as expressed in Lecture No. 35 in his *New Introductory Lectures on Psychoanalysis*.

To the discussion leader: Above have been listed twenty-two topics for reports. Should this number exceed that of the members of the class, it may be advisable to eliminate some of the reports and extend the length of time to be devoted to the individual report. Also, the age level of the group and their educational background may suggest that certain topics ought to be eliminated because of their difficulty.

Additional assignment for Session 15:
Read in text, pp. 190–195.

SESSION 15

Presentation of Oral Reports

1. Biographical sketch of Herman Melville, to include a consideration of what aspects of his life touched problems raised in the Book of Job.
2. Compare the early American Calvinistic idea of "Innate Depravity and Original Sin" with the theology expressed in the Book of Job.
3. Biographical sketch of Tolstoy, with emphasis on his social background and his unorthodox ideas, up to the completion of his writing *War and Peace* in 1869.
4. Complete the biographical sketch of Tolstoy, including the further development of his religious ideas from 1869 to 1910. Compare Tolstoy's suffering in his later years with the trials of Job, and the ways in which each man was affected.

For Class Discussion

How did the position of the established church in Russia in Tolstoy's time compare with the dominancy of a certain rigid approach of religious authority, as expressed by the three comforters of Job?

Assignment for Session 16:

Read text. pp. 195–199; Dostoevsky and Machiavelli.

SESSION 16

Presentation of Oral Reports

1. Biographical sketch of Dostoevsky, showing how his own experiences prepared him to deal with "the problem which has tormented me all my life—the existence of God."
2. Read, in *The Brothers Karamazov,* Book IV—"The Russian Monk"—biographical notes at the end of Chapter 1. Report on the influence of the Book of Job on the life and thought of Father Zossima.
3. Biographical sketch of Machiavelli, stressing the attitude toward religion which was current among the ruling officials in Florence at the end of the 15th and beginning of the 16th centuries.

299

4. Report on the events in the life of Machiavelli immediately preceding his writing of *The Prince*. In what way did these events parallel to some degree the experience of Job?
5. Read *The Prince*—Chapter XXV—"What Fortune Can Effect in Human Affairs, and How to Withstand Her." Compare Machiavelli's approach to an understanding of the seemingly senseless relationship between man's acts and the events that befall him, with the points of view expressed in the Book of Job.

For Class Discussion

What does Dostoevsky mean by "Elucidean nonsense"? Is this the same as our idea of "mechanical cause and effect"?

Assignment for Session 17:

Read text, pp. 199–206; Hobbes and Pascal.

SESSION 17

Presentation of Oral Reports

1. Biographical sketch of Thomas Hobbes, including Hobbes' ideas relating to causality in the workings of nature.
2. Report on Chapter XXXVI of *Leviathan*, titled "Of the Word of God, and of the Prophets," in which Hobbes discusses the many occasions in the Bible in which God appeared to various prophets and other individuals. Compare these meetings with Job's encounter.
3. Read Pascal's *Pensées*: Section VII—"Morality and Doctrine." Here Pascal asserts "that man without faith cannot know true good, nor justice." Read and report on the several paragraphs in which Pascal substantiates this view.
4. What is Jansenism? Can the Jansenist views be shown to have any relationship with the attitudes of Job's comforters?

For Class Discussion

1. How does Hobbes' idea of the function of the state compare with the function of Job's comforters in the Biblical tale?
2. Do you think there was any connection between Pascal's health and his attitude toward religion? Do you think

there was any connection between Job's physical condition and his attitude toward God? Discuss, and see what the implications are for people living today. Can modern examples of the relationship between physical condition and spiritual outlook be given?

3. Do you agree with Pascal that in order to become a complete believer you must first be a complete doubter? Do we know of people who have been doubted and then, through some special kind of experience, have become complete believers?

4. How does modern man re-enact Pascal's "wager"—that is, how does he, in his way, "bet on God?"

Assignment for Session 18:

Read text, pp. 206–211; Montesquieu and Voltaire.

SESSION 18

Presentation of Oral Reports

1. Biographical sketch of Montesquieu, showing how he was accepted as a "man of his own time," yet in his later years questioned the new, universal ideas of his philosopher contemporaries and so stepped beyond his own era.

2. Read, in *The Spirit of Laws,* the first chapter of Book I—"Of Laws in General." Discuss Montesquieu's view, here expressed, of a God who acts in accordance with specific laws.

3. Biographical sketch of Voltaire, showing how he in his own time, like Job, was seen as a person possessing some "revolutionary ideas."

4. Read *Candide* and discuss how Voltaire treated the problem of the theodicy in this book.

For Class Discussion

1. Compare the trick or device used by Montesquieu to that supposedly used by the author of Job in making unacceptable material available under the guise of something more palatable. (See text, pp. 105–106, 207–208.)

2. Compare Voltaire's idea that there were "natural" laws at work in the world, with Job's wondering about the "randomness" of events. (See text, pp. 179–210.)

3. How does Voltaire's idea of man's responsibility for his own fate compare with ideas set forth by Elihu. (Text, pp. 76–79, 210–211)?

Assignment for Session 19:

Text, pp. 211–217; Jean-Jacques Rousseau. Also: Four members of the class are to prepare a playlet for the next meeting, interpreting how it might have been if Job had been a righteous, God-fearing Frenchman, who had just been visited by a series of devastating tragedies, and the friends who came to comfort him were Pascal, Montesquieu, and Voltaire.

SESSION 19

Presentation of Dramatic Project

A man who has borne the trials of Job, is counseled from the points of view of Pascal, Montesquieu, and Voltaire. This theme is presented in a playlet form, and following it the group may discuss the issues raised, whether additional points may be made, whether the characteristic approach of each historical personage was recognizable, whether the audience agreed with the expression of the actors, and any other matters stimulated by the dramatic project.

Presentation of Oral Report

Biographical sketch of Jean-Jacques Rousseau, including his concept of the meaning of good and evil in the world.

For Class Discussion

1. Can you see any relationship between Rousseau's "inspiration" which led to his writing the prize-winning essay on the subject "Has the Progress of the Arts and Sciences Tended to the Purification or to the Corruption of Morality?", to Job's intense experience with God?
2. Why were Rousseau's ideas so reprehensible to Voltaire and the other "Encyclopedists"?
3. Having seen the playlet and heard the report on Rousseau, suggest how the relatively naive Rousseau would have taken the Elihu role in the Job drama, opposing his elders and coming forward with some positive ideas of his own.

Assignment for Session 20:
Text, pp. 217–229.

SESSION 20

Presentation of Oral Reports

1. Review Jefferson's philosophy and contrast his way of dealing with oppression to that of Job's comforters. Consider how Jefferson might counsel a man who appeared to be a victim of divine injustice.
2. *Job's Encounter* refers to man's intimate contact, even contest, with God as narrated in Hasidic literature, as an essential aspect of Judaism carried forward from the days when man first challenged God. Bring examples of such stories to class.
3. How did religion, once the concern of the state, become a private matter during the course of the American Revolution and the founding of the new nation?

For Class Discussion

1. In the philosophy of such men as Jefferson and Adam Smith, what is the responsibility of individual man to determine his own fate?
2. What motivated the American Revolutionists to rebel against the authority of England and to write the Declaration of Independence?
3. What is the concept of the Divine Right of Kings? Where do we first see it, and what is its significance?
4. What are the two widely separated approaches to God which are illustrated in the Book of Job? (See text, p. 227–228.)

Assignment for Session 21:
Read text, pp. 229–233.

SESSION 21

Presentation of Oral Reports

1. Biographical sketch of Freud, describing his own religious background and training.
2. Summarize Freud's approach to religion as expressed in

Lecture No. 35 in his *New Introductory Lectures on Psychoanalysis.*

For Class Discussion

1. What does Freud's essay have in common with Job's lament?
2. What kind of religion is Freud talking about in this critical essay?
3. With what important aspects of man's religious experience does Freud fail to deal in this essay?
4. In our study of modern thinkers from Melville to Freud, who have been influenced in greater or lesser degree by the Book of Job, it may have been remarked by many that in the lives of most of them there has been an extraordinary experience of some kind that had the effect of transforming a man of talent into something much more: a person of deeper perception, fuller understanding, and greater creativity. We may note what some of these experiences were. As many as possible should come from the group, and the leader may add.

Tolstoy: long bouts with illness and in later life adoption of a new form of religious understanding which led to his excommunication from the Orthodox Church.

Dostoevsky: epilepsy, and five years in prison living "like a person buried underground," without "one single person within reach with whom I could exchange a cordial word."

Machiavelli: In 1512, with the restoration of the Medicis to power, Machiavelli's public career came to an end. He was deprived of his office and exiled for a year. He then was unjustly accused of conspiring against the new government, was imprisoned and tortured on the rack. After his release from the dungeon and his retirement from public affairs, he began to live a hidden life by night in his study, where he was able to give himself over to "conversations" with the illustrious dead, Dante, Livy, Aristotle and Polybius. It was at this period in his life that he composed his principal work on politics—*Discourses upon the First Decade of Livy, and The Prince.*

Hobbes: Publication of *Leviathan* cost him an action against him by Parliament, after which he was never able to get permission to publish anything on ethical subjects. Many of his writings could be made public only after his death.

Pascal: The mystical conversion about which we read in our text (pp. 201–202) and the long and agonizing struggles against ill health.

Voltaire: Endured prison terms in the Bastille as punishment for having written certain satires which were unacceptable to the ruling powers in France. Also, a period of voluntary exile from his beloved country, after a long prison term.

Rousseau: The inspirational experience described in our text, (p. 212) and many other shocking mental and emotional experiences related in his *Confessions,* one of the world's great autobiographies.

5. What is the meaning of an "encounter with God" as applied to modern man?

Assignment for Session 22:

Read Chapter IX in the text, "Job Comes to Broadway," pp. 234–254.

SESSION 22

The title which John Ciardi, teacher and poet and poetry editor for *The Saturday Review* selected for his essay on Archibald MacLeish's *J. B.* was "The Birth of a Classic." He describes the play as great poetry, great drama, and great stagecraft. The distinction Ciardi makes between drama and stagecraft is one which concerns us here, as we ask ourselves what elements in this modern "classic" are directly borrowed from the Biblical book, and which belong to the contemporary playwright-poet. Ciardi writes in *The Saturday Review* of March 8, 1958:

"By drama one must intend a gathering of intellectual, spiritual and physical forces about the lives of characters who move those forces and who move within them to a conclusion that echoes within us to the root of our values. By stagecraft one must intend the manipulation of the illusions of the stage for momentary effect."

How does the Book of Job answer to Ciardi's definition of drama?

(The Biblical book certainly gathers together those forces of which Ciardi speaks: the intellectual, as personified in the theological views expressed; the spiritual, in the aching suffering and yearning of Job and the response of his God; and the physical, in the actual events of the drama which motivate the action and impel the characters to deal with those basic issues which echo in the value systems of men of our own time.)

How does the Book of Job serve MacLeish in providing "stagecraft"?

(Stagecraft is a modern concept—at least its current interpretation must concern itself with the momentary effect upon the audience in our own times. This MacLeish understands in contemporary terms. The Book of Job, as we read it, certainly provides high moments of exaltation, suspense, and deeply moving emotion. But on the whole, there is much repetition, lengthy speeches, little activity on the stage. Adaptation of all this, as modern taste requires, was MacLeish's own concept, based as it was on the inspiration of the vibrantly meaningful drama of Job.)

What special qualities do the figures of Mr. Zuss and Nickles, and the device of showing the story of Job as an act in a great circus ring, show?

(Unlike the characters of God and Satan in the Book of Job, the carriers of the Prologue in the modern version are basically human. Their supra-human qualities appear only as possibilities when they assume masks, props of a play that have been strewn around, one a God-mask and the other a Satan-mask. The masks enable these characters to act in a non-human way. It may be seen as almost a play on the Prologue in Job, where the characters of God and Satan are seen not in divine terms, but through the eyes of humans. And when MacLeish accepts this humanistic view of the senseless tormenting of man by unconcerned deity, then man must of necessity be seen as a mere amusement for such deities. How apt then is the metaphor of the circus ring!)

In the Book of Job, Job's wife has very little part in the drama. What is her role in the MacLeish version, and why is her part built up?

(One possibility may be that the modern American reader or play-goer finds it difficult to conceive of a man who, having suffered so much, would be able to accept his fate with only the words: "Blessed be the name of the Lord." Some part of him must necessarily rebel, even though he cannot bring himself to voice these rebellious feelings. In the Biblical book we wonder how Job can hold fast to his integrity in the face of all that has occurred. In MacLeish's play we have the bitterness that we must feel was a part of Job's response, even if not an expressed part, and we have that bitterness enunciated by the voice of Sarah, J. B.'s wife. Sarah represents that part of J. B. which is torn by doubt. J. B. and Sarah can no longer exist together in this agony of destruction. They must be separated, so that what she stands for cannot force J. B., at last, to "curse God and die." It is interesting to note that in the series of twenty-one drawings on the Book of Job made by William Blake, Job's wife is with him from the beginning to the end, always at his side, even when he is in the depths of his misery, and even when he reaches his highest moment in the encounter with God. But this is a different woman from MacLeish's Sarah. She is less a real woman than an ideal one, more a presence than anything else. One sees in the serenity of her face that she is something more, which the Biblical tale does not tell us about, but that something beyond Job's ordinary humanness, which enables him to survive what to most men would have been unendurable.)

How do you understand the meaning of the return of J. B.'s wife to J. B. at the end of the Broadway play?

(See text, pp. 242–243. This view may be compared to the Biblical tale, where there is no mention made of the return of Job's wife, only that his sisters and brothers returned "and all who had known him before." That his wife is not specifically mentioned may be interpreted as suggesting that the Biblical concept of a wife was that of a person who could almost be said so much to be a part of man, so that neither the separation nor the reunion had to be specifically pointed out. Genesis 2:21–22 states: "So the Lord God caused a deep sleep to fall upon the man, and while he slept took one of his ribs and closed up its place with flesh; and the rib which the Lord God had taken from the man he made into a woman and brought her to the man." Biblical man did not need to have this relationship pointed out to him, for it was Adam who said "This at last is bone of my bones and flesh of my flesh; she shall be called Woman, because she was taken out of Man." But modern man, who no longer holds this concept of woman, needs to see her in a somewhat different light.)

What are Mr. Driver's objections to the play J. B.?

(See text, p. 244.)

Comment on Mr. Driver's conclusion: "There is, in the final tally, not much religion and not much drama. But there is theatre all over the place. And it will hold your interest all evening, and longer. Your discussion of it will probably make more sense than it does."
How does Bible scholar Samuel Terrien observe the difference between the character of J. B., and that of Job?

(See text, p. 246.)

What problem arises, according to Dr. Henry Pitney Van Dusen, when Biblical scholars comment on a modern play based on the Bible?

(See text, pp. 247–249. It might also be well to point out here that it is important to understand the nature of the work of Biblical critics, but one must also be able to accept the view that there are other valid interpretations of Biblical writing and modern writing that stem from Biblical inspiration. The purely scholarly point of view can be as narrow as the purely literary view or the purely historical view. The important recognition is that a work of literature or art can be better appreciated when it is seen from as many viewpoints as possible, which is, of course, the aim of our study of the Book of Job.)

Reinhold Niebuhr suggests that Archibald MacLeish does not believe in a personal God. On what does he base this view? Do you feel that the view is justified?

(See text, p. 250.)

What "deep need," in the eyes of Louis Finkelstein, does J. B. fill?

(See text, p. 251.)

What conclusions do you draw from the fact that the play
J. B. has been the subject of so much interest and controversy?

Before leaving the subject of Job's influence on modern man
in the areas of literature and philosophy, mention should be
made of the sequel to the Book of Job written by American poet
Robert Frost, and titled *A Masque of Reason.* Anticipating
Archibald MacLeish's *J. B.* by a decade, Frost also underlines
the eternal significance of this Biblical book. Set in dramatic
form, the poem-play purports to be "Chapter forty-three" in
the Book of Job, taking place on Judgment Day. God appears,
looking exactly as He does in the pictures of William Blake,
and apologizes to Job for the difficulties He has caused him.
An interesting explanation of God's purpose, as Frost with his
well-known wry humor suggests it, follows:

God, speaking to Job:

> I've had you on my mind a thousand years
> To thank you some day for the way you helped me
> Establish once and for all the principle
> There's no connection man can reason out
> Between his just deserts and what he gets.
> Virtue may fail and wickedness succeed.
> 'Twas a great demonstration we put on.
> I should have spoken sooner had I found
> The word I wanted. You would have supposed
> One who in the beginning *was* the Word
> Would be in a position to command it.
> I have to wait for words like anyone.
> Too long I've owed you this apology
> For the apparently unmeaning sorrow
> You were afflicted with in those old days.
> But it was of the essence of the trial
> You shouldn't understand it at the time.
> It had to seem unmeaning to have meaning.
> And it came out. I have no doubt
> You realized by now the part you played
> To stultify the Deuteronomist
> And change the tenor of religious thought.
> My thanks are to you for releasing me
> From moral bondage to the human race.

The only free will there at first was man's,
Who could do good or evil as he chose.
I had no choice but I must follow him
With forfeits and rewards he understood—
Unless I liked to suffer loss of worship.
I had to prosper good and punish evil.
You changed all that. You set me free to reign.
You are the emancipator of your God,
And as such, I promote you to a saint.

What is Frost trying to say about the relationship of God and man here?

Assignment for Session 23:

Read text, pp. 255–259, Chapter X, "An Interpretation of Job by a Depth Psychologist." For those especially interested in this subject, the suggestion may be made to read *Answer to Job*, by C. G. Jung (Meridian Books, 1960).

Should there be sufficient time and interest, *A Masque of Reason* might be presented to the class as a reading. It should take less than half an hour to present, and might be assigned at this time for presentation at the final session of the class. Four characters are required: Job, his wife, God, and Satan.

SESSION 23

The question may well be asked by the student of modern psychology, "What has psychology to do with religious questions, with the relationship of man to his God?" Psychology, as most people understand the meaning of the word, is the science which treats of the mind in any of its aspects; it is the systematic knowledge and investigation of the phenomena of consciousness and behavior. Questions about God seem to belong to the much less scientific field of theology, where, as we have discovered, investigation is intensely subjective, since there are really no "facts" to deal with. A science, such as psychology, must deal with "facts," and if God is something more than a fact, He is also something less than a fact, as modern science regards a fact. And Job, whose origin has been studied by scholars of several centuries, has not been proved to have been a historical personage; neither is it possible to say for certain whether the story of Job was even Israelitish in origin. Paltry basis for scientific investigation, one might suggest.

Psychology, in its modern, scientific sense, is a new area of investigation. It has been less than two centuries since a Scottish physician named Cullen introduced the term "neurosis" to apply to illness without organic substance. In the interim between then and now, the ways in which man behaves, and the factors responsible for his behaving in certain ways and not in others, have been studied and observed from many viewpoints. While most of the investigations were based on observable phenomena, either in man or in animals, it remained for Freud, as we have read, to discover the importance of the role of that unobservable element in man's total make-up, the unconscious.

It was Freud, also, who recognized the importance of religion as one factor in man's experience which influenced his behavior. Freud questioned, as did Job long before, the "assertions made by religion that it could give protection and happiness to men, if they would only fulfill certain ethical obligations." (Quoted on p. 229 of the text.) He further went on to say that "Earthquake, floods and fires do not differentiate between the good and devout man, and the sinner and unbeliever. ... Dark, unfeeling, and unloving powers determine human destiny; the system of rewards and punishments, which, according to religion, governs the world, seems to have no existence." (Ibid, p. 230.) What Freud was saying is almost what Job was expressing in his laments. It was necessary for Freud, in his understanding of those forces which affect so profoundly man's response to his own experiences, to take into account man's experience of God, as he saw it within the boundaries of the traditional religion to which he had been personally exposed and which was current in the late nineteenth and early twentieth century in central Europe. Freud's era put forth certain dogmatic religious concepts, which Freud attacked. Nevertheless, the need for religious understanding and for a feeling of relatedness to what is understood as God continues to be a part of man's psychic make-up, changing as it does according to the times in which he lives and his own particular circumstances.

Jung, in his book, *Answer to Job*, does not question the "fact" of God, any more than he questions the "fact" of Job. He objects to the factual, or physical approach, saying that "physical" is not the only criterion of truth: there are also *psychic* truths which can neither be explained nor proved nor contested in any physical way. If, for instance, a general belief existed that the river Rhine had at one time flowed backward from its mouth to its source, then this belief would in itself be a fact even though such an assertion, physically understood, would be deemed utterly incredible. Beliefs of this kind are psychic facts which cannot be contested and need no proof. Religious statements are of this type. *(Answer to Job,* p. 14.) He goes on to say that religious statements frequently conflict with observed physical phenomena, and he suggests that the reason is that these religious statements are not based upon perception through the five senses, but rather upon an unconscious perception which demonstrates itself through what he calls "confessions of the psyche," and which a theologian might call "faith." It is that which we know, without knowing how we know it.

We might then ask ourselves the following question:

Would it have been possible for Job to have come to the realizations to which he did at last come, without first having had the physical suffering and the loss of his family, friends, and prestige, and without having had the conversations with his friends?

(This ought to provoke lively discussions on both sides, for the question of whether an individual must learn everything through his own personal experience has been a troubling one which concerned philosophers in the past and which has been dealt with increasingly by educators of our own day. The question should not be left without calling attention to the consideration that it is not only the experiences man has which transform his life, but also the attitude he has toward those experiences and the attempts he makes to extract meaning from them.)

In Answer to Job, *Jung points out that the Biblical God, Yahweh, had continually to be praised as being just, as possessed of a justice that could not be called into question, and that this was his most characteristic trait. Why do you suppose that people of the Bible, like the comforters of Job, for example, made such a point of constantly reiterating their confidence in God's justice?*

(Jung says that the Bible tells of a God who made covenants with the people of Israel, and with such individuals as Abraham (Gen. 15:18), Moses (Ex. 34:27), Isaac (Gen. 18:19), Noah (Gen.9:8–16), and David (Psalms 89–28, 34, 35) to act in a certain just way, rewarding man for his righteousness and that He was a God who watched jealously over the fulfillment of laws and contracts. Yet this God broke His own oath. Admitting that Job was "a righteous man," He nevertheless permits Job to be robbed of his herds, his servants to be slaughtered, his sons and daughters to be killed, and Job himself smitten with sickness and brought to the brink of the grave. To rob him of peace altogether, his wife and old friends are set loose against him, all of whom say the wrong things. Seeing these conflicting qualities in God, His worshippers felt it necessary to praise Him for His justice on the one hand, while on the other hoping that this praise would serve as a constant reminder that justice was indeed the predominant aspect of His nature.)

The opposites in God's nature, Jung believes, are indicated in many places in the Bible. He finds in the covenant with Noah, that the rainbow is a symbol of this duality. Why should this symbol so well express the different aspects of God?

(Again, to quote from *Answer to Job*, [p. 37], God "instituted the rainbow as a token of the covenant. If, in the future, he summoned the thunder-clouds which hide within them floods of water and lightning then the rainbow would appear, reminding Him and His people of the contract. The temptation to use such an accumulation of clouds for an experimental deluge was no small one, and it was therefore a good idea to associate it with a sign that would give timely warning of possible catastrophe."

Jung sees God as the totality of opposites, containing all that is good and great in man as well as all the pettiness, jealousy, ambition, the power-striving nature, which man himself possesses. Can you give an example from the Book of Job which shows God's apparent need to display his might before man?

(In the 38th and 39th chapters of the Book of Job, God demolishes Job completely with His recitation of the wonders of which He is capable. Job, humbled, grovels speechless before his God. But the mighty One is not yet satisfied. He continues in Chapters 40 and 41 with His overpowering descriptions of Behemoth and Leviathan, impressing over and over again upon Job how weak and puny he is in comparison with his Maker.)

313

Jung finds something less than complimentary in Job's statement to God when he says in Chapter 42:2, before his final capitulation: "I know that thou canst do all things, and that no purpose of thine can be thwarted." What possible meaning can you see in this statement?

(It is not only the acknowledgement that God is all-powerful and that nothing is beyond His greatness, but it is also the awareness that He can behave in ways incomprehensible to man, and that man can do nothing about this, but to acknowledge this aspect of God to himself and resign himself to it.)

In what way does man reflect the essential nature of God, in the view of Jung?

(Jung finds the same polar tension in man, as man personified by Job has seen in God. See text, p. 259.)

In what ways is Job unchanged by his encounter with God?

(He sees the same God as he did at the start, a God whose important attribute is justice, yet a God who has to be appeased for fear that other, darker qualities may manifest themselves. And Job is a righteous man throughout. He holds fast to his integrity until the very end, and it is questionable if, even in his confession, he does not fully maintain his awareness of his position in relation to God.)

In what ways is he changed?

(This is a question which is difficult to answer, because it is the question of what personal experience does to all of us. Perhaps we do not, through personal experience, learn anything we could not have learned from books, but experience produces a different *kind* of knowledge, an awareness that carries with it a depth of feeling or conviction that gives what we know a vastly different meaning.)

Assignment for Session 24:

Read text, Chapter XI, "Job's Message for Our Times," pp. 260–264. Also, bring to class any questions which you would like to discuss concerning the Book of Job.

As we conclude our study of the Book of Job, we ask ourselves whether the problems that were raised in the Book were also answered in it. We may conjecture, too, whether the countless scholars and philosophers, writers and artists, and the thoughtful readers who have perused its pages, have been able to find a message in the Book which could be communicated to others or which could be helpful to them in their own lives. If we have not learned very much about the absolute qualities of good and evil in the centuries since Job was first committed to writing, perhaps we have learned this: that the *why* in the question "why do the good suffer and the evil prosper" is not such a very important word. As soon as we stop beating our breasts crying why, why, why, we may begin to ask: "to what purpose is this apparent lack of relationship directed?" Recognizing that there is no answer to the torturing "why," we may then go forward to live in a world where conflicting principles may be accepted as coexisting.

At the beginning of our study we were as perplexed as Job to account for the necessity of the power of evil, personified by Satan, to assert itself for no apparent reason. We watched its effect upon Job, standing by helplessly because it seemed impossible to understand by any laws of reason or logic. Perhaps we have been able to grow, along with the titanic figure of Job, to the point where we, too, have stopped looking for the "cause" of evil in the world. Perhaps we have come to realize that if such a cause does exist, it lies in the essential, unchangeable nature of things.

With this in mind, how can one who has grown up in the scientific spirit of our time, approach the problem of the theodicy?.

(See text, p. 261.)

What difficulties do some modern religious leaders have with the individualistic approach of psychology and the relativistic approach of the physical sciences?

(See text, pp. 261–262, and the discussion in this *Guide* for Session 23.)

While it may be true that man often expresses the wish for a utopian state of affairs where good is clearly defined and evil is banished from the borders of the land, we may find it interesting to note that in most literature concerning "utopias," it develops, in the minds of the authors at least, that what man anticipated as the greatest good in terms of an ideal society turned out in practice to be full of unanticipated evils. What does this seem to suggest about the relationship between good and evil?

(That good and evil must be seen as relative—what is good for one person or one class or one era may be evil for its counterpart. Within the confines of an apparently ideal situation the seeds of its opposite exist. Too much freedom may breed anarchy, as too much restriction may breed revolution. The most secure peace, then, is perhaps the uneasy truce between good and evil, with man recognizing the necessity for the existence of both in his life and in his world.)

What is the final picture of God with which we are left after reading the Book of Job?

(This question will be answered in an intensely personal way, as will the next question:)

What is the final picture of Man with which we are left to conclude our reading of the Book of Job?

At this time there should be an opportunity for the members of the group to bring up for discussion those questions which they themselves have prepared for this last session on the text of *Job's Encounter.*

In the second session of this group the suggestion was made that the students should consider the following question: "How does the introduction of Satan help to explain Job's misfortunes?" Each student was to write a paragraph on this question from his own point of view, and these were to be reserved by the discussion leader. Now is the time for the leader to bring out these paragraphs, and to select several to read to the group asking individuals to comment upon the ideas contained, stating whether they agree or disagree. The names of the writers should not be divulged; and it will be especially interesting if when the leader reads a paragraph, he calls for a comment on that paragraph from the person who originally wrote it. The development of views ought to be apparent to all. At the end of the session, the leader could then distribute the paragraphs to the people who wrote them, with the suggestion that they read them over and consider whether their thinking on this question has undergone a change during the course of this study.

For those groups who will have an additional session, Session 25 should consist of the presentation of Robert Frost's *A Masque of Reason*; and a discussion of the reading.

SELECTED BIBLIOGRAPHY

Bronowski, J. and Mazlish, Bruce. *The Western Intellectual Tradition*. New York: Harper and Brothers, 1960.

Ciardi, John. "The Birth of a Classic," *The Saturday Review*, March 8, 1958.

Damon, S. Foster. *William Blake: His Philosophy and Symbols*. New York: Peter Smith, 1947.

Dante Alighieri. *The Divine Comedy*. Vol. 21 of *Great Books of the Western World*. Robert Maynard Hutchins, ed., Chicago: Encyclopaedia Britannica, Inc., 1952.

Dostoevsky, Fyodor Mikhailovich. *The Brothers Karamazov*. Vol. 52 of *Great Books of the Western World*.

Freehof, Solomon B. *Reform Jewish Practice*. Cincinnati: Hebrew Union College Press, 1944.

——— *Reform Jewish Practice*. Vol. 2. Cincinnati: Hebrew Union College Press. 1952.

Freud, Sigmund. *New Introductory Lectures on Psychoanalysis*. Vol. 54 of *Great Books of the Western World*.

Fromm, Erich. *Psychoanalysis and Religion*. New Haven: Yale University Press, 1950.

Frost, Robert. *A Masque of Reason*. New York: Holt Rinehart & Winston, Inc., 1945.

Ginsberg, Louis. *Legends of the Jews*. 7 vols. Philadelphia: The Jewish Publication Society of America, 1947.

Goethe, Johann Wolfgang von. *Faust*. Vol. 47 of *Great Books of the Western World*.

Hall, Calvin S. and Lindzey, Gardner. *Theories of Personality*. New York: John Wiley and Sons, Inc., 1957.

Hobbes, Thomas. *Leviathan*. Vol. 23 of *Great Books of the Western World*.

Hone, Ralph E., ed. *The Voice Out of the Whirlwind: The Book of Job*. San Francisco: Chandler Publishing Co., Inc., 1960.

Hutchins, Robert Maynard, ed. *Great Books of the Western World*. 54 vols. Chicago: Encyclopaedia Britannica, Inc., 1952.

James, William. *The Varieties of Religious Experience*. London: Longmans, Green and Company, 1928.

Jewish Encyclopaedia. Articles on "Biblical Exegesis" and "Job." New York: Funk and Wagnalls Company, 1904.

Jung, C. G. *Answer to Job*. New York: Meridian Books, Inc., 1960.

MacLeish, Archibald. *J. B.* Boston: Houghton Mifflin Company, 1956.

Machiavelli, Nicolo. *The Prince.* Vol. 23 of *Great Books of the Western World.*

Melville, Herman. *Moby Dick.* Vol. 48 of *Great Books of the Western World.*

Milton, John. *Paradise Lost.* Vol. 32 of *Great Books of the Western World.*

Montesquieu, Charles. *The Spirit of Laws.* Vol. 38 of *Great Books of the Western World.*

Pascal, Blaise. *Pensées.* Vol. 33 of *Great Books of the Western World.*

Pfeiffer, Robert H. *Introduction to the Old Testament.* New York: Harper and Brothers. 1941.

Rousseau, Jean-Jacques. *The Social Contract.* Vol. 38 of *Great Books of the Western World.*

Tolstoy, Leo. *War and Peace.* Vol. 51 of *Great Books of the Western World.*